Third Edition

Improving Schools Through Action Research

A Reflective Practice Approach

Cher Hendricks

Georgia Institute of Technology

PEARSON

Boston Columbus Indianapolis New York San Francisco Upper Saddle River
Amsterdam Cape Town Dubai London Madrid Milan Munich Paris Montreal Toronto
Delhi Mexico City São Paulo Sydney Hong Kong Seoul Singapore Taipei Tokyo

Vice President and Editorial Director: Jeffery W. Johnston
Vice President and Publisher: Kevin Davis
Vice President, Director of Marketing: Margaret Waples
Senior Marketing Manager: Joanna Sabella
Senior Managing Editor: Pamela Bennett
Senior Project Manager: Mary M. Irvin
Production Manager: Laura Messerly
Senior Art Director: Jayne Conte
Cover Designer: Suzanne Duda
Cover Art: Fotolia
Project Coordination: Murugesh Rajkumar, PreMediaGlobal
Composition: PreMediaGlobal
Printer/Binder: Courier/Westford
Cover Printer: Courier/Westford
Text Font: 11/13 ITC Garamond Std

Credits and Acknowledgments for materials borrowed from other sources and reproduced, with permission, in this textbook appear on the appropriate page within the text.

Every effort has been made to provide accurate and current Internet information in this book. However, the Internet and information posted on it are constantly changing, so it is inevitable that some of the Internet addresses listed in this textbook will change.

Library of Congress Cataloging-in-Publication Data

Hendricks, Cher.
  Improving schools through action research : a reflective practice approach /
Cher Hendricks.—3rd ed.
     p. cm.
  Includes bibliographical references and index.
  ISBN-13: 978-0-13-286864-8 (alk. paper)
  ISBN-10: 0-13-286864-4 (alk. paper)
  1. Action research in education—Handbooks, manuals, etc. I. Title.
  LB1028.24.H46 2013
  370.72—dc23

                                                      2011050897

3 4 5 6 7 8 9 10 V092 16 15 14 13

ISBN 10: 0-13-286864-4
ISBN 13: 978-0-13-286864-8

PREFACE

I had my first experience with action research (AR) in 1999 when, as a quantitative researcher and faculty member trained in inferential statistics methodology, I was asked to teach a course in action research. With no training in action research—and knowing there was a pervasive attitude among those in my field that action research wasn't "real" research—I was not excited about the prospect. My goal was to plod through the course, adapting my knowledge of empirical research and fitting it in where I could, and then hope I would never again be asked to teach the course.

But a few weeks into that first action research course, it was clear to me that the teachers I was working with were becoming thoroughly invested in the process of investigating their practices. Further, as I reflected on the best way to facilitate those teachers' studies, I realized that, although the process of AR shared some elements of a more traditional, empirical research framework, there was more to teaching and facilitating the process than simply teaching what I already knew and leaving out the statistics part. Instead, the process of action research involved careful analysis and understanding of the context of classrooms and schools—something that had to be tightly controlled in all the studies I'd conducted before. I saw also that through the collection and analysis of multiple forms of data (including qualitative data), validity and credibility of the studies could be even greater than that of many of the tightly controlled quantitative studies in which I'd engaged.

During that first course, I became a voracious reader of literature on action research. I was surprised to learn how long action research had been connected to K–12 education, and I was intrigued with the work of action researchers in the United Kingdom, New Zealand, and Australia who have been using AR for decades not only to improve their practice but as a vehicle for social justice as well. It was also a delight to watch the teachers in that first group get excited about studying and improving their work. At the end of the semester, there was a clear sense of empowerment among those teachers, and a number of them stayed in touch with me after the course was over to tell me how they were continuing, though often informally, to use AR strategies for their professional development.

A remarkable thing happened as I completed that first action research course: I found I didn't want to teach any course other than action research. This shift in interest caused a shift in role as well. In past courses, my role had been to bring students (all K–12 educators) into my world of academic research. In the AR course, my role was to take myself into the world of practicing educators and show them ways to investigate systematically their professional practice. This was a comfortable shift for me, largely because I consistently saw the positive ways educators were changed when they engaged in action research. I also began to see school improvement as a natural outcome when educators conducted AR. Many of the teachers, administrators, and support staff I've worked with have positively affected their schools and school districts, even when their initial studies focused on issues particular to one classroom or school.

As I've used each edition of this textbook with master's and doctoral students—and based on feedback from other professors who have used this book—I have attempted to improve it. Some of the changes reflect my own personal growth. For example, in this edition I have added *Time to Reflect* activities to stimulate readers' thinking about their values, assumptions, goals, biases, and actions. Reflection cannot be separated from the action research process; it requires understanding oneself and a commitment to align actions with that understanding. This edition has a much deeper focus on reflective and reflexive inquiry. Readers are also encouraged to collaborate with peers or a critical friend to support honest, deep reflection. Though action research can be conducted on one's own, it can be a much richer experience and lead to more growth when the process is shared with someone who is as equally committed as you are to professional growth and ongoing improvement.

I was unsure thirteen years ago whether there would ever be a second edition, much less a third, of this text. At that time, there was still quite a bit of debate about whether AR was "real" research, particularly in a political climate that focused on *scientifically based* research and had its own exclusionary way of defining that term. I am pleased that action research not only has survived, but also has established itself as a legitimate research field. This happened, I believe, because practitioners as well as a number of academic researchers have continued to engage in action research despite its critics. Action research studies are published in journals, the number of action research courses for preservice and inservice teachers continues to grow, and books on the topic have proliferated.

Action research is a powerful tool for studying and improving one's practice. It doesn't require skills educators do not already possess. Caring, conscientious educators reflect on their practice and work to improve it. That kind of reflection is at the heart of action research, and throughout this book, that's what you will be asked to do. I hope you will come to see the power of AR, and if you do, that you will share what you learn with others. In sharing, you gain a voice as a practitioner and as a researcher. It was the voices that came before yours that helped establish the legitimacy of action research. I hope you will add your voice, for our best chance of improving schools through research is to put educators in charge of the process.

APPROACH AND FEATURES

Based on my belief that caring, professional educators continuously reflect on their practice and seek to improve it, the action research approach of this textbook focuses on educators engaging in deep, critical reflection. A major part of that critical reflection is closely examining one's history and experiences, beliefs, expectations, and biases and how they affect action. One of the most powerful ways to engage in critical reflection is to work with a critical friend, and so in this edition I've added *Time to Reflect* activities throughout the chapters that include prompts to stimulate reflection; educators are encouraged to work through the reflection activities in discussion with a critical friend.

In addition to the *Time to Reflect* activities, chapters include additional activities to help educators through each step of the action research process—from choosing a topic and generating research questions through data analysis and reporting results and conclusions. Beginning in Chapter 2, each activity includes a research paper component, and the end result of completing each component is a full-length research paper that documents the action research study. Other features of the book include detailed strategies for (1) reviewing and synthesizing the literature and writing a literature review, (2) collecting, triangulating, and analyzing quantitative and qualitative data (including how to display results graphically), (3) drawing conclusions from results, and (4) writing in APA (6th edition) style. Examples are provided throughout the book that document the ways teachers, principals, counselors, administrators, and support staff can improve their practice through action research. Also, numerous Internet resources—including links to action research networks, professional organizations, and journals—are provided for educators in these and other educational roles.

NEW TO THIS EDITION

Changes to this edition include:

- A discussion about ways conducting action research can professionalize teaching, particularly in the current accountability climate.
- A focus on engaging in ongoing reflection throughout the action research cycle as a way to understand how one's history and experiences affect beliefs, biases, and actions. Unlike the previous editions of this text, in this third edition, the focus is not on the different types of reflection but rather, as explained in Chapter 2, ways "educators think about and make sense of their practice and how to improve it, connect their thinking and knowing to an ethical stance that focuses on what they believe and what they value, and take action in the direction of those values."

- An emphasis on working with a critical friend throughout the action research process as a way to stimulate reflective and reflexive thinking, challenge assumptions, and discuss and confront biases in a safe, trusting environment.
- *Time to Reflect* activities that include probing questions that encourage educators to examine continuously their beliefs and how those beliefs shape action.
- Links to new and/or additional journals, professional organizations, university and school district networks, research articles, and videos that focus on educational action research.
- A more thorough explanation of how to analyze qualitative data, including the processes of compiling, disassembling, reassembling, and interpreting data utilizing thematic analysis.
- Instructions on how to format a research paper using the latest APA guidelines (6th edition).

ACKNOWLEDGMENTS

I would like to express my gratitude to the reviewers of this text for their invaluable comments and insights: Miguel Licona, New Mexico State University; Louis Berry, University of Pittsburgh; Kathryn Castle, Oklahoma State University; J. Sabrina Mims-Cox, California State University–Los Angeles; and Eleni Elder, Tennessee State University.

BRIEF CONTENTS

CONTENTS

1

Research Methods in Education

Chapter Goals

- Explain the ways various research methodologies—quantitative, qualitative, and action research—advance knowledge in education.

- Describe the origin, types, and processes of educational action research.

- Illustrate how action research can be used to effect school change and school improvement.

- Provide activities to demonstrate the ways in which quantitative, qualitative, and action research differ, and familiarize readers with published action research studies.

Although this is a textbook on action research, it is important to begin with a discussion of the different types of research used in education, and thus this chapter begins with a brief explanation of various methodologies that can be employed to advance knowledge in the field of education. The uses of quantitative and qualitative methods of research are explained, and the ways in which practitioners, through action research, contribute to knowledge in education are described. The focus of this chapter is on action research and its origin, history, and processes. Activities are presented to illustrate the differences among research methodologies and to provide an opportunity to read published action research studies conducted by educational practitioners.

WAYS RESEARCH ADVANCES KNOWLEDGE ABOUT EDUCATION

Educational research is conducted to advance our understanding of a variety of issues and can focus on basic knowledge—such as the way the brain processes information—or on more applied concerns geared toward determining the effectiveness of certain actions (teaching or discipline strategies, for example). In education, research is used to develop theory, test hypotheses based on theory, study relationships among variables, describe educational phenomena, and determine whether actions result in desired outcomes, to name just a few of the many uses of educational research. In these varied pursuits, both quantitative and qualitative methodologies are employed to test hypotheses and answer research questions. In studies that focus on hypothesis testing and studying relationships among variables, researchers often use quantitative, statistical methods to analyze data. In studies with purposes such as developing theory or describing educational phenomena, qualitative methods are typically employed. Mixed methods research, which combines both quantitative and qualitative approaches, has been advocated because it may provide "a better understanding of research problems than either approach alone" (Creswell & Plano Clark, 2011, p. 5; also see Creswell, 2011). In other studies, such as action research projects that concentrate on investigating whether actions result in desired outcomes, both qualitative and quantitative methodologies (mixed methods) are often used.

Quantitative Research

To understand how quantitative research methods are used to advance knowledge in education, it is necessary to consider the traditional **epistemology** associated with quantitative research, which contends that reality is fixed and can be captured and understood (Denzin & Lincoln, 2011). The purpose of quantitative research is to test hypotheses and to generalize results of hypotheses tests beyond the individuals and settings that were part of the research study. In order to make such generalizations, quantitative researchers attempt to draw random samples of individuals to be studied, which then allows them to generalize results to the larger population from which the sample was drawn. For example, a quantitative researcher who randomly chooses 300 fourth-grade students from a large metropolitan school district to be in a study can generalize the results of that study to all fourth-grade students in that district. Another requirement for broad generalization is that the researcher controls as many

---

epistemology: A branch of philosophy concerned with the nature of knowledge and the relationship between the knower and the known.

contextual variables in the setting as is possible. Thus, the researcher may utilize strategies such as using only predetermined, valid, and reliable measures to assess participants or scripting intervention methods so that all individuals in experimental groups receive precisely the same instruction. When contextual variables are adequately controlled and inferential statistical methods are used to test differences between groups (or relationships among variables), a researcher using quantitative methods can say with varying degrees of certainty whether differences or relationships found are chance differences or real differences. When differences or relationships are large enough, a researcher using quantitative methods can say with a certain amount of confidence that the differences or relationships are real. When differences are small, however, the researcher is unable to conclude whether the differences or relationships are real or are due to a chance occurrence.

Qualitative Research

An assumption in quantitative epistemology is that reality is fixed, whereas in qualitative research reality is something that may be estimated but never fully captured (Denzin & Lincoln, 2011). Although researchers who use qualitative methods set out with different purposes as they conduct their studies, the general purpose in qualitative research is to understand and interpret phenomena as they occur in natural settings. As Denzin and Lincoln explain, in qualitative research, the focus is on processes "that show how social experience is created and given meaning" (p. 8). Researchers who use qualitative methods generally spend time in the field observing, talking to people, and analyzing artifacts and products of the setting under study. Researchers seek to make meaning from the information gathered from these multiple sources, but the purpose is simply to understand the setting, not to generalize findings beyond it. Thus in a qualitative study, those who are studied are chosen purposively rather than randomly. Also, the context is examined, rather than controlled, and findings are presented in light of the "interactive, complex systems" of the lived-in world (Rossman & Rallis, 2012, p. 9).

Action Research

The purpose of action research is for practitioners to investigate and improve their practices. This is a process of self-study; thus a teacher engaged in action research may, for example, study ways to increase student learning in his or her class, focusing on his or her intentions, methods, and desired outcomes as part of the investigation. In terms of epistemology, in action research, knowledge is connected to one's practice (Noffke, 2009). As McNiff and Whitehead (2010) explain, the methodology of action research allows practitioners to create their own "living educational theories of practice" (p. 9). In action research, practitioners systematically look at ways to deal with issues they are close to, such as instructional practices, social issues of schooling, collaboration with colleagues, or supervision of staff. Rather than choose participants randomly or systematically, they work with the individuals (students, colleagues, teachers, staff, parents) around whom their everyday practices revolve. Context is not controlled but is studied so that the ways in which context influences outcomes can be understood. Data from a variety of sources, including qualitative and quantitative measures, are collected and analyzed for the purpose of informing practice. Thus all results feed back into the action research cycle so that the study is continuous, flexible, and constantly evolving.

Educational researchers use a variety of methods—both qualitative and quantitative—to investigate problems in education. The methods used are determined by the purpose of the study. If, for example, a researcher wishes to compare two different instructional methods for teaching students how to assess cause-and-effect relationships, and if the researcher wants to generalize results to a population represented by the sample in the study, using quantitative research methods would be a logical choice. If, however, a researcher wants to understand how a teacher's communication with students affects their participation in the cause-and-effect learning activities, qualitative research methods would be best suited for the investigation. In some studies, researchers utilize both quantitative and qualitative methods as they investigate educational issues. Table 1.1 illustrates the ways in which quantitative, qualitative, and action research methods differ.

When practitioners—teachers, administrators, school counselors, media specialists—conduct action research studies in their settings, they often rely on qualitative data collection methods because they are interested in the contextual variables in their settings and the ways in which context influences the outcomes of their studies. Practitioners do frequently analyze quantitative measures, such as test scores, number of discipline referrals, or course averages, but these quantitative data are just one source of evidence that is analyzed with other qualitative sources of data such as observations and interviews. Further, although quantitative measures are often part of the data collected in practitioner studies, inferential statistical methods are almost never used in data analysis because (1) generalizing or inferring results beyond the study is not the goal, (2) the sample is chosen purposively instead of randomly, and (3) samples in practitioner studies are not usually large enough for statistical analysis to be useful.

TABLE 1.1   Differences Among Quantitative, Qualitative, and Action Research

	Quantitative Research	Qualitative Research	Action Research
Investigator/ Role	Higher education faculty/ personnel, graduate students. Investigator is an objective observer who studies others.	Higher education faculty/ personnel, anthropologists, graduate students. Investigator studies others through immersion in the research setting.	Teachers, administrators, school-support personnel. Students and/or higher education faculty are sometimes utilized as coinvestigators. Investigator studies self and others.
Purpose	To test hypotheses related to educational theories.	To understand and interpret phenomena in natural settings; to generate hypotheses.	To identify and study a problem in an individual's work or school setting.
Audience	Higher education faculty/ personnel, graduate students.	Higher education faculty/ personnel, graduate students.	There is not always an intended audience, though there is great potential for educators to learn from each others' experiences through the sharing of action research outcomes.
Participants	A random sample chosen from a large population is desired.	A purposive sample is chosen.	Purposively chosen participants based on the intentions of the study. The researcher is also considered a participant.
Types of Data Collected	Objective, quantitative data such as test scores are often utilized. Data from surveys and questionnaires are also used.	Analysis of artifacts, observations, interviews.	Data from a variety of sources are desired. Observations, work samples or student artifacts, interviews, journal entries, and videotapes can be utilized.
Ways the Research Advances Knowledge	With a random sample and control of contextual variables, broad generalizations can be made based on the outcome of the study.	Interpretations of data help to understand the phenomenon under study.	Results inform practice. Through action research, educators reflect and act, continually improving their practice.

Because qualitative and practitioner studies study context—rather than control it—and are less focused on generalizable knowledge than quantitative studies, there has been some debate about their usefulness for advancing knowledge about educational practices. However, because qualitative and practitioner researchers engage in studies that focus on the ways context impacts certain outcomes, it is reasonable to conclude that their results are applicable to settings with similar contexts. Further, applicability of results in qualitative and practitioner studies can be increased when detailed descriptions of the setting, participants, and context are provided. The number of action research studies that are being published in academic journals suggests that research by practitioners is a credible and valuable source of knowledge in education. As Dinkelman (2003) explains, "Although more traditional educational researchers debate the academic rigor of [teachers'] self-study . . . its rapid acceptance in the research literature has been nothing short of astonishing" (pp. 10–11).

McNiff and Whitehead (2010), in fact, have called for a change in the way educational theory is conceptualized, so, as they explain, "it is no longer seen as the domain only of academics, whose job is to produce theory, to be applied by practitioners to their practices" (p. 2). Research as a domain for both practitioners and academics has been supported by a number of educational theorists, and in 1999, the National Academy for Education (NAE) proposed that support be given for collaborative research projects between professional educators and professional researchers, making both accountable for improving education. Although there remain a number of barriers to structuring the type of collaborative research endeavors suggested by the NAE and others (e.g., Buysse, Sparkman, & Wesley, 2003; National Research Council, 1999; Palinscar, Magnusson, Marano, Ford, & Brown, 1998), it is clear that many educational researchers desire for both practitioners and researchers to construct knowledge about education so that a clear connection can be made between what we know and what we do (Buysse et al., 2003; Elliot, 2009).

All educational research—whether conducted by teachers, administrators, evaluators, university faculty, or others interested in studying educational issues—has the potential to enhance knowledge about teaching and learning. Dissemination of research findings, through sharing with colleagues, presenting at conferences, or publishing in teaching magazines or academic journals, adds to the knowledge base in education, and practitioners and university faculty alike are able to make real contributions to the knowledge base whether they use qualitative methods, quantitative methods, action research, or a combination of methods to investigate educational concerns.

In Activity 1.1, two research articles on using collaborative learning strategies are presented for comparison. The study by Michael DuBois, a middle school science teacher, is an example of an action research study in which qualitative methods were employed. The study by Mastropieri, Scruggs, and colleagues, a team of university professors and researchers, is an example of a study that used quantitative data to compare differences between experimental and control groups. The purpose of Activity 1.1 is to show ways in which the various types of research contribute to the educational knowledge base. The sections of this chapter presented after Activity 1.1 describe the origin, types, and processes of action research, which is followed by an explanation of the ways action research can be used for school improvement.

ACTIVITY 1.1
Comparison of Articles on Cooperative Learning

To gain a better understanding of the ways in which different types of research are used to generate knowledge in education, read and analyze the following two articles that use these different methods. The full text of both articles can be accessed online through ERIC at the addresses listed.

DuBois, M. (1995). Conceptual learning and creative problem solving using co-operative learning groups in middle school science classes. In S. Spiegel, A. Collins, & J. Lappert (Eds.), *Action research: Perspectives from teachers' classrooms*. Tallahassee, FL: Southeastern Regional Vision for Educators. Retrieved November 21, 2011, from the ERIC website: http://www.eric. ed.gov/ERICWebPortal/contentdelivery/servlet/ERICServlet?accno=ED403138. [ERIC # ED403138]

Mastropieri, M. A., Scruggs, T. E., Norland, J. J., Berkeley, S., McDuffie, K., Tornquist, E. H., & Connors, N. (2006). Differentiated curriculum enhance-ment in inclusive middle school science: Effects on classroom and high-stakes tests. *Journal of Special Education, 40* (3), 130-137. Retrieved November 21, 2011, from the ERIC website: http://www.eric.ed.gov/ERICWebPortal/ contentdelivery/servlet/ERICServlet?accno=EJ758174. [ERIC # EJ758174]

Note: If you have any difficulty with the links above, go to the ERIC website (http://www. eric.ed.gov/) and search by the ERIC numbers, which are listed with the preceding articles: ED403138 and EJ758174. Once the ERIC reference is found, click on the ERIC Full Text link.

Once you have read both the articles answer the following questions:

1. What differences and similarities exist between the two articles in terms of the authors' reasons for conducting their respective studies?
2. Describe the ways in which participants were chosen in each study. What reasons did the authors give for the choice of participants?
3. Compare the types of data collected in each study. How were these data sources used to answer research questions?
4. How were results reported in each article? Describe differences and similarities in reporting methods.
5. How do the authors of each study explain their intentions for future research based on their findings (see *Discussion* sections)?
6. In what ways does each article contribute to the educational knowledge base?

THE ORIGIN OF ACTION RESEARCH

In the 1930s, Kurt Lewin first described the theory of action research. His early research focused on workplace studies comparing methods for training factory workers. Lewin viewed action research as a spiraling process that included reflection and inquiry on the part of its stakeholders for the purposes of improving work environments and dealing with social problems (Burns, 1999). One of the tenets of his theory was that democratic workplaces produce employees who take ownership of their work, which increases both morale and productivity. This idea became connected to Dewey and Count's progressive education movement, as Clem Adelman (1997) explains, because Lewin had created the methods schools needed to become the driving force of democratic change within a community. Although it would be years before action research found its way to the classroom and to schools, Lewin is credited with the formalization of the theory and principles of action research.

While Lewin was developing his theory of action research, the Progressive Education Association was studying the ways in which **progressive education** was superior to traditional education in *The Eight Year Study*. Dewey challenged the emphasis placed on scientific methods in the study of education, asserting that practitioners should be directly involved in the process of research (Burns, 2010). However, as Schubert and Lopez-Schubert (1997) explain, there were a number of research flaws with *The Eight Year Study*, including a lack of true reflection in early studies (although Tyler, the evaluator for *The Eight Year Study*, did realize the importance of teacher reflection in school research) and use of mechanized research strategies that devalued the practical inquiry of teachers. These problems, exacerbated by the push at that time toward rigorous scientific studies in the field of education, prevented action research from taking hold (Burns, 2010). Schubert and Lopez-Schubert explain that the initial goals of action research have only recently begun to be realized, especially since the initiation of the teacher-as-research movement in United Kingdom in the 1970s and 1980s, inspired by Lawrence Stenhouse, who recognized teacher reflection as an important type of research.

In 1970, Stenhouse founded the Center for Applied Research in Education at the University of East Anglia in England with the objective of demystifying the practice of research and making it more useful and accessible to teachers. Cochran-Smith and Lytle (1993) explain that Stenhouse encouraged teachers to conduct their own research with the goal of improving their practices—an idea that was radical in its time because its impetus was Stenhouse's claim that researchers needed to justify themselves to practitioners rather than insist practitioners

progressive education: A child-centered approach to teaching and learning that focuses on the development of socially engaged intelligence. Progressive education seeks both to positively impact individual development and to foster social justice.

justify themselves to researchers (Stenhouse, 1981). As Rudduck (1988) articulates,

> Stenhouse was critical . . . of inequality in relation to teachers and research. There were, in his view, two cultures—the culture of academic researchers, who are served by research, and the culture of practitioners, who are ruled by research or merely ignore it. He saw a need to analyze the structures that govern the production and distribution of research knowledge and that determine the right to engage in research acts. His aspiration was to bring educational research to the orbit of the practitioner's world. (pp. 35–36)

In Stenhouse's view, a basic flaw in the traditional thinking of academic researchers was that academic research devalued teacher judgment (Fishman & McCarthy, 2000). Stenhouse's idea was that the theory proposed by academic researchers was of little use unless teachers were able to test it. His position was that academic researchers and teachers had to work together for research to be meaningful and beneficial. Stenhouse (1981) asserted,

> There is in the field of education little theory which could be relied upon by the teacher without testing it. Many of the findings of research are based on small-scale laboratory experiments which often do not replicate or cannot be successfully applied in classrooms. Many are actuarial and probabilistic, and, if they are to be used by the individual teacher, they demand situational verification. . . . The teacher has grounds for motivation to research. We researchers have reason to excite that motivation: without a research response from teachers our research cannot be utilized. (pp. 109–110)

Pushing for systematic, self-critical teacher research based on these ideas, Stenhouse initiated a large action research movement in the United Kingdom. Unlike earlier action research movements—which were unsuccessful largely due to the inability of the movement to get beyond a number of critics who supported scientific, empirical research studies—the phenomenon inspired by Stenhouse and his colleagues was successful and has endured. A number of action research proponents have influenced its growth in the last few decades. Many of these individuals are listed on the timeline in Figure 1.1, which reveals the development of the action research movement in the United States and abroad. (Note: See Carr, 2006, for a different historical accounting of the action research movement that is particularly relevant to those interested in the philosophical and methodological underpinnings of action research.)

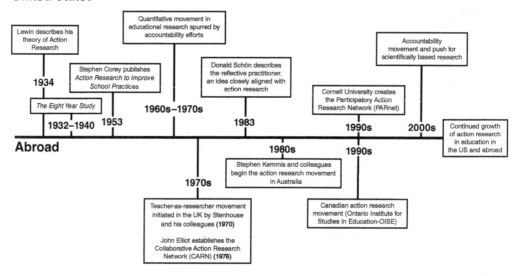

FIGURE 1.1 Action research timeline.

Today large action research networks exist in the United Kingdom, Australia, Canada, and the United States. Educational action research journals (e.g., *Educational Action Research* and *Action Research*) have been established, and many academic journals now publish action research studies. In addition, a variety of school district action research networks have been created that encourage teachers to conduct action research and provide resources for teachers interested in conducting action research. The lists at the end of this chapter provide information on many of these action research sources as well as additional reading materials on the fascinating progression of the action research movement.

THE ACTION RESEARCH PROCESS

Stenhouse (1981) described action research as a systematic, self-critical inquiry. *Systematic* means that a certain structure, or set of steps, is utilized in the action research process. Action research theorists and practitioners follow a systematic set of procedures, though these procedures can vary slightly depending on individual preferences. For example, Kemmis and Wilkinson (1997) describe the action research process utilizing these steps: plan, act and observe, reflect, revise the plan, act and observe, reflect, and so on. Cole and Knowles (2009) describe similar steps that include developing a focus, gathering information, making sense of information through analysis and reflection, and acting based on findings. For Kemmis and Wilkinson, as well as Cole and Knowles, the process of action research does not have an end. Rather, it is an unending reflective process that is graphically displayed

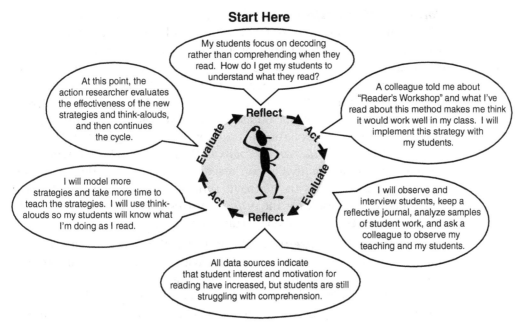

FIGURE 1.2 The action research process.

in the shape of a spiral with each systematic step leading to the next step and continually beginning anew. As Mills (2011) explains, the various models of action research share common elements such as identifying a problem, collecting and analyzing data, and then "some form of 'action' that invariably 'spirals' the researcher back into the process repeatedly" (p. 17).

The action research process that will be described in this book follows the principle of systematic inquiry based on ongoing reflection. The process is a series of steps in which the action researcher reflects, acts, and evaluates. After evaluation, the process continues with reflection, action, and evaluation. Thus the process shares the idea of spiraling, consistent with the notion that action research is an ongoing process that individuals use to constantly improve their practices. Figure 1.2 provides an example of how this process is utilized in action research.

TYPES OF ACTION RESEARCH

Various types of action research have been identified and described, illustrating the different purposes, goals, and values of the different branches of study. Three types of action research—collaborative, classroom, and participatory—are defined and described here. Understanding the following terms will help educators become informed action researchers and allow them to think about the type of action research that most closely aligns with their own goals, purposes, and values.

Collaborative action research   A system of action research in which multiple researchers from school and university settings work together to study educational problems. Collaboration among teachers and administrators may occur as well as collaboration among school personnel and university researchers. The goal of this type of research is to utilize the expertise of the collaborators and to foster sustained dialogue among educational stakeholders in different settings. An example of collaborative action research is the *SafeMeasures Collaborative Action Research Program*, through Main Street Academix, a student-led collaborative action research project that brings together students and teachers to improve school climate (see http://www .msanh.com; also look for the *Safe Measures* YouTube video available on the MainStreetAcademix YouTube channel).

Classroom action research   A form of action research that is conducted by teachers in their classrooms with the purpose of improving practice. It values the interpretations that teachers make based on data collected with their students. Although it is frequently a solo endeavor, collaboration among classroom teachers can occur. To see an example of a classroom research network, visit the Madison (WI) Metropolitan School District classroom action research site (https://staffdevweb .madison.k12.wi.us/node/232).

Participatory action research   A social, collaborative process of action research. The goal is to investigate reality so that it can be changed. This type of action research is considered to be emancipatory (the action researcher is able to explore practices within the limits of social structures), critical (the action researcher's goal is to challenge alienation, unproductive ways of working, and power struggles), and transformational (changing both theory and practice). The work of Flores-Kastanis, Montoya-Vargas, and Suárez (2009); Kemmis and McTaggart (2000); and Kemmis (2006) provides in-depth information on participatory action research. An example is *Voices of Youth in Chicago Education* (VOYCE), a student collaborative that partners with the community to research issues such as dropout prevention. (See www.voyceproject.org/research-findings-solutions. Also look for the YouTube video on the VOYCEProject channel.)

Although these and other types of action research—such as emancipatory action research, critical action research, and teacher research—are commonly referred to in the literature, Noffke (2009) has proposed a different way to categorize studies, preferring the terms *professional*, *personal*, and *political*. Noffke suggests that these fluid, overlapping dimensions provide a less hierarchical structure than the categories listed earlier, which can be seen as having different levels of value or worth. The point is that all action research, when conducted systematically by educators who wish to know more about themselves and how to improve their practice, has value, regardless of the particular type or orientation.

THE IMPORTANCE OF ACTION RESEARCH FOR IMPROVING SCHOOLS

Educational action research is a system of inquiry that teachers, administrators, and school support personnel can use to study, change, and improve their work with children and in schools. Through the action research process, educators are able to generate knowledge about their practice and share that knowledge with their colleagues. Practices that Fullan (2002, 2010) suggests are key elements of producing lasting and sustainable change in schools. Further, as Allen and Calhoun (1998) explain, the promise of action research is its capacity to help individuals, small groups, or even entire school faculties increase their understanding and improve their practice. In terms of using collaborative models of action research for school change, Allen and Calhoun state:

> For those seeking whole-school improvement—both in terms of student learning and in terms of the conditions of the professional workplace—action research places disciplined inquiry (i.e., research) in the context of focused efforts to improve the quality of the school and its performance (i.e., action). The integrity of the process for site-based school improvement lies in the union of the "researchers" and "action takers," for action research is conducted by those persons responsible for bringing about changes. (pp. 706–707)

Calhoun (2002), however, expresses the need for the development of systems to provide the time, support, and professional development activities necessary to encourage and sustain action research as a process of school improvement. With this support, action research becomes the guiding force behind professional development, allowing practitioners to study their own practices and take charge of developing their professional work as educators.

There are a number of ways action research leads to school improvement. The educators with whom I have worked have expressed how action research improves schools and professionalizes the work of

- **Teachers**, by allowing them to investigate ways to deal with issues related to student achievement, classroom management, students with special needs (such as the gifted, exceptional, or limited English proficient), and motivation.

- ***Media specialists***, by giving them the opportunity to study methods to increase interest in reading, utilization of the media center, use of technology for student and teacher research, and teaming with teachers to develop and teach lessons.
- ***Coaches***, because they can examine ways to increase skills in sport, evaluate the effectiveness of their coaching styles, increase persistence and perseverance, and include students with special needs in athletics.
- ***Counselors***, by giving them the tools to study the usefulness of counseling programs (e.g., character education, bullying prevention, student advisement, career counseling), ways to identify students who need advocates, and ways to effectively communicate with teachers, students, and parents.
- ***Principals***, who can encourage and evaluate action research by their teachers and who can conduct their own school improvement studies related to school climate, professional development, school–community relations, working with parents, curricular programs, student achievement, attendance, and discipline.
- ***District administrators***, who can focus on issues such as the usefulness of professional development activities, student achievement, curriculum reform, training and induction of new school administrators, and teacher and administrator recruitment and attrition.
- ***Teachers of the arts, speech pathologists, and support teachers***, who can investigate the ways they teach and interact with students, effective teaching strategies, motivation, achievement, and individual gains.

This list is not meant to be exhaustive. These are just a few of the many ways action research can be used to improve classrooms and schools. Keep in mind that regardless of the various roles that exist in educational settings, the process of action research is the same—only the research problems are different. This means that teachers who learn to use action research to improve classrooms are able to use the same *process* of action research if they one day become a school or district administrator. Also, experienced action researchers are able to pass their knowledge—both of the process of action research *and* what was learned in the study—to colleagues, mentored individuals, and supervisors.

By using action research to study problems such as those mentioned, educators can improve what occurs in classrooms and schools. Action researchers have the potential to impact students in a number of exciting ways, and they have the potential to learn a great deal about themselves in the process. There are several benefits of becoming an action researcher. The teachers, administrators, counselors, and media specialists whose action research studies I have facilitated describe a number of benefits of the process. They explain that conducting action research

- Professionalizes the work of educators because it puts them in charge of improving their practice and their professional development.
- Encourages educators to work collaboratively.
- Gives educators a voice in the field, allowing them to disseminate their findings so that others can learn from their experiences.
- Encourages educators to rethink the ways they evaluate their work and the work of students, increasing the likelihood that they will use multiple forms of measurement that are credible and useful and that can stand up to scrutiny.
- Provides educators with rich sources of data that can be used to improve classrooms and can ultimately lead to school improvement.
- Revitalizes educators' professional lives because it makes work exciting, fun, interesting, and rewarding.
- Allows educators to develop the ability to articulate the choices they make and the methods they use, even if those methods are challenged.
- Helps educators get to know students, both academically and personally, which increases mutual understanding and respect among students, parents, teachers, and administrators.

Many of these benefits are supported in the action research literature. Anderson, Herr, and Nihlen (1994, 2007), for example, assert that participating in action research can stimulate collegiality, empower educators, and give school personnel a voice in decision making in educational policy and change. Further, they suggest that engaging in action research allows educators to become creators of their own knowledge about teaching and learning rather than only consumers of others' research. As Smiles and Short (2006) explain, educators gain *voice* with other educators and are able "to immediately use understandings from research to inform teaching" (p. 133). Based on comments from teachers with whom she worked, Burns (1999, 2010) concluded that conducting research on their practice increased teachers' personal insight and self-awareness, helped them grow personally and professionally, gave them a method for coming up with solutions to institutional demands, and allowed them to have an opportunity to systematically reflect on the educational decisions they made.

In addition to these benefits, Elliot (2010) asserts that due to top-down mandates of policy makers who wish to make educational outcomes more predictable (via accountability measures, for example) and the ways in which these mandates deprofessionalize teaching, educators who wish to reclaim their professionalism can no longer view action research as optional. Elliot explains that educators "can either strive to empower themselves to make and create change through action research, or simply hand responsibility for change over to policy makers and educational managers" (p. 2). He supports the view of action research as a type of ethical inquiry that allows teachers to reflect on their educational values and the ways in which their teaching can reflect those values, a process that ultimately empowers educators and professionalizes their field.

BECOMING FAMILIAR WITH THE LANGUAGE AND PROCESS OF ACTION RESEARCH

The purpose of this text is to help educators carry out each step of the action research cycle as they engage in studies of their practice. Each of the remaining chapters describes a specific phase of the process based on the reflect–act–evaluate method: reflecting on practice to select an area to study, connecting theory to action through a review of related literature, planning and implementing the project, gathering information, making sense of collected information, and writing the final action research report. Before delving into the steps of the process in detail, though, it is important to familiarize yourself with the language of action research. A good way to get started is to read several action research studies, an activity that introduces the language, methods, and intricacies of action research. Reading action research studies is a good way to get an overall sense of what a project entails and the ways in which action research leads to school improvement and teacher empowerment. Also, reading studies conducted by others in the field of education helps generate research ideas for your own action research investigation.

The goal of Activity 1.2 is to provide you the opportunity to read action research studies conducted by other educators. Studies can be found in many educational journals and on a number of websites. Reading articles and summarizing them in terms of the reflective practices that initiated the studies, the actions taken by educators, and the methods used to evaluate actions will help to bring the action research cycle to life.

ACTIVITY 1.2
Reading Action Research Studies

Locate three action research studies to read and summarize. Choose articles that describe action research studies that were actually conducted rather than articles about action research. Good journals and websites include *Educational Action Research*, the *International Journal of Scholarship of Teaching and Learning*, *The Reading Teacher*, *Networks: An Online Journal of Teacher Research*, the *Ontario Action Researcher*, the Madison Metropolitan School District Classroom Action Research site, the Action Research Lab at Highland Park High School, and the Teachers Network Leadership Institute Fellows. The resource lists at the end of the chapter contain detailed website information for these and other sites where action research studies can be located. After reading each study, write a response to each of these prompts:

1. Describe the reflections given at the beginning of the article that led the researcher to conduct the particular action research study (what problem was identified by the researcher, and why was it important?).
2. Describe the actions that were taken by the researcher during the study (what did the researcher do to investigate the problem identified during the reflection process?).
3. Describe the evaluation techniques used by the researcher (what types of data were collected, and how were they analyzed?).
4. Describe the researcher's reflections at the conclusion of the article (what did the action researcher learn, and what did he or she intend to do next?).

After reading the three articles, explain the ways in which the authors' studies can impact school improvement and lead to educator empowerment.

Summary

This chapter revealed the ways in which various forms of research—quantitative, qualitative, and action research—can be used to advance knowledge about educational practices. The focus of the chapter, however, was on action research, a method practitioners can use to study and improve their practice. Introduced by Kurt Lewin as a process to investigate workplace issues and social problems, action research was slow to be accepted as a useful form of educational research but is now embraced as a valuable way to study classrooms and schools for school improvement. The spiraling reflect–act–evaluate process of action research was described, and three types of action research—collaborative, classroom, and participatory—were introduced. A number of benefits of educational action research were presented including professionalizing the work of teachers, encouraging collaboration, and giving practitioners the opportunity to add to the educational knowledge base.

Additional Reading Materials

Atweh, B., Kemmis, S., & Weeks, P. (Eds.). (1998). *Action research in practice. Partnerships for social justice in education.* London: Routledge.

Carr, W. (2006). Philosophy, methodology, and action research. *Journal of Philosophy of Education, 40*(4), 421–435.

Carson, T. R., & Sumara, D. (Eds.). (1997). *Action research as a living practice.* New York: Peter Lang.

Corey, S. M. (1953). *Action research to improve school practices.* New York: Teachers College Press.

Elliot, J. (1978). What is action research in schools? *Journal of Curriculum Studies, 10,* 355–357.

Elliot, J. (1991). *Action research for educational change.* Philadelphia: Milton Keynes/Open University Press.

Kemmis, S. (1993). Action research and social movement: A challenge for policy research. *Education*

Policy Analysis Archives, 1. [Available online at http://epaa.asu.edu/epaa/v1n1.html]

Kemmis, S. (2006). Participatory action research and the public sphere. *Educational Action Research, 14,* 459–476.

Noffke, S., & Somekh. B. (Eds.). (2009). *The SAGE handbook of educational action research.* Thousand Oaks, CA: SAGE.

Schön, D. (1987). *Educating the reflective practitioner.* London: Jossey-Bass.

Action Research Resources

University, Regional, and School District Action Research Sites

ActionResearch.net (UK)
www.actionresearch.net/

Action Research at Queen's University (Canada)
http://resources.educ.queensu.ca/ar/

Action Research in the Grand Erie School District (Canada)
http://schools.gedsb.net/ar/

The Action Research Laboratory at Highlands Park High School (Illinois, USA)
http://hphs.dist113.org/Academics/Pages/
    ActionResearch.aspx

Action Research Network
http://actionresearch.altec.org/

Action Research Network in Alberta (Canada)
www.uleth.ca/education/research/arnia

Action Research Network Ireland
www.eari.ie/index.html

Amphitheater (AZ) School District Collaborative Action Research (USA)
www.amphi.com/departments--programs/
    career-ladder/collaborative-action-research-
    %28car%29-2011-2012.aspx

Brown University—Voices from the Field
www.alliance.brown.edu/pubs/voices

Catholic Action Research Network (US)
http://researchandaction.wordpress.com/
    ar-research-projects/

Center for Collaborative Action Research—Pepperdine University (USA)
http://cadres.pepperdine.edu/ccar

Clark County (NV) Action Research Project (USA)
http://ccsd.net/AARSI/Research/action_research.php

Collaborative Action Research Network (CARN) (UK)
www.esri.mmu.ac.uk/carnnew/

Fairfax County (VA) Public Schools Teacher-Researcher Network
www.fcps.edu/plt/tresearch.htm

Kirkwood (Missouri) Teacher Action Research
http://www.kirkwoodschools.org/parents/
    curriculumheader/actionresearch/

Madison (Wisconsin) Metropolitan School District Classroom Action Research
https://staffdevweb.madison.k12.wi.us/node/232
http://oldweb.madison.k12.wi.us/sod/car/search.
    cgi (for papers/abstracts)

New Zealand Collaborative Action and Research Network
www.litarts.canterbury.ac.nz/NZCARN.shtml

Rochester (New York) Teacher Center for Teacher Research (USA)
www.rochesterteachercenter.com/teacher
    research.htm

Shawnee Mission (KS) School District Action Research (USA)
www.smsd.org/custom/curriculum/action
    research.htm

Teacher Research at George Mason University (USA)
http://gse.gmu.edu/research/tr

Teachers Network Leadership Institute (USA)
http://teachersnetwork.org/TNLI/research/

Journals

Action Learning: Research and Practice
http://www.tandf.co.uk/journals/titles/14767333.asp

Action Research
http://arj.sagepub.com/

Educational Action Research
http://www.tandf.co.uk/journals/reac

The International Journal for the Scholarship of Teaching and Learning
http://academics.georgiasouthern.edu/ijsotl/
  index.htm

The Journal for Social Action in Counseling and Psychology
http://jsacp.tumblr.com/

The Journal of Scholarship on Teaching and Learning
https://www.iupui.edu/~josotl/

Networks: An Online Journal for Teacher Research
http://journals.library.wisc.edu/index.php/
  networks

The Ontario Action Researcher
http://www.nipissingu.ca/oar

Participatory Learning and Action
http://www.planotes.org/

ARTICLES ON SPECIAL EDUCATION ISSUES

Atkinson, C., Regan, T., & Williams, C. (2006). Working collaboratively with teachers to promote effective learning. *Support for Learning, 21*(1), 33–39.

Brigham, M., & Hartman, M. C. (2010). What is your prediction? Teaching the metacognitive skill of prediction to a class of sixth- and seventh-grade students who are deaf. *American Annals of the Deaf, 155*(2), 137–143.

Brookhart, S., Andolina, M., Zuza, M., & Furman, R. (2004). Minute math: An action research study of student self-assessment. *Educational Studies in Mathematics, 57*(2), 213–227.

Carnahan, C. R. (2006). Photovoice: Engaging children with autism and their teachers. *Teaching Exceptional Children, 39*(2), 44–50.

Cushing, L. S., Carter, E. W., Clark, N., Wallis, T., & Kennedy, C. H. (2009). Evaluating inclusive educational practices for students with severe disabilities using the program quality measurement tool. *Journal of Special Education, 42*(4), 195–208. doi:10.1177/0022466907313352

Dymond, S. K. (2001). A participatory action research approach to evaluating inclusive school programs. *Focus on Autism and Other Developmental Disabilities, 16*(1), 54.

Dymond, S., Renzaglia, A., Rosenstein, A., Chun, E., Banks, R., Niswander, V., et al. (2006). Using a participatory action research approach to create a universally designed inclusive high school science course: A case study. *Research and Practice for Persons with Severe Disabilities (RPSD), 31*(4), 293–308.

Hammel, J., Finlayson, M., & Lastowski, S. (2003). Using participatory action research to examine outcomes and effect systems change in assistive technology financing. *Journal of Disability Policy Studies, 14*(2), 98–108.

Jones, M. (2006). Teaching self-determination: Empowered teachers, empowered students. *Teaching Exceptional Children, 39*(1), 12–17.

Kroeger, S., Burton, C., Comarata, A., Combs, C., Hamm, C., Hopkins, R., & Kouche, B. (2004). Student voice and critical reflection. *Teaching Exceptional Children, 36*(3), 50–57.

Moore, R. A., & Brantingham, K. L. (2003). Nathan: A case study in reader response and retrospective in miscue analysis. *The Reading Teacher, 56*, 466–474.

Mortensen, S. (2002). Action research on cognitive rescaling. *Journal of Special Education Technology, 17*, 53–58.

Norwich, B., Griffiths, C., & Burden, B. (2005). Dyslexia-friendly schools and parent partnership: Inclusion and home-school relationships. *European Journal of Special Needs Education, 20*(2), 147–165.

Schoen, S. F., & Bullard, M. (2002). Action research during recess. *Teaching Exceptional Children, 35*, 36–39.

Schoen, S. F., & Nolen, J. (2004). Action research: Decreasing acting-out behavior and increasing learning. *Teaching Exceptional Children, 37*(1), 26–29.

Schoen, S. F., & Schoen, A. A. (2003). Action research in the classroom: Assisting a linguistically different learner with special needs. *Teaching Exceptional Children, 36*, 16–21.

ARTICLES ON EARLY CHILDHOOD AND ELEMENTARY EDUCATION ISSUES

Baumann, J. F., Hooten, H., & White, P. (1999). Teaching comprehension strategies through literature: A teacher-research project to develop fifth graders' reading strategies and motivation. *The Reading Teacher, 53*, 38–51.

Buchanan, B. L., & Rios, J. M. (2004). Teaching science to kindergartners: How can teachers implement science standards? *Young Children, 59*(3), 82–87.

Bukowiecki, E. M., & McMacklin, M. C. (1999). Young children and narrative texts: A school-based inquiry project. *Reading Improvement, 36*, 157–166.

Capobianco, B., & Lehman, J. (2006). Integrating technology to foster inquiry in an elementary science methods course: An action research study of one teacher educator's initiatives in a PT3 project. *Journal of Computers in Mathematics and Science Teaching, 25*(2), 123–146.

Cardno, C. (2006). Leading change from within: Action research to strengthen curriculum leadership in a primary school. *School Leadership & Management, 26*(5), 453.

Espiritu, E., Meier, D. R., & Villazana-Price, N. (2002). A collaborative project on language and literacy learning: Promoting teacher research in early childhood education. *Young Children, 57*, 71–74.

Griffin, M. L. (2002). Why don't you use your finger? Paired reading in first grade. *The Reading Teacher, 55*, 766–774.

Hyland, N., E., & Noffke, S. E. (2005). Understanding diversity through social and community inquiry: An action-research study. *Journal of Teacher Education, 56*(4), 367–381.

Keaton, J. M., Palmer, B. C., Nicholas, K. R., & Lake, V. E. (2007). Direct instruction with playful skill extensions: Action research in emergent literacy development. *Reading Horizons, 47*(3), 229–250.

Knight, S. L., Wiseman, D. L., & Cooner, D. (2000). Using collaborative teacher research to determine the impact of professional development school activities on elementary students' math and writing outcomes. *Journal of Teacher Education, 51*, 26–38.

Kremenitzer, J. P., & Myler, T. (2006). Collaboration between teacher educator and kindergarten teacher: A 4-year action research study to improve our own professional practices. *Childhood Education, 82*(3), 165–170.

Loertscher, D. (2006). Living the hero's quest: Character building through action research. *Teacher Librarian, 33*(3), 40–41, 66.

Schmidt, P. R., Gillen, S., Zollo, T. C., & Stone, R. (2002). Literacy learning and scientific inquiry: Children respond. *The Reading Teacher, 55*, 534–548.

Souto-Manning, M., & Mitchell, C. H. (2010). The role of action research in fostering culturally responsive practices in a preschool classroom. *Early Childhood Education Journal, 37*(4), 269-277. doi:10.1007/s10643-009-0345-9

Tancock, S. M., & Segedy, J. (2004). A comparison of young children's technology-enhanced and traditional responses to texts: An action research project. *Journal of Research in Childhood Education, 19*(1), 58–65.

ARTICLES ON ISSUES FOR ENGLISH LANGUAGE LEARNERS

Buck, G., Mast, C., Ehlers, N., & Franklin, E. (2005). Preparing teachers to create a mainstream science classroom conducive to the needs of English-language learners: A feminist action research project. *Journal of Research in Science Teaching, 42*(9), 1013–1031.

Burnham, J. J., Mantero, M., & Hooper, L. M. (2009). Experiential training: Connecting school counselors-in-training, English as a second language (ESL) teachers, and ESL students. *Journal of Multicultural Counseling and Development, 37*(1), 2–14.

Cohen, L., & Byrnes, K. (2007). Engaging children with useful words: Vocabulary instruction in a third grade classroom. *Reading Horizons, 47*(4), 271–293.

Hu, G. (2005). Using peer review with Chinese ESL student writers. *Language Teaching Research, 9*(3), 321–342.

McCall-Perez, Z. (2000). The counselor as advocate for English language learners: An action research approach. *Professional School Counseling, 4*(1), 13–22.

Patten, K. B., & Craig, D. V. (2007). iPods and English-language learners: A great combination. *Teacher Librarian, 34*(5), 40–44.

Zainuddin, H., & Moore, R. (2004). Engaging preservice teachers in action research to enhance awareness of second language learning and teaching. *Teacher Education and Practice, 17*(3), 311–327.

ARTICLES ON SOCIAL STUDIES ISSUES

Bednarz, S. W. (2002). Using action research to implement the National Geography Standards: Teachers as researchers. *Journal of Geography, 101*, 103–111.

Chant, R. H. (2009). Developing involved and active citizens: The role of personal practical theories and action research in a standards-based social studies classroom. *Teacher Education Quarterly, 36*(1), 181–190.

Dils, A. K. (2000). Using technology in a middle school social studies classroom. *International Journal of Social Education, 15*, 101–112.

Dixon, D. A. (2001). The three R's of school-university collaboration: Re-engaging classroom teachers by reframing social studies research. *Journal of Social Studies Research, 25*, 47–53.

Fallace, T. D., Biscoe, A. D., & Perry, J. L. (2007). Second graders thinking historically: Theory into practice. *Journal of Social Studies Research, 31*(1), 44–53.

Kosky, C., & Curtis, R. (2008). An action research exploration integrating student choice and arts activities in a sixth grade social studies classroom. *Journal of Social Studies Research, 32*(1), 22–27.

STUDIES ON MATH AND SCIENCE ISSUES

Agnello, M. F., & Carpenter, P. (2010). Integrating geospatial technologies, action research, and curriculum theory to promote ecological literacy. *Multicultural Education & Technology Journal, 4*(3), 188–197. doi:10.1108/17504971011075183

Bonner, P. J. (2006). Transformation of teacher attitude and approach to math instruction through collaborative action research. *Teacher Education Quarterly, 33*(3), 27–44.

Briscoe, C., & Wells, E. (2002). Reforming primary science assessment practices: A case study of one teacher's professional development through action research. *Science Education, 86*, 417–435.

Capobianco, B. M., Lincoln, S., Canuel-Browne, D., & Trimarchi, R. (2006). Examining the experiences of three generations of teacher researchers through collaborative science teacher inquiry. *Teacher Education Quarterly, 33*(3), 61–78.

Goldston, M. J., & Shroyer, M. G. (2000). Teachers as researchers: Promoting effective science and mathematics teaching. *Teaching and Change, 7*, 327–346.

Martin-Dunlop, C. (2006). Science learning environments and action research. *Science Scope, 30*(1), 44–47.

Oliver, M. (2011). Teaching and learning evolution: Testing the principles of a constructivist approach through action research. *Teaching Science, 57*(1), 13–18.

Otto, C. A., Luera, G. R., & Everett, S. A. (2009). An innovative course featuring action research integrated with unifying science themes. *Journal of Science Teacher Education, 20*(6), 537–552. doi:10.1007/s10972-009-9146-7

Zaikowski, L., & Lichtman, P. (2007). Environmental research puts science into action. *The Science Teacher, 74*(4), 47–51.

Zollman, A. (2009). Students use graphic organizers to improve mathematical problem-solving communications. *Middle School Journal, 41*(2), 4–12.

STUDIES ON MEDIA CENTER ISSUES

Dickinson, G. K. (2005). How one child learns: The teacher-librarian as evidence-based practitioner. *Teacher Librarian, 33*(1), 16–20.

Howard, J. K., & Eckhardt, S. A. (2005). Why action research? The leadership role of the library media specialist. *Library Media Connection, 24*(2), 32–34.

Kearns, J. (2006). Living the hero's quest: Character building through action research. *School Library Journal, 52*(5), 168.

Martin, J., & Tallman, J. (2001). The teacher-librarian as action researcher. *Teacher Librarian, 29*, 8–10.

STUDIES ON ISSUES IN MIDDLE GRADES EDUCATION

Brough, J. A., & Irvin, J. L. (2001). Parental involvement supports academic improvement among middle schoolers. *Middle School Journal, 32*, 52–61.

Keiser, J. M., Klee, A., & Fitch, K. (2003). An assessment of students' understanding of angle. *Mathematics Teaching in the Middle School, 9*(2), 116–119.

McLaughlin, H. J., Watts, C., & Beard, M. (2000). Just because it's happening doesn't mean it's working: Using action research to improve practice in middle schools. *Phi Delta Kappan, 82*, 284–290.

Niday, D., & Campbell, M. (2000). You've got mail: "Near-peer" relationships in the middle. *Voices from the Middle, 7*(3), 55–61.

Peterson, S. S., Rochwerger, L., Rigman, J., & Wood, K. (2006). Cross-curricular literacy: Writing for learning in a science program. *Voices from the Middle, 14*(2), 31–37.

Schwartz, T. A. (2004). Writing and neighborhood voices: "It depends on where you grow up at." *Voices from the Middle, 12*(1), 16–22.

STUDIES IN MUSIC AND ART EDUCATION

Adderley, C., Kennedy, M., & Berz, W. (2003). "A home away from home": The world of the high school music classroom. *Journal of Research in Music Education, 51*(3), 190–205.

Cain, T. (2008). The characteristics of action research in music education. *British Journal of Music Education, 25*(3), 283–313. doi:10.1017/S0265051708008115

Conway, C. M., & Borst, J. (2001). Action research in music education. *Update: Applications of Research in Music Education, 19,* 3–8.

Gamwell, P. (2005). Intermediate students' experiences with an arts-based unit: An action research. *Canadian Journal of Education, 28*(3), 359–383.

Heid, K. (2007). Seeing feelings through shared art making. *Kappa Delta Pi Record, 43*(3), 110–116.

Hutzel, K. (2007). Reconstructing a community, reclaiming a playground: A participatory action research study. *Studies in Art Education, 48*(3), 299–315.

McKay, S. W. (2006). Living the questions: Technology-infused action research in art education. *Art Education, 59*(6), 47–51.

Miller, B. A. (1999). Learning through composition in the elementary music classroom. *Bulletin of the Council for Research in Music Education, 142,* 87–88.

Pitri, E. (2006). Teacher research in the socioconstructivist art classroom. *Art Education, 59*(5), 40–45.

STUDIES IN PHYSICAL EDUCATION

Barker-Ruchti, N. (2002). A study journey: A useful example of action research. *Journal of Physical Education New Zealand, 35,* 12–24.

Barney, D., & Strand, B. (2006). Appropriate practices in elementary physical education: Create a foundation for physical education majors. *Teaching Elementary Physical Education, 17*(5), 20–23.

Couturier, L. E., Chepko, S., & Coughlin, M. A. (2005). Student voices—What middle and high school students have to say about physical education. *Physical Educator, 62*(4), 170–177.

Ovens, A. (2004). Using peer coaching and action research to structure the practicum: An analysis of student teacher perceptions. *Journal of Physical Education New Zealand, 37*(1), 45–60.

Perry, C. (2004). Getting beyond technical rationality in developing health behavior programs with youth. *American Journal of Health Behavior, 28*(6), 558–568.

Vecchiarelli, S., Prelip, M., Slusser, W., Weightman, H., & Neumann, C. (2005). Using participatory action research to develop a school-based environmental intervention to support healthy eating and physical activity. *American Journal of Health Education, 36*(1), 35–42.

ARTICLES ON ISSUES IN SCHOOL COUNSELING

Bundy, P. (2006). Using drama in the counseling process: The "Moving On" project. *Research in Drama Education, 11*(1), 7–18.

Guiffrida, D. A., Douthit, K. Z., Lynch, M. F., & Mackie, K. L. (2011). Publishing action research in counseling journals. *Journal of Counseling and Development, 89*(3), 282–287.

Hunt, B., & Trusty, J. (2011). Special section: Counseling research and publishing in JCD. *Journal of Counseling and Development, 89*(3), 259–260.

Kidd, S., & Kral, M. (2005). Practicing participatory action research. *Journal of Counseling Psychology, 52*(2), 187–195.

Luck, L., & Webb, L. (2009). School counselor action research: A case example. *Professional School Counseling, 12*(6), 408–412.

Niles, S. (2003). Career counselors confront a critical crossroad: A vision of the future. *Career Development Quarterly, 52*(1), 70–77.

Rowell, L. (2005). Collaborative action research and school counselors. *Professional School Counseling, 9*(1), 28–36.

Rowell, L. (2006). Action research and school counseling: Closing the gap between research and practice. *Professional School Counseling, 9*(5), 376–384.

STUDIES ON USING ACTION RESEARCH FOR SCHOOL CHANGE AND IMPROVEMENT

Calhoun, E. (2002). Action research for school improvement. *Educational Leadership, 59*, 18–24.

Cardno, C. (2006). Leading change from within: Action research to strengthen curriculum leadership in a primary school. *School Leadership & Management, 26*(5), 453–471.

Crocco, M. S., Faithfull, B., & Schwartz, S. (2003). Inquiring minds want to know: Action research at a New York City professional development school. *Journal of Teacher Education, 54*, 19–30.

Diana, T. J. (2011). Becoming a teacher leader through action research. *Kappa Delta Pi Record, 47*(4), 170–173.

Glisan, E. (2010). Time for professional renewal and reflection. *Foreign Language Annals, 43*(2), 179–180.

Goodnough, K. (2008). Dealing with messiness and uncertainty in practitioner research: The nature of participatory action research. *Canadian Journal of Education, 31*(2), 431–457.

Gross, R. R. (2002). Research-driven school improvement. *Principal Leadership, 2*, 35–40.

Hahs-Vaughn, D., & Yanowitz, K. L. (2009). Who is conducting teacher research? *Journal of Educational Research, 102*(6), 415–424, 480.

Halbert, J., & Kaser, L. (2002). Inquiry, eh? School improvement through a network of inquiry. *Education Canada, 42*(2), 19.

Hayes, B., Hindle, S., & Withington, P. (2007). Strategies for developing positive behaviour management: Teacher behaviour outcomes and attitudes to the change process. *Educational Psychology in Practice, 23*(2), 161–175.

Loertscher, D. (2008). Schoolwide action research for professional learning communities: Improving student learning through the whole faculty. *Teacher Librarian, 36*(1), 49.

Maher, M., & Jacob, E. (2006). Peer computer conferencing to support teachers' reflection during action research. *Journal of Technology and Teacher Education, 14*(1), 127–150.

Price, J., & Valli, L. (2005). Preservice teachers becoming agents of change: Pedagogical implications for action research. *Journal of Teacher Education, 56*(1), 57–72.

Rust, F., & Meyers, E. (2006). The bright side of the moon: Teacher research in the context of educational reform and policy-making. *Teachers and Teaching: Theory and Practice, 12*(1), 69–86.

Sappington, N., Baker, P. J., Gardner, D., & Pacha, J. (2010). A signature pedagogy for leadership education: Preparing principals through participatory action research. *Planning and Changing, 41*(3), 249–273.

Senese, J. C. (2002). Energize with action research. *Journal of Staff Development, 23*, 39–41.

St. John, E., McKinney, J., & Tuttle, T. (2006). Using action inquiry to address critical challenges. *New Directions for Institutional Research, 130*, 63–76.

Varga, A., Koszo, M., Mayer, M., & Sleurs, W. (2007). Developing teacher competences for education for sustainable development through reflection: The environment and school initiatives approach. *Journal of Education for Teaching: International Research and Pedagogy, 33*(2), 241–256.

Warrican, S. (2006). Action research: A viable option for effecting change. *Journal of Curriculum Studies, 38*(1), 1–14.

JOURNALS THAT PUBLISH ACTION RESEARCH

Journal of Research in Childhood Education
www.tandfonline.com/toc/ujrc20/current

Educational Studies in Mathematics
www.springerlink.com/content/102875

English Journal
www.ncte.org/journals/ej

Journal of Physical Education, Recreation & Dance
www.aahperd.org/publications/journals/joperd/

Journal of Research in Science Teaching
onlinelibrary.wiley.com/journal/10.1002/%28I
SSN%291098-2736

*Journal of Research on Technology in
Education*
www.iste.org/learn/publications/journals/jrte.aspx

Journal of Teacher Education
http://jte.sagepub.com

Learning & Leading with Technology
www.iste.org/learn/publications/learning-and-
leading.aspx

Mathematics Teaching in the Middle School
www.nctm.org/publications/mtms.aspx

Professional School Counseling Journal
www.schoolcounselor.org/content.asp?
contentid=235

Studying Teacher Education
www.tandf.co.uk/journals/titles/17425964.asp

Teacher Education Quarterly
www.teqjournal.org

Teacher Librarian
www.teacherlibrarian.com

Teaching Children Mathematics
www.nctm.org/publications/tcm.aspx

Teaching Exceptional Children
http://journals.cec.sped.org/tec/

The Quarterly (National Writing Project)
www.nwp.org/cs/public/print/doc/resources/
quarterly_archives.csp

The Reading Teacher
www.reading.org/General/Publications/Journals/
RT.aspx

Young Children
www.naeyc.org/yc/

Journal Issues on Action Research

Educational Leadership, 59(6) (2002)
www.ascd.org/publications/educational-leader
ship/mar02/vol59/num06/toc.aspx

English Education, 32(2) (2000)
www.ncte.org/journals/ee/issues/v32-2

Language Arts, 77(1) (1999)
www.ncte.org/journals/la/issues/v77-1

*Teachers and Teaching: Theory and
Practice, 12(1) (2006)*
www.tandfonline.com/toc/ctat20/12/1

2

Generating Research Ideas Through Reflection

Chapter Goals

- Explain the ways reflection can be used to generate ideas for action research.
- Describe the history and definitions of reflection in educational practice.
- Define the processes of reflective and reflexive inquiry and how

they can be used throughout the action research cycle.

- Provide reflection activities that reveal ways to align action research studies with personal goals and values.

The goals, benefits, and reflect–act–evaluate process of action research were presented in Chapter 1. This chapter focuses on reflection, as both an initial step and an ongoing process of action research. In this chapter, the history of reflection in education is described, reflective and reflexive inquiry strategies are defined, and the act of reflection—at the beginning and throughout the process of action research—is discussed. Presented first are three examples of the reflective process that demonstrate how educators use reflection to generate ideas for action research studies.

In the three reflection examples, the educators reflect on their practice as they consider their values and goals and focus on desired outcomes.

Reflections such as those presented in the examples are a starting point for generating research ideas. For example, Danetta's reflection leads to the study of the ways in which educational disparity based on race can be examined and rectified. Jack's reflection can direct him to study methods that can help students connect with literature. Susan's reflection targets how to build a sense of community among teachers at her school.

Reflection Example 1

Danetta, an elementary school guidance counselor, considers how to best serve a small group of students with recurring behavior problems. She reviews the students' files and then observes them in and out of class both formally and informally over several weeks, which leads her to question whether these students, who are all Hispanic, are being disciplined differently than the African American students who make up a large majority of the student body.

Reflection Example 2

Jack, a middle school reading teacher, becomes frustrated with his students' apathy toward reading. As a child, Jack had little opportunity to read outside of school and was, in fact, a slow reader throughout elementary school. In sixth grade, his teacher, Ms. Gonzales, sparked his interest in reading, first by working with him every day after school on his reading skills, and then by supplying him with books such as *I Am the Cheese* and *The Chocolate War* by Robert Cormier. From sixth grade through high school, Jack devoured books, which helped him succeed in school and earn a scholarship to college. The first college graduate in his family, Jack attributes his success to reading. In college, he decided to become a middle school language arts teacher so that he, like Ms. Gonzales, could help students develop a love of reading. Now in his second year of teaching, Jack questions his ability to foster a love of reading in his students. In his first year of teaching, he existed strictly on survival mode, making sure he covered the required material and kept his kids in line. Now, more confident in his classroom management skills but disillusioned by a mandated curriculum that focuses on the mechanics of language arts rather than on reading and writing, Jack wants to find a way to cover the required material, get his kids excited about reading and writing, and open their worlds through literature.

Reflection Example 3

Susan, a fourth-year high school principal in a small rural school, is concerned with the lack of community she senses in the educators at her school. In the last few years, many teachers have retired and their jobs have been filled with young teachers just out of college. The result is a teaching pool that is made up of about half who are older, experienced teachers and half who are younger teachers just a few years older than the senior class. Although Susan had hoped that the more experienced teachers would step in to mentor the new teachers, this has not happened. In actuality, the experienced teachers tend to eat lunch together, talk with each other between classes, and sit together at faculty meetings, whereas the younger teachers socialize after school hours but stay in their classrooms working independently during school hours. Susan plans to create a professional learning community, using *Critical Friends Groups*, and requires all teachers to participate.

THE HISTORY OF REFLECTION IN EDUCATION

Most educators have been exposed to the idea of reflection, perhaps even so much so that the term elicits little personal meaning. The term *reflective practitioner* is extensively used in education literature. Zeichner and Liu (2010) explain that during the 1980s reflection became a popular trend in teacher preparation, though the authors stress that it became little more than a "slogan . . . to frame and justify what [teacher educators] were doing in their programs" (pp. 68–69). Although the idea of reflection is pervasive in education, there remains some debate about what it is and what purpose it serves. Bullough and Gitlin (2001) suggest that too often the push for teachers to become reflective practitioners who study their practice results in ". . . only empty slogans [that] boil down to nothing more than a plea to 'think hard' about what they are doing and why they are doing it" (p. 13). Reflection involves more than simply thinking about practice, though, and in order to understand the process of reflection and its role in action research, it is important to consider the history of reflection in education.

John Dewey described the act of reflection in *How We Think* (1910, 1933). Dewey (1933) explained that reflective thinking is a process directed at seeking a conclusion through inquiry. This definition of reflection goes beyond the notion that reflection is merely thinking about a problem. Instead, thinking about a problem is a first step of reflection. Norlander-Case and colleagues (1999) stress the problem-solving nature of Dewey's definition of reflection, asserting that for Dewey true reflection could occur only when an individual is confronted with a problem, recognizes it, and then attempts to resolve the problem rationally.

In her synthesis of research on reflective inquiry, Lyons (2010) explains that although Dewey is considered the "master theorist of reflective thinking" (p. 14), few educators embraced the concept until Donald Schön's *The Reflective Practitioner: How Professionals Think in Action* was published in 1983. Schön's early work was based on his studies of reflective practices of individuals in fields other than education. Later, he expanded his work to include the reflective practices of teachers, and in this work, Schön proposed that teachers learn in large part as they reflect on their everyday practices (Sparks-Langer & Colton, 1991). The impact of Schön's writings on reflection was huge. As Lyons explains, "Schön's work launched unprecedented interest in reflective practice, revised curiosity about the earlier work of John Dewey on reflective inquiry, and erupted a widespread experimentation with reflection for many professional practitioners—that continues today" (p. 14).

Following Schön, the writings of Paulo Freire, an educator from Brazil whose work teaching the poor to read and write resulted in banishment from his country, have been brought into the dialogue on reflection. A central idea in Freire's *Pedagogy of the Oppressed* (1970, 1997) is that "a neutral, uncommitted, and apolitical education practice does not exist" (Freire, 1997, p. 39). Flores-Kastanis, Montoya-Vargas, and Suárez (2009) explain that Freire's work called for authentic participation of educators in a reflective, inquiry-based process. It was only through reflection that educators could engage in the kind of critical work that would lead to liberation and freedom from oppression. Although this kind of critical stance may seem outside the realm of teachers' practices, dynamics of power—such as top-down accountability mandates or lack of equal access to quality education—are always at work in the lives of educators.

In synthesizing the history of reflective practice in education, Lyons (2010) suggests that Dewey viewed reflective inquiry as thinking, Schön saw it as a way of knowing, and Freire defined it as a type of critical consciousness. The common element is that of *action*, that is, the actions one takes to understand his or her practice, to improve it, or to advocate for social justice. Another way to consider reflection is as a habit of mind—through reflection, educators think about and make sense of their practice and how to improve it, they connect this thinking and knowing to an ethical stance that focuses on what they believe and value, and they take action in the direction of those values.

REFLECTION IN ACTION RESEARCH

As explained in Chapter 1, action research is an ethical inquiry that allows educators to reflect on their educational values and the ways in which their teaching can reflect those values (Elliot, 2009). Thus the process of action research is, in and of itself, a process of reflection. When educators reflect as part of the action research cycle, they have the opportunity to develop new knowledge about teaching and contribute to the knowledge base on best practices (Zeichner & Liu, 2010). The reflective inquiry that is at the heart of action research can professionalize the work of educators by encouraging them to collaborate, by giving a voice to those who engage in the practice, and by providing educators with opportunities to examine the professional purposes and possibilities of their work (Lyons, 2010).

In describing the power of reflection, Bolton (2010) states that the process "challenges assumptions, ideological illusions, damaging social and cultural biases, inequalities, and personal behaviors" (p. 3) that may marginalize others. In examining these areas, practitioners, Bolton explains, can engage in inquiry about what they believe and value, what they know and don't know, and what they value and what they actually do. Reflecting on values and actions can be difficult, particularly when discrepancies are revealed. It is important to understand that engaging in deep reflection can reveal your hidden assumptions and biases, as well as disconnections between what you say you value (your espoused values) and what you actually do (your enacted values).

Consider the reflection examples at the beginning of this chapter. Danetta, in reflecting about possible differences in the way Hispanic students are disciplined at her school, will need to examine her own biases and assumptions related to race as well as what she may believe about her colleagues. Although this can be an uncomfortable prospect, examining values, biases, and hidden assumptions is needed for responsible, ethical practice (Bolton, 2010). Considering what you say you believe in light of the decisions you make is an important part of the reflective process in action research. If Danetta says she believes her colleagues want to make fair discipline decisions about Hispanic students but realizes she is putting practices in place that might publicly bring to light their biases, she will need to consider the possibility that the actions she takes may reveal her hidden assumptions and her true intentions. She might ask herself *What's most important—equity for the students or revealing my colleagues' biases? Do I simply desire to uncover the poor practices of my colleagues, or do I really want to help students?* Asking questions such as these can help a practitioner choose actions that align with his or her values.

Hidden assumptions and biases do not exist only in action research studies that are clearly about social justice or equity. Jack (Reflection Example 2) and Susan (Example 3) will both need to engage in reflection to consider their beliefs, assumptions, and intentions. As Rossman and Rallis (2012) suggest, educators can ask themselves what they feel and believe about the topics they wish to study, whether they feel passionately about them (or some aspect of them), and if they are open to solutions or possibilities, they have not yet considered. If Jack pursues his study without examining the underlying assumptions of his research goal (which, for example, could be a passion about making kids lifelong lovers of reading), he could pursue a course of action that takes him away from what may be in the best interest of his students. Jack will need to consider what he knows about his students, what is in *their* best interest, and whether making all children as passionate as he is about reading should be the goal of his study. He may also need to examine how much his resistance to the mandated curriculum is affecting his study goals. Susan may need to examine whether what she envisions as an effective school community (a Critical Friends Group or CFG) is a vision shared by her teachers. If teachers simply enact her vision and engage in the CFG because Susan expects it, is Susan really creating the kind of open, professional community she wants among her colleagues?

One way to examine assumptions and values is through **reflexive inquiry**. Rossman and Rallis (2012) define reflexivity as "a bending back" (p. 47) that requires introspection and a consideration of the ways in which

---

reflexive inquiry: Considering past experiences and actions in order to understand how they impact present and future actions and thoughts.

your history and experiences affect what you think, believe, and value. Cole and Knowles (2009) explain that through reflexive inquiry, educators connect their personal lives with their professional careers. In describing differences between reflective and reflexive processes, Cole and Knowles state:

> Reflective inquiry is an ongoing process of examining and refining practice, variously focused on the personal, pedagogical, curricular, intellectual, societal, and/or ethical contexts of professional work. . . . Reflexive inquiry . . . is reflective inquiry situated within the context of personal histories in order to . . . understand personal (including early) influences on professional practice. (p. 2)

Based on this definition, reflexive practice can provide educators with a framework for knowing where they have come from in order to understand where they are going and the decisions they make as educators. Reflexive inquiry places present thoughts and actions in the context of past thoughts, actions, and history. Placing reflexive inquiry in the context of the pressures teachers face—due to the accountability and standards movements, for example—Bullough and Gitlin (2001) suggest that when teachers understand themselves and the contexts in which they teach, they are better able to answer the question, "Can I be who I am in the classroom?" (p. 44).

Answering this question helps educators align their core values with the actions they take. As McNiff and Whitehead (2006) explain, "The basis for many practitioners' research is that they are trying to live in the direction of their educational values" (p. 19). And, in fact, the reflective and reflexive inquiry that are part of conducting action research often leads to moments of insight that help educators determine when they are not acting according to their values. For example, if Susan, the principal described in Reflection Example 3, truly values creating a sense of community among the teachers at her school, through reflective and reflexive inquiry she may determine that mandating all teachers participate in a Critical Friends Group would remove teachers' voices from the conversation about how best to create their own community.

In Activity 2.1, questions and prompts are presented to stimulate thoughtful consideration of the ways in which your history and experiences have influenced you as an educator. These experiences, which you will examine through reflexive inquiry, have shaped and defined what your educational core values are. Understanding connections between experiences and values can help uncover assumptions, biases, and differences between what you say you value (your espoused values) and what you actually do (your enacted values)—a good first step before engaging in action research.

When reflecting in action research, there are several considerations to be made. First, reflection must be tied to action, which requires going

ACTIVITY 2.1

Engaging in Reflexive Inquiry as a Way to Know Yourself as an Educator

This activity focuses on one main question: "What are your core values as an educator?" Engage in reflexive inquiry and then describe the experiences you have had as a student and educator that have shaped your core values.

To stimulate your thinking, consider these prompts:

- What were your best and worst experiences as a student (at any level)?
- What were your best and worst experiences as an educator?
- What were your family's values/beliefs about education?
- Before you took your first job in education, what were your professional hopes, dreams, or aspirations? What did you think it would be like to be an educator?
- What type of educator do you/did you want to be?
- Which of your professional goals have you reached? Which goals are still ahead of you?
- What is your personal vision as an educator?
- In terms of your life as an educator, what do you want to be remembered for?

You may choose to work with a partner or group to discuss what your reflexive inquiry has revealed and what has shaped your core values as an educator.

beyond merely thinking about experience. Action that follows experience is a key element in reflection. Thus for a principal to be truly reflective, she must go beyond thinking about the problem of teacher attrition in her school; she must consider actions that will help her understand and deal with the attrition problem. Second, reflection is a meaningful and important part of a practitioner's professional development. Reflection allows the educator to consider issues and problems relevant to his or her own practice and then act in ways to study or resolve those issues, guiding his or her own development as a professional educator. Third, self-understanding is an important part of the reflective process because it allows an educator to focus on the ways in which experiences and values affect actions.

The process of action research begins with systematic, critical reflection. Reflection helps identify a problem to investigate, and, by considering biases, assumptions, and values through reflexive inquiry, practitioners can attempt to align values and actions in their research studies. It is important to note, however, that reflection does not end once a research problem is identified. Reflection is the first step in choosing an area to study, but reflection is also an ongoing activity engaged in throughout the study.

REFLECTING TO IDENTIFY A RESEARCH FOCUS

As you begin reflecting on your practice and the issues you face as an educator to identify an area for your action research study, remember to frame your reflections in terms of the *actions* that you can take to proactively study the issue and the *outcomes* you would like to occur. When educators are first beginning reflective activities, they sometimes focus on big issues such as "Is there a difference in the way we treat Hispanic and African American students with discipline problems?" "Why don't students like to read?" and "Why does our school lack a sense of community among teachers?" The problem with focusing on big issues is that they are not outcome and action oriented. That's not to say the issues listed cannot be studied at all. In fact, each of the previous questions, which are broad topics based on Danetta's, Jack's, and Susan's reflection examples from the beginning of the chapter, can easily be focused into a good action research study:

- Danetta asked teachers in her school to make observations to determine whether Hispanic and African American students were being disciplined differently. If observations do indicate a disparity, action can be taken: Teachers can collaborate to determine how to enforce consistent discipline procedures. Once a method is established, action is taken, and the teachers can evaluate the effectiveness of the action. The desired outcome is equitable treatment of all students in the school.
- Jack has identified the outcomes he desires: to cover required material, to get kids excited about reading and writing, and to open students' worlds through literature. In order to determine whether those outcomes can be met, he must seek actions that he can undertake (e.g., starting a Reader's and Writer's Workshop in his class).
- In her reflection example, Susan has identified a desired outcome (building a sense of community among teachers) and actions to take to reach that outcome (having teachers engage in Critical Friends Groups). As she engaged in reflexive inquiry, she decided mandating CFGs wasn't the solution she was looking for, so she decided to bring teachers together to discuss their perceptions of the current sense of community among teachers, what their needs are in terms of building a sense of community, and their ideas for changing the community.

In these examples, broad, general research questions have been narrowed to focus on specific actions and outcomes. As you begin thinking about a topic to study, remember to concentrate your reflections in an area or areas where you can make a change (action-focused) and then examine the effects of this change (outcome-focused).

Provided here is an example of a middle school principal's reflection of a problem he has faced as an administrator. Roy offers a well-articulated reflection, focusing on a specific issue that is important to him, the actions he is considering taking to study this issue, and the outcomes he hopes to see. Notice, too, elements of Roy's story—autobiographical information that includes his history, beliefs, and values—that show the reflexive nature of his thinking.

As a new administrator several years back, I was amazed at the lack of good teaching skills I observed in some teachers. These were experienced teachers who had a difficult time with class-room management, time on task, communication with parents, and content knowledge in their subject areas. As a teacher, I had assumed that all teachers were experts at what they did. As I have matured as an administrator and an educator, I recognized that I made judgments about the skills of teachers based upon my own experience as a teacher. As I further reflected on this prob-lem, I realized that many teachers never go to graduate school. Many teachers are satisfied with having an undergraduate teach-ing degree and have no desire to further their education. While I realize that the decision to further one's education is a personal one, I am concerned about the benefits lost when teachers do not seek to further their knowledge.

As a principal, I want to raise the standard of teacher knowl-edge at my school. My problem is how to raise the standard. This is important to me because in this age of accountability, I am the one held accountable for the results of my school. But even more important to me is the issue of my personal accountabil-ity. I am an educator because it is my calling. I do this because I want to help children. I am committed to providing the students with whom I am charged a quality education. In order to provide this quality education for students, we must have quality teachers. Teachers must further their education either formally or informally to provide students with quality.

My area of focus is to research the use of teacher study groups at my school. In the study groups, teachers will read lit-erature on topics related to the development of good teaching practices and strategies. The study groups will meet to discuss this literature, much in the same way that individuals discuss books in book clubs. The prospect of creating study groups creates its own set of problems. When will teachers have the time to participate in groups? Who will set up the groups? What topics will teachers study? Where will the resources be found for teachers to use in the study groups? What will be the impact on students as a result of teachers participating in study groups? The study group concept and these related questions will be the focus of my school-based action research study.

As you engage in reflection to determine a research focus, consider your personal history, beliefs, assumptions, and values as well as those perplexing, intriguing, and difficult issues that you face daily as an educator. As research topics are identified, continue to engage in reflective and reflexive inquiry to clarify your understanding and beliefs about the topic, actions that might be taken, and outcomes that are desired.

Figure 2.1 includes notes I jotted after engaging in a passionate debate with doctoral students about scripted reading instruction, an instructional

March 10. I had an interesting conversation with several doctoral students tonight about scripted instruction. During our conversation, I became aware that several of the students, who are teachers and administrators, think there is a lot of value in scripted instruction, especially in schools with low achievement. As I think about this now, I realize my argument to them (that scripted instruction is counter to treating teachers as professionals) may have fallen on deaf ears. I am passionate about empowering teachers, but I'm not in the trenches facing an accountability movement.

March 17. We had another discussion on scripted instruction today, but in the last week, as I considered that I, too, used scripted instruction years ago as a special education teacher, I have really had to try to come to terms with two competing values: First, in my experience, scripted instruction works. But forcing teachers to use scripted instruction takes away their autonomy and may prevent them from engaging in the teaching activities they think are most effective. I guess as we continued the conversation tonight, we were in fact engaged in a sort of collaborative reflection. Each person shared his/her perspective on the issue, though I felt like a real outsider. There was consensus among the teachers and the administrators that scripted instruction does increase test scores and does help the majority of new teachers who struggle in teaching reading when left to their own devices. When I brought up the issue of teacher autonomy, I was the only person in the conversation passionate about it. Everyone else agreed autonomy is important, but they felt student achievement is more important. This took us to another conversation on the preparation of teachers and their ability to take control of studying their effectiveness. We had no resolution, but I definitely have a better understanding of the reasons schools are embracing scripted instruction. I think, too, the others may be thinking about how scripted instruction takes away teaching autonomy. I don't think values have changed but for my part I have to admit that my values get messy in light of the realities educators face. There are issues here of social justice, which I hadn't considered before—the right of students to learn to read and the right of teachers to be treated as professionals. I can't help feeling that social justice is where my argument is based, even though I have to keep in mind that my own history includes teaching with scripted instruction, and teaching very successfully. My core value as an educator is that I do whatever it takes to help students succeed. In my past, I used scripted instruction to do that. Now that my work focuses on facilitating educators' study of their practice through action research—and now that I have seen how incredibly powerful it is for empowering teachers—I must try to find a way to reconcile—or at least hold on to—these two competing values.

FIGURE 2.1 Reflective notes from scripted instruction conversation.

method used widely in public elementary schools in Georgia that involves teachers following completely scripted lesson plans to teach reading. This example shows the ways I have reflected on my own practice and on my work with educators. As I engage in reflection, I find that I often reflect inwardly and reflexively, considering first my educational values and beliefs. As I continue to reflect, which takes place over the course of several days, I tend to think about ways my experiences as a teacher, and often even as a student, may be influencing the directions I choose to follow.

The reflection displayed in Figure 2.1 illustrates the reflective notes I made after several conversations with graduate students engaged in their own action research studies. As I reviewed these notes, I began planning my own study to determine how best to facilitate educators' alignment of values and actions. This led to a yearlong action research study with doctoral students. As they planned and carried out their action research projects, I investigated my practice in facilitating and directing their studies. I focused on having them in engage in ongoing reflective and reflexive inquiry about educational core values and the alignment of those values with the purposes of their studies and the actions taken in those studies.

REFLECTIVE JOURNALS

One tool I often use when reflecting is a journal. Other methods are useful as well, including having conversations with others (engaging in collaborative reflection) and recording those conversations. A reflective journal is a place to store information that comes from private, internal thoughts and from conversations with others. In recording reflections and actions, educators are able, as Stevens and Cooper (2009) explain, to clarify their thoughts, reflect critically, develop their professional identity, and examine deeply held assumptions. Cole and Knowles (2009) refer to journaling as a way to "pause, reflect, reenergize" (p. 49), which they view as a necessary activity in the sometimes frenetic world of teaching.

One way to begin the action research process is to start a journal. A journal can be kept in a looseleaf notebook, a diary, a composition book, or as an electronic journal on a computer. Journal writing can be used at the beginning of a study as a research focus is identified. In addition, writing in a journal throughout an action research study is a good way to record observations, ideas, challenges, successes, and failures and it provides a way to keep track of the reflective and reflexive inquiry processes an educator engages in as values, assumptions, goals, and actions are continuously examined. Several suggested journaling techniques are offered for consideration here:

- Write information as soon as you can. It isn't always possible to stop what you are doing and write in your journal, but as soon as you get a break, write a few notes to help jog your memory later when you have more time to think, reflect, and write.
- Hobson (2001) suggests jotting quick notes on lesson plans, sticky notes, or in a notebook. Even writing a word or two can help you remember important occurrences, thoughts, or concerns.
- Set aside time each day to review the notes you have jotted down that day. As you review the notes, expand them in detail in your journal.
- Utilize prompts to jumpstart your writing. These questions by McNiff and Whitehead (2006) may be useful: "What is my concern? Why am I concerned? What experiences can I describe to show why I am concerned? What can I do about it? What will I do about it?" (p. 9). Additional prompts are provided in Activity 2.2.
- Remember that context is critical in action research. Include contextual information in your journal entries. For example, don't just write, "Several teachers approached me angrily about the new attendance policy for the school." Instead, provide context information such as, *The teachers who were angry seem to frequently come to my office with complaints about my management as principal of this school. In an incident last week and in today's incident, I get the feeling that these teachers are quick to react to management that they feel is "top down." Mrs. J., who is typically the leader in these confrontations, stated today, "We are tired of being micromanaged with these policies that we have no voice in making." However, teachers have had a say during faculty meetings about creating and enforcing school policies. Mrs. J., though, has missed three of the last five meetings.* One method for journaling this way is to use a double-entry journal (Harris, Bruster, Peterson, & Shutt, 2010). In a double-entry journal, use two columns—one labeled *Observations* (what happened) and the other labeled *Reactions* (how you feel about what happened, how you might explain it, questions that remain, etc.).
- Include in your journal entries actions you might consider taking and outcomes you wish to occur. The principal in the previous example could include *actions* and *outcomes* this way: *I need to better communicate with this group of teachers, especially Mrs. J. And perhaps I need to conference with Mrs. J., privately, explaining my management style and goals for this school and eliciting from her the management style she uses as a teacher, the management style she desires from a principal, and her goals for the school* [actions]. *I want this school to have a positive climate for teachers and students, and I want teachers to feel valued as decision makers* [outcomes].

- Review your journal as often as you can. Don't simply add to your journal without referring to events you have already recorded. Reviewing your journal occasionally will allow you to see themes and patterns that may be important. In order to see developmental patterns, make generalizations, and formulate hypotheses from reflections, Hobson (2001) suggests writing dates and times on each entry to keep track of chronology of events.
- When engaged in collaborative reflection with colleagues, digitally record or audiotape the discussion (with your colleagues' permission). This becomes a record of the group reflection, and if it is transcribed (put into printed form), the written record can be used to document the activity.
- Use technology in collaborative reflection activities. Online bulletin boards, chat room discussions, and communication via email and/or listservs provide a number of ways to encourage collaborative reflection among educators. Using technology provides all members of the community an opportunity to participate in the discussion, and written records can be generated from each of the sources listed here. A benefit of using technology in this way is that people who are reluctant to talk during face-to-face discussions are often much more comfortable contributing their ideas and opinions electronically.

REFLECTING WITH A CRITICAL FRIEND

Journals are a means for capturing reflective and reflexive inquiry; engaging in reflection with a critical friend can be a powerful way to stimulate those reflective and reflexive processes. The term *Critical Friends Group* (CFG) was introduced early in this chapter in Susan's reflection (Reflection Example 3). It is important to understand that the CFG *process* involves a learning community made up of educators who collaborate to improve their practices, a model of professional learning advocated by the National Reform Council (see www.nrsfharmony.org for more information). Although a CFG is a good place for groups of practitioners to engage in critical reflection, it is not necessary to be in a CFG to reap the benefits of working with a critical friend.

In their review of critical friends research, Baskerville and Goldblatt (2009) offer several definitions of the term, including Costa and Kallick's (1993) explanation that a critical friend is someone who can be trusted; who asks difficult, challenging questions; who offers alternative ways of looking at a problem; and who provides a constructive critique. They further state, "A critical friend takes the time to fully understand the context of the work presented and the outcomes that the person or group is working toward. The friend is an advocate of that work" (p. 50). Other critical friends elements described by Baskerville and Goldblatt include the friend as someone who understands the ways assumptions may affect or serve as justification for practice (Hill, 2002) and a critical friendship as one built on common values and trust (Swaffield, 2005). Finding a critical friend you trust, who is an advocate of the work you do, and who will ask provocative questions about your assumptions, values, and biases can greatly enhance your reflective and reflexive inquiry throughout the action research cycle.

Because reflective and reflexive inquiry are important parts of the entire action research cycle, throughout the remainder of this book, *Time to Reflect* activities are included to stimulate your thinking about how the actions you take and choices you make throughout each step of your action research study connect to your values and assumptions. When you see a *Time to Reflect* activity or set of questions, take time to engage in reflection, work with a critical friend through the activities, and document reflections in your journal.

The last part of this chapter is focused on using reflection to identify a research focus. The importance of critical reflection that focuses on actions and outcomes was described, and methods for documenting reflection, both at the beginning of and throughout the study, were presented. Activity 2.2 presents prompts that will help you identify a research focus through reflecting on practice.

ACTIVITY 2.2
Reflecting to Identify a Research Focus

Choose a way to document your reflections. Journaling provides a written record of reflection and is perhaps the simplest method of documenting reflection. Other methods involve documenting reflections by audio or video recording them. If you choose either of these methods, it may be necessary to add written documentation transcribed from the recordings. Once you have chosen a method to document your reflections (written, electronic, recorded journal), respond to the following prompts:

1. There are a number of potential action research studies that could be conducted on your practice, and several broad topics are presented here:

student achievement	behavior/discipline	school climate
mentoring	teacher attrition	attendance
counseling programs	inclusion	team teaching
collaboration	needs of at-risk students	dropout prevention
motivation	extracurricular participation	media services
technology	professional development	parental involvement

Think about which of these topics are issues in your work as an educator. Provide a documented reflection on the two topics (either from this list or on other topics of your own choosing) that you are most interested in or about which you feel the most passionate.

(continued)

2. Add to your documented reflection the outcomes you desire regarding these two topics and the actions you might take in pursuit of those outcomes.

3. Choose one of the topics as your area of research focus. Expand your reflection by engaging in reflexive inquiry (refer to your responses from Activity 2.1). As part of your reflexive inquiry, think about these questions posed by Rossman and Rallis (2012):

   • What assumptions do you make about this topic?
   • What opinions do you have about this topic?
   • What preconceptions, prejudices, or biases do you bring to the study of this topic?
   • What assumptions do you have about those who will participate in your study (e.g., your students or colleagues)?

Group/collaborative/critical friend activity: Work with a critical friend or in a small group to discuss your potential areas of focus. Brainstorm potential areas of study based on the issues each group member is dealing with in his or her professional setting. Share assumptions about the topic as well as core values. Each person should describe ways in which values are (or are not) in alignment with the direction of the study and the actions that may be taken in the study. Within the group, use Taggart and Wilson's (2005) questioning strategies: (a) help each group member narrow the research focus, (b) discuss alternatives to potential actions, (c) define pertinent issues related to the focus, and (d) clarify beliefs and values.

Research paper activity: Use your documented reflection to write a brief introductory paragraph on your area of research focus. Write the reflection in first person. Include in the focus the desired outcome and the actions you are considering taking. Write a brief description of your educational role (teacher, principal, administrator) and your setting (grade level, subject area, etc.). Include relevant information about the reflective process(es) you used to identify the focus, and illustrate the ways these processes reflect your core educational values. Use a heading such as *Reflection* or *Research Focus* for this paragraph.

NOTE: The symbol ✍ is used in Activity 2.2 to indicate that this is a journal activity. Throughout the remainder of the text, when the symbol appears in a chapter activity, it signifies that journaling will be part of the activity. The symbol 🤝 indicates a group or collaborative activity. The symbol 📄 is used to alert you to the fact that the activity can be expanded to become part of a research paper. If you are writing a research paper for a course, presentation, or publication, or as a professional growth activity, follow the directions next to the research paper icon. This symbol will be used throughout the remaining chapters of the textbook.

Summary

The purpose of this chapter was to explain the ways in which reflective inquiry is used in the process of action research. The history of reflection in education was presented, and ways reflective and reflexive inquiry can be used in action research studies were described. In addition, methods were presented for documenting reflective inquiry. A goal of this chapter was to illustrate the power of reflective processes not only in the action research cycle but also in the everyday practices of educational practitioners. Now that an area of research focus has been identified, the next step is to learn more about it through reviewing related literature. Reviewing the literature, a process of connecting theory to practice, is the focus of Chapter 3.

Connecting Theory and Action

Reviewing the Literature

Chapter Goals

- Explain the professional, intellectual activity of reviewing literature in order to connect theory and action.
- Describe methods of searching for literature to review.
- Illustrate ways to choose, evaluate, and synthesize published research and to use it to inform practice.
- Suggest ways to organize and write the literature review.
- Provide writing activities that take practitioners through various steps of the literature review process.

The activities in Chapter 2 involved reflecting on practice to identify an area of research focus. With the topic (focus) identified, it is now time to learn more about it so that activities, interventions, or innovations (actions) can be planned that can help achieve the desired outcomes. Reviewing literature is important for a variety of reasons. First, reviewing literature on the topic under investigation provides an opportunity to learn what is already known about the topic. Second, in reviewing related literature one can learn about other researchers' (both practitioners' and university researchers') successes and failures using various interventions, which can help identify useful practices that can be incorporated into the study plan. It should be noted that the focus of this chapter is on writing a review of literature, which is a necessary part of writing an action research paper or a report. If the creation of a paper is not the goal of your study, you may wish to use the strategies in this chapter simply to locate and synthesize research findings so that the study you plan is connected to best practices found and described in the literature.

REVIEWING LITERATURE AS A PROFESSIONAL, INTELLECTUAL ACTIVITY

Reviewing the literature is an important step in conducting educational research regardless of whether quantitative, qualitative, or action research methodologies are employed. In quantitative research, a literature review must be conducted after research questions have been identified but before hypotheses have been generated. The reason for this is that hypotheses must be theory-driven, and theory is not known or completely understood until literature pertinent to that theory has been thoroughly studied. Because the goals of qualitative and action research are different from the goal of quantitative research, the purpose of literature review is also somewhat different. In qualitative research, which has as its goal understanding and theory building, reviewing the literature may occur at the beginning or end of the study as the researcher attempts to link what was learned in the qualitative investigation with what is known from the literature.

In educational action research, the literature review is completed before beginning the study but after initial research questions are identified, which helps in the planning and implementation of actions and interventions taken. A practitioner who spends time reading studies relevant to his or her own investigation is able to clarify the goals of the study and to discover new strategies that seem to have great potential in the investigation. Insight can be gained regarding ways to collect and evaluate data for the project. At the least, new information is learned that increases knowledge and understanding of the topic being studied. Becoming informed allows the practitioner to connect existing best practices to the actions he or she chooses to take. In addition, as Phillips and Carr (2010) explain, the literature review "is vital in grounding the assumptions, results, and conclusions of [the] research in the broader context of professional inquiry" (p. 52).

The study and review of published research to inform practice is an important and valued activity in many professions. Medical researchers, scientists, and other professionals familiarize themselves with knowledge in their fields before conducting research. Trial lawyers review case law before going to trial. Being well informed means these professionals are less likely to make mistakes in their studies (or trials), and they are more likely to engage in work that is important and valuable. Although often not seen as a valuable professional activity for educators, reviewing educational research is an important and necessary activity for practitioners' professional development. Consider the argument made by Fecho (1992), a secondary English teacher and action researcher, who explains that if teachers do not read educational theory and participate in ongoing classroom research, they diminish their potential to be seen as professionals and intellectuals. The point here is that teachers have a responsibility both to engage in reading educational research and to carry out research in their own classrooms, an idea supported by Calhoun (2002). Through the combination of these activities, theory and action are connected, and teachers create what Fecho calls a "distinctive interpretive community" of professionals with a collective voice that can be heard and can effect change (p. 266).

The National Board for Professional Teaching Standards (NBPTS) also clearly indicates that teachers should engage in research on their own practice, and they include the expectation that teachers study professional literature and base their practitioner studies on findings from research. For example, the Early Childhood/Generalist Standards state that

> [Accomplished early childhood teachers] may also conduct research in their classrooms or collaborate with other professionals to examine their practice critically...they may conduct systematic classroom-based inquiry to solve problems or answer questions related to their teaching practice. They select from theories, emerging practices, current debates, and promising research findings those that could improve their practice...They stay current with and evaluate professional and other literature and curricular materials along with the issues affecting families and schooling in their community. (NBPTS, 2001, p. 60)

The NBPTS standards for other subjects and grade levels include similar language, indicating the value of reviewing literature and learning from published research to inform educational practices.

So how exactly does reviewing the literature help a practitioner engaged in action research? To answer that question, consider this example: Jack, our middle school reading teacher from Chapter 2, wants to study the effectiveness of using reading clubs to increase students' engagement with literature. Reviewing literature about reading clubs can help Jack identify their potential benefits. Literature on reading clubs might also provide information about activities that make them successful and unsuccessful. If, for example, other studies have found that reading clubs with more than eight participants are difficult to manage, it would be sensible for Jack to plan for the club to have fewer than eight students or to create several clubs with eight or fewer members in each. Reviewing published research may also help in identifying ways to observe and measure student engagement.

TIME TO REFLECT

Review the reflection you wrote for Activity 2.1 as well as the assumptions, opinions, preconceptions, and biases you have about your research topic. Then, consider the following reflection questions (consider discussing them with a critical friend) and as you reflect, make notes in your journal:

- As an educator, do you value research conducted by those outside the classroom (such as university/academic researchers)? Do you value research conducted by your peers?
- How open are you to learning from practitioner and academic research?
- How might reviewing the literature challenge the assumptions you have about your topic as well as those you have about educational research?
- What will you do if the literature does challenge your current beliefs or expectations about your topic?
- How open are you to critically examine both what you believe about your topic and what you will learn about it as you review the literature?

SOURCES OF TOPIC-SPECIFIC LITERATURE

Various sources, such as books, journal articles, and conference papers, may be used as resources when reviewing literature. In some cases, educational books are especially useful in the process of reviewing the literature. For example, Jack, the teacher who is interested in starting a reading club, might find Harvey Daniels's (2002a) book *Literature Circles: Voice and Choice in Book Clubs and Reading Groups*; Day, Spiegel, McLellan, and Brown's (2002) book *Moving Forward with Literature Circles;* or Daniels and Steineke's (2004) book *Mini-Lessons for Literature Circles* to be good resources for learning how to structure an effective reading club. In addition, though, Jack would also want to read research related to the implementation of book clubs. Journal articles (and possibly papers presented at professional conferences) and action research studies on book clubs could be reviewed to determine what other researchers and educators have found in their studies about using book clubs in classrooms. Thus, whereas Daniels's book on literature circles would inform Jack about strategies for forming a reading club, journal articles and action research studies would inform him of others' results when they implemented reading clubs in their settings.

Sources of literature vary in terms of ways they are useful in the process of action research. Usefulness can depend greatly on the type of literature chosen to review. For example, in searching for literature on reading clubs, Jack is likely to find books on reading clubs as well as articles in the form of reviews of literature, opinion pieces, teaching suggestions, and research studies. These different types of literature vary in their usefulness for informing Jack's own study on reading clubs. Books that explain ways to set up reading clubs can be helpful, particularly if the book's author(s) have based their suggestions on extended experience with implementing reading clubs. Reviews of literature, which largely contain information about other researchers' findings on reading clubs, could also be helpful to Jack because literature reviews contain a number of references, and references of those studies that closely resemble what Jack hopes to accomplish can be located and reviewed. Finding a well-written, complete, recent literature review on reading clubs could save Jack a lot of time reviewing the literature because it would provide a review of (and a list of) much of the reading club literature.

Opinion pieces and teaching suggestions are generally less helpful when reviewing literature because they are typically written based on experience and anecdotes and contain little or no data to support the authors' contentions or suggestions. Research studies, however, can be helpful for informing educators' action research studies. Unlike opinion pieces and teaching suggestion articles, research studies—whether quantitative, qualitative, mixed, or action research—are based on the authors' actual structured studies of particular topics. Research studies include data to support results, and they can provide various forms of helpful information regarding ways to implement reading clubs, ways to measure outcomes, and ways to analyze sources of data. One note of caution, however: Some research studies, particularly quantitative studies that involve use of inferential statistics to analyze data, can be difficult to understand. One strategy I use when reviewing studies such as these is to read the article several times and make notes or highlight the basics: What was the research question or hypothesis? What was the intervention? What types of data were collected? What were the results? What conclusion did the author(s) make about the intervention? The most difficult part for me is sifting through the results, especially when complicated inferential statistical methods have been employed. However, even in a sea of numbers and statistical jargon, an author usually will clearly state the results. For example, you might run across results that look something like this:

> According to the first ANOVA test, end-of-year reading scores significantly differed for students across the three reading conditions ($F = 26.34$, $p < .05$). Mean scores were 87.23 (SD = 12.45) for the literature circle group, 81.54 (SD = 15.66) for the literacy center group, and 74.39 (SD = 26.88) for the traditional instruction group.

Although some of the information, such as use of analysis of variance (ANOVA) and inclusion of F-values and p-values, may be unclear, the other information provided is easier to understand. Three groups were compared—a group that learned via literature circles, one that learned in literacy centers, and one that received traditional instruction—and scores were highest for students in the literature circle group, followed by students in the literacy center group and those in the traditional group. There was about a 6-point difference between the two non-traditional instruction groups and about a 13-point difference between the literature circle and traditional groups.

Some published research studies may contain so much technical statistical information that they are not very useful for informing practitioner research. In working with practitioner researchers, the decision is often made to forgo review of extremely technical articles because understanding them requires the specialized knowledge and skills of individuals who have been trained in quantitative analysis. A good rule to use when determining whether to include a technical article is to ask the question, "Does this study contain the kind of information that can help inform my practice as an educator?" If the answer is yes, but you lack the prerequisite knowledge to understand the article without assistance, ask a person skilled in quantitative analysis (such as the school district assessment coordinator, a colleague who has taken statistics courses, or a university faculty member) to help you make sense of the article.

SEARCHING FOR LITERATURE TO REVIEW

There are a number of ways to find topic-related literature to review, and many resources are available online, which increases the availability of sources. It is *not* recommended, however, to find information by conducting a search using an Internet search engine. Searching this way may result in a number of websites that include information on the research topic, but the quality of the information is unknown. Also, much information found this way will not be the type of information that is useful when reviewing literature. One exception is *Google Scholar* (http://scholar.google.com/), a web search engine that indexes scholarly research. Though it rarely links to full-text articles (except for those that are freely accessible), it can be useful for finding sources that can then be accessed through a library or database.

A better way to search for articles on issues in educational research is to use a computerized database such as *ERIC*, *ProQuest*, and/or *EBSCOhost*. These three databases can be accessed from any computer with Internet access. However, accessing ProQuest and EBSCOhost through a university library will yield a greater number of free, full-text online articles because college and university libraries typically subscribe to a number of full-text journals. If you access an online database without going through a library, there is a greater chance you will have to pay to read and/or receive journal articles.

Another way to access journal articles is through journal websites. *Early Childhood Research and Practice* (http://www.ecrp.uiuc.edu/) is one journal that makes full-text articles available at its website. Table 3.1, which can be found at the end of this chapter, provides a list of educational journals that can be accessed via the web. While some of these journals make available all articles free to the public, others may provide only tables of contents, abstracts, or a limited number of free articles per issue.

Another way to find resources on a research topic is to check with the school or school system media specialist to determine which journals are available in the school media center. Media specialists in P–12 schools often subscribe to a number of journals for teachers' and administrators' use, and these journals can be reviewed for relevant articles. Although it is a bit more time-consuming than using a computer database, browsing through hard copy journals often can result in locating relevant articles that inform the educator's action research study. However, to save time, ERIC can be utilized to search for articles in the particular journals available in the media center. This process will be described in more detail in the next section of this chapter.

When using online databases, searches are conducted using keyword descriptors. Keywords or descriptors are terms related to the topic of interest. Jack, our example teacher, could start with the keyword *reading club* as he begins his database search. Searching using this term will result in a list of articles in which this keyword is found. Searching other databases is a similar process of looking for matches based on keywords or descriptors.

ERIC

The ERIC homepage can be accessed online at www.eric.ed.gov/. Instructions for using ERIC are available by clicking on the *Help* tab in the top right corner of the page. Figure 3.1 displays the ERIC homepage. You can begin a basic keyword search from the homepage by entering keyword descriptors of interest in the box that says *Search Term(s)*.

Entering the keyword descriptor *reading clubs* will search the database for all articles and papers that include the phrase. When I searched the database for *reading club*, 442 results were returned (see Figure 3.2). Results can be further narrowed by choosing options on the left menu (*Narrow Your Search*), which allows you to choose author, thesaurus descriptor, date of publication, audience the article was written for, source/journal where the article is published, education level of the study participants or subjects, and publication type (e.g., journal article, book, opinion paper). Figure 3.3 displays articles when results were narrowed to the education level *Middle Schools*. Narrowing the search to reading clubs at the middle school level resulted in 33 potential sources.

Clicking on the article title of the matching document opens a new screen that has more detailed information about the document, including an abstract and information on how to obtain the document. The EJ or ED number is called the ERIC accession number and is used to identify each document.

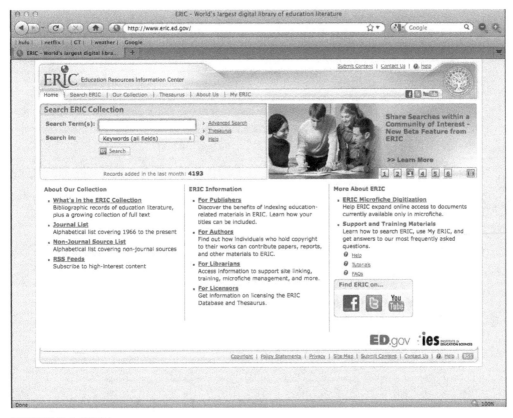

FIGURE 3.1 ERIC homepage.

Thus, each ERIC document has its own unique EJ or ED accession number. An accession number that begins with EJ is an ERIC journal article, which means it has appeared in a published journal. An accession number that begins with ED is an ERIC document, which means it could be a teaching guide, conference paper, opinion article, project description, or technical report. More often, research study articles will have EJ accession numbers. Although research studies sometimes have ED accession numbers, particularly those that are conference papers, be advised that a research article with an ED number has not necessarily been scrutinized through peer review, a method by which articles are evaluated by experts in the field before they are published.

Earlier it was mentioned that it is possible to use ERIC to search for articles in particular journals. This can be done by using the *Advanced Search* feature, which is available on the ERIC homepage under *Search ERIC*. After clicking on *Advanced Search,* enter keyword descriptors, place the name of the journal in one of the search term boxes, and change the search field to *Source Journal*. Figure 3.4 shows a search of the keyword descriptor *reading clubs* in the journal *The Reading Teacher*. This strategy can be helpful

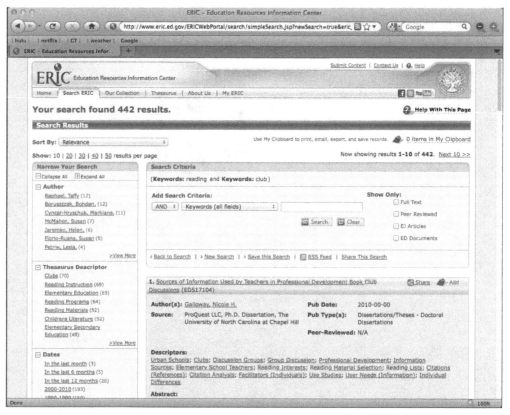

FIGURE 3.2 ERIC search results page.

for an educator who has access to certain journals either personally or through a school library or media center and wishes to determine whether any topic-specific articles are available in those journals. This strategy makes it unnecessary to conduct manual searches through stacks of journal issues.

ERIC searches can be expanded and narrowed by utilizing various search tools. As explained previously, results can be limited by adding additional search terms, limiting publication dates and publication types, and searching for articles in particular journals. ERIC searches can be expanded by using the online *Thesaurus* feature. Clicking on *Thesaurus* on the ERIC homepage provides access to the various terms related to keywords, which can expand a search by increasing related search terms. Detailed information on how to use the *Thesaurus* feature is included in the *Help* section on the ERIC homepage.

ProQuest

ProQuest is an online database that provides access to full-text journal articles. When ProQuest is used to search the ERIC database, many of the matches are available for immediate viewing as either an HTML file or a PDF file. Many

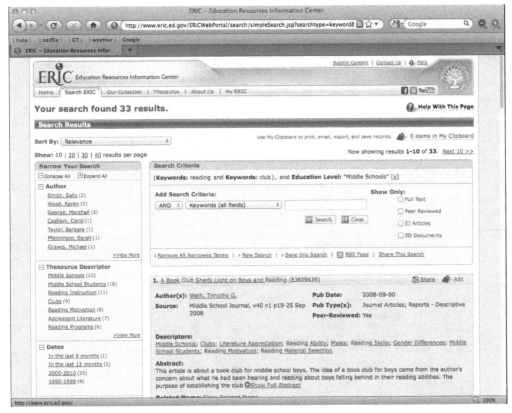

FIGURE 3.3 Limiting results in the ERIC database.

university libraries and some public libraries subscribe to ProQuest, and it is necessary to go through a library website to use the database. University students can typically access the ProQuest database from home by going through their university library's website. The process of searching ProQuest is similar to searching the ERIC database. Keyword descriptors are used, and various fields can be searched to find matching articles.

Next to each located article title are icons that indicate its available format. The summary icon ⊞ indicates that the abstract is available for the article. Thus, clicking on this icon will bring up a screen that contains only the abstract of the article. The page icon 📄 indicates that the text of the article is available in HTML format. Finally, the page image icon 🔲 indicates that the article is available in PDF format, which means that it can be read only using Adobe Acrobat Reader. This reader can be downloaded free from the Adobe website (www.adobe.com/Acrobat).

There are several ways to expand and limit searches using ProQuest. Just as in using the ERIC database, keyword descriptors can be added to limit matches or removed to expand matches. Limiting searches can also be accomplished by selecting certain fields to be searched (as described when

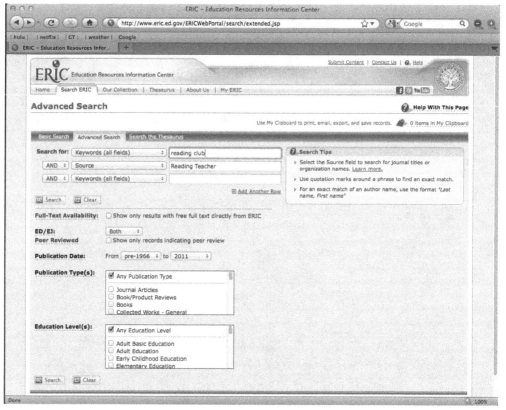

FIGURE 3.4 Searching ERIC for articles in particular journals.

searching the ERIC database), limiting searches to full-text-only documents, limiting searches to documents that were peer-reviewed (those that were reviewed and then recommended for publication by scholars from the author's field), and limiting searches to documents published during a certain year or range of years. ProQuest also allows narrowing of results by source type (e.g., scholarly journals, books), publication title, and subject (which allows for both including and excluding terms from the search). Clicking on the tab labeled *Help* will bring up a help screen that provides detailed information on ways to search for articles using the ProQuest database. ProQuest provides online tutorials for additional assistance as well as user guides available at www.proquest.com under the tab *Support & Training*.

EBSCOhost

The EBSCOhost database is similar to ProQuest in that the only way to access a full-text article through it is to access the database through a university or public library that subscribes to its services. EBSCOhost is different from ProQuest because full-text ERIC documents (rather than only ERIC journal articles) are available through EBSCOhost. Searching EBSCOhost is similar to searching using ProQuest. Keyword descriptors are entered to begin the search, and searches can be limited and expanded in the same way that ProQuest searches can be limited and expanded.

The benefit of using EBSCOhost is that many full-text ERIC documents that are not available through ProQuest are available through EBSCOhost. In addition, many full-text journal articles are also available through EBSCOhost in both HTML and PDF formats. Clicking on the document title will open up a summary screen that provides the abstract of the article as well as the full text of the article, if available. In addition, icons near the top of the screen can be clicked to change the viewing format (HTML or PDF) if different formats are available. Additional support for EBSCOhost, including video tutorials via *YouTube*, is available online at http://support.epnet.com/index.php.

Documents Not Available Full-Text

Searching only for articles that are available with full text can significantly limit the number of matches found, and it can result in missing relevant articles that could greatly enhance the quality and usefulness of the literature review for informing educational practices. Journal articles that are not available full-text may be available in hard copy form in a university or public library, where they can be copied at minimal cost. University students can also use their library's interlibrary loan system to order from other libraries journal articles (as well as books) that are not available in their local library. At most institutions, interlibrary loan is a free service, and often articles and books are delivered within a week of the request. Most interlibrary loan systems also use electronic delivery to speed up delivery time of articles, which means that articles can sometimes be delivered electronically in 48 hours. The point here is to make sure not to discount articles that aren't immediately accessible. Accessing full-text articles is quick and relatively simple, but limiting a literature review only to articles that can be accessed immediately is counter to what thoughtful practitioners do. Instead, search for those books and articles that are relevant, are of high quality, and seem best able to inform the educational practices that will be investigated.

CHOOSING, EVALUATING, AND SYNTHESIZING REVIEWED LITERATURE FOR ACTION RESEARCH STUDIES

The process of reviewing literature involves choosing relevant literature that can help to inform the action research study, evaluating the literature in terms of what it means and how information can be used, and synthesizing information so that major points or themes from the literature are used to guide the action research study. Reviewing literature is not a process of listing related articles or summarizing individual articles or books in separate paragraphs (which is actually an annotated bibliography). Instead, the process is one of finding themes in the literature that can be used to inform the action research study and organizing the themes in a logical, coherent way.

Choosing Literature

The previous section of this chapter provided guidelines for finding literature to review. However, after sources are located, the next step is to determine whether they are useful for guiding the action research study. The process of choosing literature takes time and patience. First, once sources are located, they should be skimmed quickly to determine whether they contain relevant information that can help serve as a link between the research problem described in the reflection and the actions that will be implemented and studied (refer to Activity 2.2 from the previous chapter). Consider Jack's research problem, which is to determine whether reading clubs can be used to increase students' engagement with literature. In his initial search for literature to review, he locates two books and eight articles, which are listed here.

Baer, A. L. (2003). I can, but I won't: A study of middle school reading engagement. *Ohio Reading Teacher, 36*(1), 27–36.

Daniels, H. (2002a). Resource for middle school book clubs. *Voices from the Middle, 10*(1), 48–49.

Daniels, H. (2002b). *Literature circles: Voice and choice in book clubs and reading groups.* Portland, ME: Stenhouse.

Daniels, H. (2003). How can you grade literature circles? *Voices from the Middle, 11*(1), 52–53.

Day, D., & Kroon, S. (2010). "Online literature circles rock!" Organizing online literature circles in a middle school classroom. *Middle School Journal, 42*(2), 18–28.

Drogowski, P. P. (2006). Between pages, personalities, and pizza: A middle school book club. *School Library Monthly, 23*(4), 32–34.

Kong, A., & Fitch, E. (2002). Using book club to engage culturally and linguistically diverse learners in reading, writing, and talking about books. *The Reading Teacher, 56*(4), 352–362.

Moeller, V. J., & Moeller, M. V. (2007). *Literature circles that engage middle and high school students.* Larchmont, NY: Eye on Education.

Seyfried, J. (2008). Reinventing the book club. *Knowledge Quest, 36*(3), 44–48.

Whittingham, J. L., & Huffman, S. (2009). The effects of book clubs on the reading attitudes of middle school students. *Reading Improvement, 46*(3), 130–136.

After this closer look at sources, the next step is to carefully read each to further determine its relevancy. In Jack's case, the articles by Kong and Fitch (2002) and Whittingham and Huffman (2009) are the only true research studies—which means they contain sections on identification of the problem, a review of relevant literature, a description of methods used, results of analysis of collected data, and conclusions based on those results. Several articles provide information about how the authors have created book clubs. The Daniels article on grading book clubs might be useful as Jack plans his book club intervention. A benefit of this article is that it was written by Harvey Daniels, an expert on literature circles and author of the book on literature circles Jack has chosen to review. The "Resource for Middle School Book Clubs," also written by Daniels (2002a), is also of interest to Jack because it specifically deals with the age group with whom he is working.

The process of choosing sources for the literature is one of constant decision making. What should be kept? What should be disregarded? How can a search be expanded if, in choosing articles, too few sources remain? In Jack's case, his search has thus far resulted in finding two books—Daniels (2002a) and Moeller and Moeller (2007)—and just a handful of articles that are only peripherally related to the direction of his action research study. This, however, is a normal part of the literature review process. Searches must be limited and expanded depending on whether too few or too many sources are found. The next thing for Jack to do is complete another search using different search terms. Articles on literature circles may be helpful, and Jack also may decide to expand his search using the keyword descriptor *increasing reading engagement.* When more matching sources are found, each article should be skimmed and the most relevant sources should be kept. Then a more in-depth reading of each article should occur to determine whether to keep the source or throw it out. In addition, reference lists in the articles should be scanned to determine if relevant titles are included. If potential sources are found this way, the articles or books must be obtained and read to determine whether they are good literature review sources.

Evaluating Literature

In choosing sources for the literature review, an initial evaluation is made regarding the relevance of the source for informing the action research study. However, once sources are chosen, they must be further evaluated to determine the ways in which the reviewed information can be used to guide the action research process. Questions to ask in evaluating the literature include the following:

- *Relevance* Does the source provide information that can help inform my action research study? For example, does it provide information about ways to structure the intervention or innovation I am interested in trying? Does it provide conclusions made by other researchers on the intervention I want to implement? What can I learn from the source that can help me in the planning of my action research study?
- *Credibility* Does the source seem credible? If the source is not a research study, are the claims and/or suggestions made by the author based on his

or her extensive experience? If the source is a research study, are the results of the study supported by data and do the research methods seem sound?

• ***Similarity***   Is information in the source based on the study of a setting that is similar to mine? Is it based on the study of participants (teachers, students, etc.) who are similar to the participants who will be in my study?

TIME TO REFLECT

Once you have located relevant research and read it, consider the following reflective questions. You may wish to discuss them with your peers or a critical friend. Write about your reflections in your journal.

- What surprised you in the literature? What challenged your assumptions? What aligned with what you believed before you reviewed the literature?
- How open were you to what you reviewed, particularly when your assumptions or preconceptions were challenged?
- How confident are you that you have chosen literature that will best help you meet your desired outcome?
- Now that you have read literature on the topic, reexamine your desired outcome and the actions you plan to take. Consider (and write about) areas where you see misalignment among your espoused values, the outcomes you desire, the actions you plan to take, and the literature you have chosen to inform your study.

Synthesizing Literature

Once sources have been chosen based on their relevance, credibility, and similarity to the action research study being planned, the next step is to synthesize information. Synthesizing involves connecting information into a coherent, integrated whole, and this process cannot occur until all relevant sources have been thoroughly read. In reading sources, common themes or topics typically emerge, and it is around these topics that a synthesized literature review is written. One common mistake in writing a literature review is to organize the review by sources, which results in a review that is simply a list of the information from each source. Instead of organizing by sources, the review should be organized by topic.

In Jack's case, several topics may emerge as he reads his sources, such as ways to structure reading clubs, the reading–writing connection, ways students talk about books in reading clubs, the history of literature circles and book clubs, and the positive impact of reading clubs. Identifying these as topics means several different sources have included information in each of these areas. As topics are identified, a determination must be made regarding the relevance of each topic for informing the action research study being planned. For example, Jack wishes to implement a reading club to get his students excited about literature. As Jack considers the topics he has located from his sources, he may decide three seem most relevant. Because he has little experience with reading clubs, it is important to him to read all he can on how best to structure one. Thus, one topic he will review is the structuring of reading clubs. Also, because he wants to learn all he can about the positive ways reading clubs impact students (and to see if the literature supports his belief that reading clubs can get students excited about reading), he will review this topic, too. A third topic he is interested in is the reading–writing connection because his students are even more apathetic about writing than they are about reading. For the purpose of this particular study, Jack chooses not to include information on the history of book clubs and literature circles because these topics do not, at this stage of his study, provide the kind of relevant information he needs to plan his own reading club.

The process of identifying topics and then choosing those that are most pertinent is part of synthesizing information. Once related topics are chosen, they are organized and expanded into subtopics, and then a cohesive, synthesized literature review is written. This process is explained in more depth in the following section of the chapter.

ORGANIZING AND WRITING THE LITERATURE REVIEW

A simple yet effective way of organizing the literature is to make an outline using the topics and subtopics that have been identified from the sources. In the previous example, Jack narrowed his literature review topics to three subjects: the structure of reading clubs, the positive effects of reading clubs, and the reading–writing connection. Next, he must determine how best to present the information—he must choose a logical sequence for the information. As he considers the structure, Jack begins an outline, organizing the topics in the way that seems to make most sense. Next, he looks back to the literature to determine the subtopics associated with each main topic. For example, in reading his sources, Jack determines that there are several positive effects of reading clubs—improving reading comprehension, encouraging collaborative learning, increasing motivation and desire to read, providing opportunities for discussion, allowing students or groups of students to work at their own reading levels—and that these effects can be classified as *positive student effects* (improved reading comprehension and motivation) and *positive instructional effects* (encouraging collaborative learning, providing opportunities for discussion, and allowing students to work at their own reading levels). A structure starts to develop that can be graphically displayed in a standard outline format, which is shown in Figure 3.5.

Notice in Figure 3.5 that sources have been listed next to *improved comprehension* and *improved motivation*. In creating an outline, sources

Literature Review Outline for Reading Club Study

I.   Positive effects of reading clubs
   1. Positive student effects
      a. Improved comprehension (Daniels, 2002; Day, Spiegel, McLellan, & Brown, 2002; Raphael & McMahon, 1994; Kong & Fitch, 2003)
      b. Increased motivation (Daniels, 2002; Day, Spiegel, McLellan, & Brown, 2002; O'Donnell-Allen & Hunt, 2001; Raphael, Florio-Ruane, & George, 2001)
   2. Positive instructional effects
      a. Encourage collaborative learning
      b. Provide opportunities for discussion
      c. Allow students to work at their own reading levels

II. Structure of reading clubs
   1. Selection of books
      a. Teacher selected
      b. Student selected
      c. Same/different books for each group
   2. Group structure and activities
      a. Group member roles/teacher role
      b. Scheduling meetings
      c. Fostering discussion and promoting participation
   3. Evaluation
      a. Teacher observation
      b. Student journals
      c. Self-evaluations by students
      d. Book logs
      e. Conferencing with teacher

III. Reading/writing connection
   1. Benefits
      a. Encouraging deep thinking
      b. Personal connection with the literature
      c. Connections across texts
   2. Informal writing
      a. Notes in books
      b. Journal entries
      c. Responses to prompts
      d. Letter writing to reading club members
   3. Formal writing
      a. Written book projects
      b. Letter writing to teacher
      c. Book reviews

FIGURE 3.5 Beginning literature review outline.

that support topics and subtopics can be listed on the outline, which makes it easier to use the outline to write the literature review.

In this example, Jack chose to structure the main topics beginning with the benefits of reading clubs and then moving to structuring reading clubs and finally the reading–writing connection. Although the main topics could have been ordered differently, Jack believed beginning with structuring reading clubs and then following with the benefits of reading clubs would result in a review that wasn't cohesive. Structuring the review that way would result in sloppy organization that would present the information as *This is how to create a reading club—this is why reading clubs are good—this is how to connect reading and writing in reading clubs.* In his view, starting with the benefits of reading groups, which include subtopics covered in the subsequent main topics (e.g., fostering collaboration is listed as a benefit under main topic one, and then a description of how to encourage collaboration is further discussed under main topic two) helped to focus the review and provided a way to make connections among the various topics and subtopics. In this way, the information is presented as *These are the benefits of reading clubs based on the research—these are ways to structure effective reading clubs—this is how to foster a reading–writing connection in a reading club.*

Whereas some individuals find outlining to be a simple way to prepare the structure of a literature review, others may find a prewriting strategy such as clustering (sometimes called idea mapping) to be more effective. In clustering, topics and their relationships are displayed graphically. Figure 3.6

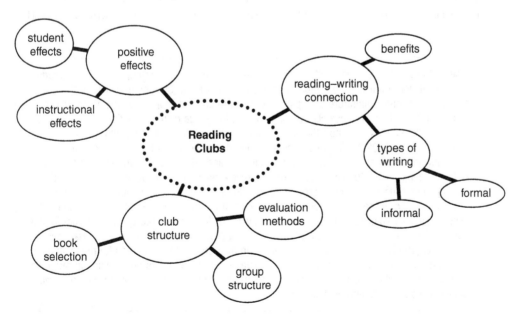

FIGURE 3.6 Reading club idea map.

illustrates how clustering could be used to design an idea map that displays reading club topics and the way in which these topics are related.

In creating an idea map, the main topic is written first (reading clubs), and then subtopics are clustered around that topic based on the ways the subtopics are related to the main topic and to each other. An idea map like the one in Figure 3.6 can be developed before an outline, or it can be developed instead of an outline. If an idea map is used in place of an outline, sources should be connected to subtopics on the graphical illustration just as they were linked to topics in the written outline in Figure 3.5.

Once the outline or idea map has been completed and sources have been linked to topics and subtopics, the next step is to write the literature review. Writing the review requires synthesis of information under each topic and/or subtopic. This means that information from each source must be connected in a way that makes sense and that flows. In addition, sources must be referenced in a scholarly format (typically APA in educational studies, but MLA is sometimes used) throughout the literature review. In Figure 3.7, a paragraph from Jack's literature review is included. Notice that the paragraph conveys information on one subtopic—the positive effect of increased reading comprehension— and that three different studies that relate to this subtopic are reviewed and cited. Notice, too, that the ways in which the studies are related or connected is made clear through transitional sentences or phrasing. For example, the fourth sentence begins "Other smaller studies also show the positive effects . . ." This phrasing lets the reader know that the

One of the positive effects of students working in reading clubs is improvement in reading comprehension. Daniels (2002) reports results from a study in Chicago in which teachers were trained to implement literature circles and reading-writing workshops in their classes. In grades 3, 6, and 8, students in these classes outperformed citywide gains in reading comprehension. Other smaller studies also show the positive effects of reading clubs on reading comprehension. Kong and Fitch (2002/2003), for example, studied the effects of a book club on students in a culturally and linguistically diverse, combined fourth- and fifth-grade classroom. Over the course of the academic year, students in the book club read eleven books that they both responded to in writing and discussed in various group settings. Comparisons of their comprehension strategies at the beginning of the year (before becoming part of the book club) and then at the end of the school year revealed gains in making predictions, verifying information, previewing, self-questioning, summarizing information, and drawing from background knowledge. A study by Raphael and McMahon (1994) resulted in similar outcomes. In their study of fourth- and fifth-grade students who were part of a book club for one to two years, the researchers noted gains in students' skills in synthesizing information, locating and discussing central themes, and taking on various perspectives when discussing literature.

FIGURE 3.7 Example paragraph from literature review on reading clubs.

previously described study by Daniels was a larger-scale study and that other smaller studies reveal similar findings regarding increased reading comprehension.

Figure 3.7 is not meant to be a template for writing paragraphs in the literature review. Instead, it is one example of how information on reading clubs' impact on reading comprehension can be presented. A number of other ways would also suffice. Jack could have begun the paragraph with an overview of the various reading comprehension strategies that have been shown to increase because of reading clubs, and then he could have followed that introduction with information from each specific source. One aspect of synthesis is determining ways to present information so that it is both organized effectively and connected to other relevant and related information.

Writing a review of the literature is a challenging task, even for individuals who have written a number of reviews for previous research studies. The task can be made much easier, however, by carefully choosing relevant literature, spending time reading each source carefully and thoughtfully, thinking about ways sources are connected, establishing topics and subtopics, and organizing topics into a structured outline. Sharing the work with a collaborator can also help, and collaborating in the process allows for discussion and refinement of topics and subtopics as well as ways to organize and present information. There are a number of Internet sites on writing literature reviews that may be helpful, including:

- ***University of Wisconsin–Madison:***

  www.wisc.edu/writing/Handbook/ReviewofLiterature.html

- ***University of Arizona:***

  www.library.arizona.edu/help/tutorials/litreviews/index.html

Pan (2004) provides a number of helpful suggestions for writing the literature review:

- In an introductory paragraph, explain the importance of your topic.
- Define major terms (e.g., early in his review of literature, Jack should explain what a literature circle is).
- Move logically between subtopics and major topics.
- Use multiple references, when possible, to support each major point in the review.
- Use as few direct quotes as possible. Remember, however, to cite your sources even when you restate findings in your own words.
- Describe your own conclusions based on what you have learned from the literature.
- Provide summaries within topic areas as well as a final summary. With the final summary, connect the literature to your area of focus.

Activity 3.1 provides steps to help you successfully write your literature review. Provided here are some tips for writing in APA style. Review Chapter 8 for additional information regarding how to cite using APA.

IN-TEXT CITATIONS AND VERB TENSE. When citing within text, use past tense or present perfect tense:

- Past tense:

Daniels (2002) reported significant gains in reading achievement.

- Present perfect tense:

Daniels (2002) has reported significant gains in reading achievement.

ACTIVITY 3.1
Reviewing the Literature

Follow the steps for searching for literature to review, choosing sources, determining topics and subtopics, and organizing and writing the literature review:

1. Use online databases such as the library catalog (to search for books) and ERIC, ProQuest, and/or EBSCOhost (to search for articles, conference papers, etc.) to search for sources related to the research topic identified in Activity 2.2. Use keyword descriptors in your search. Acquire books, articles, and other sources found in your search.
2. Skim sources and keep those that are most relevant to your study. Next, carefully read each source and determine the relevancy of each. Keep the most relevant sources.
3. If necessary, expand the search to acquire more sources. Search using new keyword descriptors and acquire sources from the reference lists of the articles, books, and other previously acquired literature.
4. Read all sources and keep those that are the most relevant, credible, and similar to the study you are planning. Once sources are chosen, carefully reread each, making notes on the topics discussed in each reference.
5. Generate a list of topics that emerged from the literature. Create an organized, structured outline of these topics and add subtopics. Next to each subtopic, list sources in which the subtopic is discussed.

Research paper activity: Use your outline to write a draft literature review. Be sure to follow APA guidelines (see Chapter 8). Synthesize so that information is provided on each topic/subtopic. Be sure multiple references/sources are described for each topic or subtopic. Use transitional sentences or phrases in your writing to connect ideas. Use a heading for the literature review such as *Literature Review, Review of Literature, Connection to Best Practices*, or another appropriate heading. Place the literature review after the reflection written in Activity 2.2.

CITING AN AUTHOR/AUTHORS. There are a number of guidelines regarding citing authors within text:

- One author:

  Daniels (2002) reported significant gains in reading achievement. Significant gains in reading achievement were noted in the study (Daniels, 2002).

- Two authors (note the difference in using *and* and &):

  Carter and Doyle (2006) described the use of storytelling narratives. Storytelling narratives are a powerful way to guide reflective practice (Carter & Doyle, 2006).

- Three to five authors:

  Cite all authors the first time the reference appears: Smith, Tripp, Kim, and Michaels (2003) found no significant differences in achievement.

  Use *et al.* after the initial citation: In subsequent studies, significant differences were found in mathematics (Smith et al., 2003).

- Six or more authors:

  Use the first author's name followed by *et al.*

- Citing different sources to support the same idea or within parentheses:

  Kimm (2003) and Jones and Little (2001) have reported significant learning gains for students involved in reading clubs.

  Significant learning gains have been reported for students involved in reading clubs (Jones & Little, 2001; Kimm, 2003). NOTE: In this case, sources are presented in alphabetic order.

- Two or more works by the same author in the same year:

  Chester (1999a) found differences in reading achievement. NOTE: The first work is noted with an *a* after the date, and each additional work from that year is noted with *b*, *c*, and so on.

- Indirect sources (used when you cite something read in another source rather than from the primary source):

  Smith (as cited in Chester, 1999) has suggested a number of strategies for improving reading achievement.

QUOTES. First, remember to use quotes infrequently. A good guideline is this: If paraphrasing would result in changing the author's intended meaning, quote the original. Be aware that this is rarely the case. Also, remember that restating is part of understanding and synthesizing the literature. If you do quote, include short quotes (fewer than forty words) in the paragraph itself. Long quotes are placed in a freestanding block with a 5-point left indent. All quotes must be accompanied by the number of the page where the quote is found in the work:

- Short quotes are included within the paragraph:

  Galvan (2007) defines reflection as "an intense self-study" (p. 23).

  Reflection has been defined as "an intense self-study" (Galvan, 2007, p. 23).

- Long quotes are freestanding blocks. Note that quotation marks are not used and that there is no punctuation after the page number and parenthesis:

  Anderson, Herr, and Nihlen (2007) explain

  > Most academic researchers assume that they are doing research on someone. That someone is generally referred to as the "subject," "informant," "interviewee," or "participant." What makes practitioner research unique is that practitioners/researchers are their own subjects or informants. They are insiders, not outsiders. (p. 8)

- If page numbers are not available, use the paragraph number for quotes:

  Trimbul (2008) describes teacher self-study as "action in power" (para. 3).

Summary

The purpose of this chapter was to explain the steps of conducting a literature review, which is a necessary step in action research that allows educators to connect what is known from research (theory and best practices) with what will be done in the practitioner's particular study. Information was provided on the steps of reviewing the literature, which include searching library catalogs and online databases for sources related to the topic under study, evaluating and choosing literature, defining topics and subtopics from the literature through synthesizing information from all sources, organizing information, and writing the review. The focus of the next chapter is on using the information learned through the review of literature to plan an intervention that will be implemented in the action research study.

TABLE 3.1   Educational Journal Descriptions, Internet Addresses, and Online Availability

Journal Title	Information Provided	Web Address	Full-Text Online
Action Research	Academic articles on the theory and processes of action research	http://arj.sagepub.com	No—TC only
American Educational Research Journal	In-depth reviews of literature on topics in education	http://aer.sagepub.com	No—TC only
The American Journal of Education	Research, theory, synthesis articles, policy, and practice	www.journals.uchicago.edu/AJE	No—TC only
American School Board Journal	Newspaper-type articles on various topics in education	www.asbj.com	Yes
Bilingual Research Journal	Issues and research on bilingual education	www.tandf.co.uk/journals/ubrj	Yes
Contemporary Educational Psychology	Academic research articles related to cognitive processes of learning	www.elsevier.com/locate/cedpsych	No—TC only
Contemporary Issues in Early Childhood	Articles about research; reviews of literature	www.wwwords.co.uk/ciec	Online only; requires subscription
Current Issues in Education	Articles related to research, practice, and policy	http://cie.asu.edu	Yes
Early Childhood Research and Practice	Research on the development and care of young children	www.ecrp.uiuc.edu	Yes
Early Childhood Research Quarterly	Research on educating children through age 8	http://www.naeyc.org/publications/ecrq	No—TC & AB only
Educational Action Research	Various forms of action research in education	http://www.tandf.co.uk/journals/reac	No—TC & AB only
Educational Evaluation and Policy Analysis	Academic articles related to evaluating educational policy	http://epa.sagepub.com	No—TC & AB only
Educational Leadership	Articles on P–12 curriculum, instruction, administration, and leadership	http://www.ascd.org/publications/educational-leadership.aspx	Selected FT; TC given
Educational Researcher	Reviews on topics related to broad educational theories	http://edr.sagepub.com/	No—TC & AB only
Educational Technology & Society	Research and commentary on the uses of technology in education	www.ifets.info	Yes
Educational Theory	Discussions of theoretical problems in education	http://www.ed.uiuc.edu/eps/educational-theory/	Archived only
Education Week	Newspaper format	www.edweek.org	Yes
The Elementary School Journal	Research on problems in the classroom	www.journals.uchicago.edu/ESJ/home.html	TC only
English Journal	Teaching ideas for middle and high school English teachers	http://www.ncte.org/journals/ej	Selected FT; TC given

(continued)

TABLE 3.1 *(continued)*

Journal Title	Information Provided	Web Address	Full-Text Online
Exceptional Children	Academic research on teaching exceptional children	http://journals.cec.sped.org/	No—current TC only
International Journal for the Scholarship of Teaching and Learning	Articles, essays, and discussions about scholarship of teaching	www.georgiasouthern.edu/ijsotl	Yes
International Journal of Education in the Arts	Research in the areas of art theory, music, visual arts drama dance and literature	http://www.ijea.org/	Yes
International Journal of Educational Policy & Leadership	Formerly the *Journal of Curriculum & Supervision*	http://journals.sfu.ca/ijepl/index.php/ijepl	No—current TC only
Issues in Educational Research	Australian journal of research on teaching issues	www.iier.org.au/iier.html	Yes
Journal for Research in Mathematics Education	NCTM journal that includes research, literature reviews, and theoretical analyses	http://www.nctm.org/publications/jrme.aspx	No—AB only
Journal of Adolescence	Articles on teaching, research, guidance, and counseling of teenagers	www.elsevier.com/wps/find/journaldescription.cws_home/622849/description#description	No—TC & AB only
Journal of Cases in Educational Leadership	Research on the preparation of educational leaders	http://jel.sagepub.com	Yes
Journal of Intellectual Disabilities	Research on the education of individuals with learning disabilities	http://jid.sagepub.com	No—TC only
The Journal of Scholarship of Teaching & Learning	Essays, academic, and action research studies related to education	www.iupui.edu/~josotl	Yes
Journal of Special Education Technology	Research, policy, and practice related to the use of technology in the field of special education	http://www.tamcec.org/jset/	No—TC & AB only
Journal of Technology Education	Research, theory, and philosophy related to educational technology	http://scholar.lib.vt.edu/ejournals/JTE	Yes
Journal of Vocational Education & Training	Articles on work-related education	http://www.tandf.co.uk/journals/titles/13636820.asp	No—TC only
Kairos	Research on teaching writing using the World Wide Web; geared toward teaching writing at the college level	http://kairos.technorhetoric.net/	Yes
Language Arts	Articles pertaining to classroom strategies, methods, reports of research at the elementary school level	http://www.ncte.org/journals/la	No—TC only

TABLE 3.1 *(continued)*

Journal Title	Information Provided	Web Address	Full-Text Online
Language Learning & Technology	Research related to teaching foreign languages	http://llt.msu.edu	Yes
Learning & Leading with Technology	Articles emphasizing practical ideas about technology in the K–12 curriculum.	http://www.iste.org/learn /publications/learning-and-leading.aspx	TC & selected FT
The Mathematics Educator Online	Literature reviews, article critiques, academic and action research	http://math.coe.uga.edu/ TME/tmeonline.html	Yes
Mathematics Teacher	NCTM journal; articles on improving math education in grade 8 and above	www.nctm.org/publications	TC & selected FT
Mathematics Teaching in the Middle School	NCTM journal; provides teaching strategies for use with middle school students	www.nctm.org/ publications	TC & selected FT
National Forum of Educational Administration and Supervision Journal	Articles related to school administration and supervision	www.nationalforum.com	Yes
National Forum of Special Education Journal	Articles related to special education issues	www.nationalforum.com	Yes
Networks: An Online Journal for Teacher Research	Educational action research studies	http://journals.library.wisc. edu/index.php/networks	Yes
On-Math. Online Journal of School Mathematics	NCTM journal; teaching resource for math teachers	http://www.nctm.org/ publications/onmath.aspx	TC & selected FT
Ontario Action Researcher	Educational action research studies in Canada	www.nipissingu.ca/oar	Yes
Phi Delta Kappan	Articles related to policy issues, research-based school reform, and controversial topics	http://www.kappanmagazine. org/	Yes
Primary Voices K–6	Articles written by teachers on teaching strategies	http://www.ncte.org/journals/ pv/issues	TC only
Reading and Writing Quarterly: Overcoming Learning Difficulties	Articles on causes, evaluation, and remediation of reading and writing difficulties	www.tandf.co.uk/journals/ titles/10573569.asp	No—TC only
Reading Online	Articles specific to methods for teaching literacy	www.readingonline.org	Yes
Research in the Teaching of English	Academic research related to teaching English	http://www.ncte.org/ journals/rte	Archived FT only
Review of Educational Research	In-depth literature reviews on educational topics in any discipline	http://rer.sagepub.com/	No—AB only

(continued)

TABLE 3.1 *(continued)*

Journal Title	Information Provided	Web Address	Full-Text Online
School Library Media Research	Research on instructional theory, teaching methods, and critical issues relevant to school library media	http://www.ala.org/ala/ mgrps/divs/aasl/ aaslpubsandjournals/slmrb/ schoollibrary.cfm	TC & FT archived
The Science Teacher	Issues related to teaching science in secondary schools	www.nsta.org/publications/ journals.aspx	Yes
Social Education	Theory and practical ideas related to teaching social studies	www.socialstudies.org/ publications/se	TC & AB only
Social Studies and the Young Learner	Practical ideas for teaching social studies K–6	www.socialstudies.org/ publications/ssyl	No
Teachers College Record	Articles on education-related issues	www.tcrecord.org	Yes
Teachers and Teaching: Theory and Practice	Research on teachers thinking, reflections, and work	http://www.tandf.co.uk/ journals/ctat	No—TC only
Teaching Children Mathematics	NCTM journal on activities and strategies for teaching math	http://www.nctm.org/ publications/tcm.aspx	TC & selected FT
Teaching English as a Second Language	Research and literature reviews related to ESL teaching	http://www.tesol.org/s_ tesol/index.asp	Yes
Teaching Exceptional Children	Articles on methods and materials for teaching exceptional children	http://www.cec.sped.org/ Content/NavigationMenu/ Publications2/ TEACHINGExceptional Children/default.htm	No—current TC only
Technological Horizons in Education (T.H.E.) Journal	Issues related to technology in education	http://thejournal.com	Yes
Technology Source	Case studies related to utilizing technology in schools	http://technologysource.org	Yes
Voices from the Field	Action research and topics related to classroom instruction (last updated 2002)	www.alliance.brown.edu/ pubs/voices	Yes
Voices from the Middle	Descriptions of classroom practices in the middle school English classroom	http://www.ncte.org/ journals/vm	No—TC only

Key: TC (table of contents), FT (full-text), AB (abstracts)

4

Initial Planning of the Action Research Study

Chapter Goals

- Explain the process of articulating research questions that are action oriented and outcome based.

- Illustrate the process of planning and implementing the intervention that will be used.

- Describe the processes of choosing research participants and engaging in collaboration.

- Describe procedures for following ethical guidelines in action research studies.

- Provide activities that guide practitioners through the planning and implementation phase of their studies, including following ethical guidelines.

After completing a review of the literature on the chosen research topic, the next step is to plan the intervention that will be used. The information learned in reviewing the literature is used to guide the creation of the implementation plan. For example, in Chapter 3, Jack, our middle school teacher interested in increasing student engagement with literature by implementing reading clubs, reviewed the literature and learned ways in which reading clubs impact student learning and motivation, the positive instructional benefits of utilizing reading clubs with students, methods for structuring reading clubs and evaluating their effectiveness, and ways to connect reading and writing activities through the reading club model. This information provides a way to structure and evaluate the effectiveness of the reading club intervention Jack will use.

At this stage of the action research process, the first step is to articulate research questions. Next, the intervention is planned based on what was learned from a review of the literature. Once the intervention plan has been formulated, participants must be chosen, and collaboration possibilities can be further explored. For many studies—particularly those that are conducted as part of a graduate or undergraduate research course—permissions must be secured to conduct the research study and collect data. Activities are provided in this chapter to help you complete each of these important initial steps in the planning process.

ARTICULATING RESEARCH QUESTIONS

The first step in planning an action research study is to clarify research questions. A primary research question that is based on the purpose of the study should be articulated at this stage. In Chapter 2, a reflection activity (Activity 2.2) was completed that included a detailed reflection on the area of research focus. The reflection also included an explanation of desired outcomes for the project. In Chapter 3, a literature review on the area of focus was conducted. At this point in the project, it is time to write a primary research question that is based on the purpose of the study described in the initial reflection statement *and* what was learned in the review of literature. It is necessary to consider both the initial reflection and the information gathered in the literature review when planning a study that is aligned with the area of focus and with best practices found in the literature. To illustrate how the process moves from reflection to theory/best practices to the intervention plan, consider this example: Rosario, a third-grade teacher, wrote this initial reflection:

> Each year I seem to spend a lot of time working with students on their writing. With my third-grade students this year, I am spending more time than ever helping students correct spelling and grammar mistakes in their written work. We seem to spend so much time on these basics that I have little time to focus on other important concepts in writing, like using compound sentences and using adverbs and adjectives to make writing more interesting. My students seem really turned off on writing. They groan when I give a writing assignment, and they act as if their monthly book reports are absolute torture. For my action research study, I would like to find a way to improve students' writing. I would also like to see a positive change in students' attitudes about writing. These goals align with my core values as an educator. I know the importance of being able to communicate through writing. This was a skill I did not possess when I graduated from high school, and I struggled in college until a caring professor offered to help. By the end

of the semester, I was earning passing grades in my English course and was getting positive comments about my papers and essays from other professors. I was so encouraged, I took a creative writing class as an elective, and there I learned how wonderful it feels to make stories come alive. I want to inspire my students just as my professor inspired me. I want my kids to enjoy writing; I want them to see it as a way to express themselves rather than as a mandatory school task. I know, too, that writing well can open a lot of doors for my students, both in school and out of school.

Rosario's reflection includes a clear statement of the problem (spending too much time with writing instruction that is not helping students' negative attitudes toward writing), plainly stated outcomes (improvement in student writing and a positive change in students' attitudes), and a link to her core educational values. In the early reflection stage, however, Rosario was not ready to write research questions. If she had simply written questions based on her reflection, they would have lacked a key element: the *action* part of the action research process. To clarify, if Rosario had written research questions before conducting the literature review, they probably would have been questions such as, "How do I improve students' writing achievement?" and "How do I improve students' attitudes about writing?" These questions provide no indication of any action (such as an instructional method) that will be taken to improve attitudes about and achievement in writing. Thus, Rosario first needed to consult the literature to review best practices that could be used to achieve her desired outcomes. This provided her with a strategy to improve students' writing achievement and attitudes about writing.

In Rosario's literature review, she read about an intervention that involves students and the teacher working together to create grading rubrics that are used for evaluating student writing. In her review, Rosario learned that in other studies, students' writing achievement and attitudes about writing increased when they were able to have a say in how their work was graded. The process of creating the rubric helped students better understand the elements of good writing and made them more responsible for the quality of their written work. Because improvement in writing, more positive attitudes about writing, and increased student responsibility and ownership of their writing were outcomes Rosario desired in her own students, she decided to study the rubric intervention in her action research study. With an intervention decided upon, Rosario wrote her primary research question: "In what ways will the process of creating and using writing rubrics increase students' writing achievement?" Rosario also had a secondary question: "How will the process of creating and using writing rubrics change students' attitudes about writing?"

By returning to her initial reflection and core values, considering the best practices information gathered in the literature review (specifically the information on the intervention using rubrics), and focusing on her desired outcomes, Rosario was able to write well-articulated primary and secondary research questions. As you begin formulating research questions for your study, remember to consider the initial purpose of your study described in your reflection, the desired outcomes of your study, *and* what you learned in your literature review as you write your research questions. Research questions should include the action that will be taken and the desired outcome. Begin by listing a primary or main research question. Next, list one or two secondary questions. As you begin your study, you do not want to focus on a lot of secondary questions. If there are too many secondary questions, it will be difficult to focus on the primary research question. Also, as the study progresses, many new questions will come up, and these questions are typically much more important in understanding the outcomes of the study than the scores of secondary questions that can be generated before the study even begins.

A number of factors should be considered as you formulate research questions. Anderson, Herr, and Nihlen (2007) explain the importance of considering the political consequences, as well as personal consequences, of pursuing certain questions. Consider Danetta, the elementary school guidance counselor introduced in Chapter 2, who was interested in studying possible disparity in the ways minority students were disciplined at her school. Pursuing this line of research—and asking tough questions related to social justice—would be difficult in certain school climates or without support and/or buy-in from colleagues and administrators. It is vitally important to consider potential political and personal pitfalls as you begin to articulate research questions. It is important, too, to examine your assumptions, preconceived notions, and biases about your topic as you reflect on the possible consequences of your study. Often, discussing questions with a few close colleagues or a critical friend can help you determine whether you've chosen a potentially problematic topic.

Several years ago, a teacher in my action research course planned to study ways to decrease the use of a certain racial slur commonly used among the young African American students at his middle school. As he discussed this idea with his principal, she described district-level issues (largely based on the biases of one or two individuals who possessed most of the decision-making power) that would make it impossible to pursue his research. Although he was committed to his topic, he realized it could mean his job if he moved forward with the study. Instead of taking that risk, he revisited his reflection, considered his core values, and decided to look for ways to increase positive, affirming communication among his students—an action much more in line with his espoused values. This new study idea allowed him to remain focused on the issue at the heart of his original research idea, but he was able to get there only by examining his assumptions and biases and being open to new possibilities.

A second factor to consider is whether you want to ask a question about the effectiveness of an intervention or innovation—such as Rosario's question, "In what ways will the process of creating or using writing rubrics increase students' writing achievement?"—or whether you want to ask a more general question that will lead to understanding or describing—such as Danetta's question, "What types of disparity in discipline exist in our school?" In some cases, you must ask a general question and answer that question before moving on to intervention questions. Danetta's question, once answered, would likely lead to a more specific question about what to do about the disparity, if it does indeed exist.

A third factor to consider relates to who gets to be part of developing the research question. Anderson and colleagues (2007) suggest that educators work collaboratively to establish research questions, which can decrease potential political problems like those discussed earlier. They explain that other benefits of collaboration at this stage include quickening the pace of the study (because work is shared), increasing visibility (which may encourage others to become involved), and improving relationships (if collaboration cuts across hierarchical lines such as student–teacher and/or teacher–administrator).

TIME TO REFLECT

Look back at the journal entries you wrote as you worked through the activities and reflections in Chapters 2 and 3. Then, consider the following reflection questions—either on your own, in a collaborative group, or with a critical friend. Note in your journal your reflections.

- Are there potential consequences of conducting your study you didn't initially consider? How might you address these now?
- Are the actions you plan to take in your study in line with your values? Are the outcomes? If there isn't alignment, what new possibilities might you consider that would still allow your study to align with your values?

Here are some additional factors to consider as you frame your primary and secondary research questions:

- Do not ask a question that can be answered yes or no.

  Poor question: Is there discipline disparity in our school?

  Better question: What types of disparity in discipline exist in our school?

- Ask questions that are researchable given your limitations.

  Poor question: Do guidance counselors in the United States experience role conflict?

  Better question: What types of role conflict are experienced by high school guidance counselors in my district [or school]?

- Ask questions that can be answered with data.

   Poor question: Is it important to teach character education?

   Better question: What are parent, student, and teacher perceptions about the importance of teaching character education?

- In intervention studies, include the intervention and the outcome (you might also want to include the setting if you can do so without sacrificing clarity).

   Poor question: Does writer's workshop affect learning?

   Poor question: Does the intervention improve students' writing?

   Better question: In what ways will the process of creating or using writing rubrics increase my third-grade students' writing achievement?

Activity 4.1 will take you through the process of writing well-developed research questions.

ACTIVITY 4.1
Articulating Research Questions

Begin by referring to your reflection, your core values, and the purpose of your action research study. Next, reread your literature review. Then do the following:

1. State your primary research question. Make sure the question is aligned with your initial reflection and your literature review. Your question should include the intervention you will use (if applicable) and the outcome you desire.
2. State no more than two secondary questions. These questions should be aligned with your initial reflection and your literature review. Include the intervention (if applicable) and desired outcomes.

(?) Has the direction of your study changed after reviewing the literature, examining assumptions, and reflecting on alignment among your values, actions, and desired outcomes? If so, rewrite your initial reflection to indicate this change and to ensure that it is aligned with your new purpose and desired outcomes. This kind of change is normal in action research.

Journal activity: As new questions emerge during your study, write them in your journal. Mark all questions so that you can find them easily. Highlight these questions in the same color, use sticky notes, or utilize another method to mark and keep track of emerging questions. Consider discussing these questions with peers or a critical friend.

Research paper activity: Write a paragraph on the purpose of your study followed by the primary and secondary questions that are the focus of your investigation. Label this section *Purpose and Research Questions* (or a similar heading). Place this section of the paper after the literature review (Activity 3.1).

PLANNING THE INTERVENTION

After writing primary and secondary research questions, the next step of the action research process is to create the intervention plan, which should be based on the best practices reviewed in the literature. In the plan, you should clearly describe the intervention you will use and its relation to the literature reviewed, and the plan should be written with enough detail so that other teachers or administrators can read the plan and use it in their settings. It is important to describe the activities included in the intervention and the length of the intervention (How long will the intervention last? How long are individual sessions? How much time will be devoted to the activities in the intervention?). Look back to Rosario's reflection and research questions in the previous section. In planning and describing her intervention, Rosario needs to explain the rubric activity that students will engage in, and she needs to provide a time frame for the study. Rosario's intervention plan might look like this:

> As described by Skillings and Ferrell (2000), when students are part of the process of creating scoring rubrics, they develop a better understanding of what counts as good work, and they are able to develop the metacognitive skills necessary to monitor their own learning and understanding. With this in mind, the students and I will collaborate in the creation of a rubric that will be used to evaluate the monthly book reports. During the first four days of the intervention, we will work on the rubric activities for approximately one hour per day. On the first day of the intervention, I will describe what a rubric is, and I will provide several examples of rubrics for students to study. Students will have copies of rubrics, and we will discuss the type of information included on a rubric. On the first day, I will also explain that we will develop a rubric together that will be used to grade book reports. On the second day, I will ask students to provide suggestions about what categories should be incorporated on the book report rubric (e.g., capitalization, punctuation, spelling, description), and I will provide guidance to ensure that certain non-negotiable categories are included. On the third day, we will work to create scoring levels in each category. On the fourth day, students will work in pairs to score their book reports from last month using the rubric. Students will discuss the way they scored their own work and their partner's work using the rubric. After this activity, we will work in a large group to discuss difficulties or questions using the rubric, and we will refine the rubric as needed. Approximately one week later, students will begin working on their October book reports. They will be instructed to use the rubric as they write their book reports. Two days before the book report due date, students will work in pairs to evaluate each other's

book reports using the rubric, and then students will have the opportunity to seek guidance from me on unclear points. Students will make any necessary revisions to their book reports before turning them in. Students will be required to turn in a rubric with their own evaluation of their book report. These rubric activities (writing the book report with the rubric, reviewing reports with partners, and turning in a completed rubric with the book report) will be required on each book report for the remainder of the school year.

Rosario's plan could also be graphically represented in a lesson plan format, as shown in Figure 4.1.

Rosario has written an understandable intervention plan that could be used by another teacher wishing to use a similar rubric activity. An initial

FIGURE 4.1 Rosario's intervention plan: Lesson plan format.

		Week 1		
Monday 9:00–9:55	*Tuesday* 9:00–9:55	*Wednesday* 9:00–9:55	*Thursday* 9:00–9:55 10:15–10:35	*Friday* 9:00–9:30
Rubric description. Students will study example rubrics. *Goal explanation:* Students and I will create a rubric that will be used to grade students' book reports.	Review of rubric description. Students will review example rubrics. Students generate ideas about what to incorporate into book report rubric.	Review of rubric description. Review of student-determined rubric categories. Students review scoring levels on example rubrics. Students develop scoring levels for book report rubric.	Review of student-developed rubric categories and scoring levels. Students work in pairs to score last month's book reports using newly developed rubric. Rubric scoring discussion/questions. Rubric refinement.	Additional time for rubric discussion and rubric refinement, as necessary.

		Week 3		
Monday 9:00–9:55	*Tuesday* 9:00–9:55	*Wednesday* 9:30–9:45 10:15–11:00	*Thursday* 9:00–9:45	*Friday*
Review of student-generated book report rubric. Students begin October book report, using rubric to write and evaluate report.	Review of student-generated book report rubric. Book report writing.	Rubric review: Using the rubric to score book reports. Students work in pairs to evaluate their partner's book report using rubric. Rubric conferencing.	Students revise book reports based on feedback on rubric scored by partner.	Book report and self-scored rubric due.

timeline is included that will help Rosario stay focused on her plan. It should be noted that the plan does not have to be laid out in precisely this way, focusing on activities of each day. Instead, this is just one way of describing an intervention. Consider, too, that the daily interruptions faced by teachers may mean that Rosario will alter the plan as she goes, but that is a typical part of the action research process that will not interfere with Rosario's completing the intervention, even if it means taking a few more days to get through the activities.

If your study does not involve an intervention or innovation, you will need to review Chapter 5 before writing the research plan. In studies that focus on understanding or describing, the research plan typically includes simply the data collection strategies that will be used to answer the broad, general research question and a timeline for collecting the data.

Once you have designed a good research plan, but before implementing the plan, you need to consider who the participants will be and how (if at all) collaboration will occur during the study.

Participants

Who will be part of your research study? Will you conduct your action research study on all students, students in one class, or a small group of students, teachers, staff, or others? In Rosario's study, her participants will be all the third graders in her class. As Rosario plans her study, she might also consider asking students' parents to participate in her study. For example, if Rosario wishes to determine whether students are more positive about completing their book report activities when rubrics are used, she could survey parents about their children's attitudes as they work on their book reports at home. She may also solicit information from parents about any comments their children have made outside of school about the rubric activity, writing the book reports, or writing in general. Parents could be a good source of information on the effects of the rubric activity beyond Rosario's classroom.

The teachers and administrators with whom I have worked frequently ask parents of students to be research participants in their action research projects. Parents can do more than simply provide a source of data. Sometimes they become part of the study itself, helping with classroom activities, planning with teachers, or offering input on interventions. When parents are asked to participate, they often become excited about their participation, which builds positive relationships between educators and parents and provides the educator with a valuable ally who is just as invested in student learning as the educator is.

As you consider who will participate in your study, remember that a participant is anyone who can contribute in any way to your study. This might include colleagues, parents, and students. Remember, too, that you are not just the researcher in your project; you, too, are a participant. Although you may believe at this early stage of the process that action research is about gathering information on others, a larger part of action research is learning about yourself.

One thing to be mindful of as you determine who will participate in your study is keeping your study manageable. If you are a teacher who has several different groups of students each day, you should think about focusing on just one class or one group of students for your first action research study. This will help to ensure your study is manageable, which will increase your ability to conduct the study effectively. Often, teachers and administrators want to include large numbers of participants in their first action research studies. However, having many participants means having to develop a more complicated research plan. It also means having more data to collect and analyze. If this is your first time conducting a study in your classroom, school, or district, focus this initial study on a small number of participants. This will help ensure that you are able to conduct your study the right way, which will allow you to learn how to do action research effectively. You will also have a better chance to develop a sense of the work and time commitments needed in the action research process. Once you are an experienced action researcher, you will be able to commit to larger projects with more participants.

Collaboration

As mentioned in Chapter 1, collaboration is an aspect of various forms of action research. In completing the reflection activities in Chapter 2, you may have engaged in reflective activities with colleagues or a critical friend, which is a collaborative act, and in reviewing literature, you may have sought the assistance of colleagues, which is also a way of collaborating. There are several benefits of continuing the process of collaboration as you plan and implement your action research study.

- *Collaboration makes the work of educators a less lonely endeavor.* Hobson (1996) and Burns (1999) express concern over the isolation many educators feel and suggest that collaborating on action research studies can serve to alleviate this sense of isolation. Hobson explains that collaboration in action research provides educators with the opportunity to work with colleagues to investigate problems and questions that have practical importance to them. Hobson, promoting the establishment of teacher research-community groups, suggests collaboration "enables teachers to celebrate their successes with each other, create and re-create ways of helping groups of children, learn more effectively, and strengthen the connections teachers have with each other" (p. 96).
- *Collaboration encourages educators to engage in ongoing professional development.* Cole and Knowles (2000) explain that "collaboration is a powerful mode for the facilitation of learning and the propelling forward of professional growth" (p. 136). Thus, when educators engage in dialogue about improving teaching practices, and when they work together

to facilitate moving conversations about best practices into their classroom activity, professional growth is a natural outcome.

• *Collaboration allows educators to gain multiple perspectives on critical educational issues.* In the action research courses I teach, I assign teachers to work in groups based on similar research interests. In a typical semester, there may be a group of teachers discussing using literature circles, another group discussing discipline programs, regular and special education teachers talking about ways to make inclusion and co-teaching work, and another group discussing educational disparities in their schools or districts. What I have found in my observations of these groups is that educators are often pleasantly surprised by the insight, experiences, and suggestions given by their peers. Colleagues can be an incredible resource when engaging in an action research project. You may find individuals who have attended inservice training on an instructional method you are interested in trying. You may find others who have read extensively on the topic you are investigating. Others may have found successful ways to deal with the research problem you wish to investigate. If you are a teacher, don't discount the possibility of collaborating with an administrator from your school or district. An administrator's broad range of experience and desire to assist teachers in engaging in best teaching practices make him or her a good ally and a good potential collaborator.

In addition to considering collaboration possibilities with individuals at your school, you may also consider working with a university faculty member or an educator from another school who you feel can assist you in your study. Cole and Knowles (2009) point out several benefits of working with outside researchers. First, levels of experiences and expertise are enhanced when outside researchers become part of your action research study. Second, university researchers often can dedicate time and even financial assistance through grants to the project. Third, a university collaborator may be able to put you in touch with others around the world who are studying the same topic you are investigating.

Yet another source of collaboration is having your participants serve as research collaborators. If you are a teacher, your students can be researchers with you. Instead of studying them, consider having them study themselves (much in the same way that you are now studying yourself in this action research process) and their classroom. If you are an administrator studying teachers, consider having the teacher-participants work with you as collaborators, rather than as participants only. As Greenwood and Levin (2007) explain,

The democratic assumption here is that every human being knows more about his or her own life situation than anyone else and that everyone, given reasonable support, is capable of contributing knowledge and analysis to a collaborative social process if we collectively are skillful enough in creating the arena for collaboration. (pp. 261–262)

Cole and Knowles (2009) suggest several ways to involve students as research collaborators, and these methods can be extended to other types of participants—parents, teachers, staff—as well. First, participants can work with you to conceptualize the study, meaning they develop the area of focus for the study while you facilitate the process. Second, participants can become co-investigators, working with you collaboratively to develop an area of research focus. Third, you can take charge of identifying the area of focus for your study and then give participants partial responsibility for planning the study. Finally, participants can also become collaborators through helping with data collection (e.g., conducting interviews or leading focus group discussions with peers), evaluating and interpreting the results of the study, and even helping plan future actions based on study results.

Another form of collaboration is teacher inquiry groups. As Singer (2007) explains, teacher inquiry groups allow educators to engage in "critical, professional conversation" because they begin with teachers' (insiders') questions, and they give teachers the opportunity to involve themselves in research related to their practices" (p. 10). In a teacher inquiry group, educators work together toward a common goal. They rely on each other's strengths, knowledge, and experiences as they study problems in their settings. Conducting action research within a teacher inquiry group has several benefits. Shosh and Zales (2005) suggest that action research conducted by inquiry groups allows teachers to make informed instructional decisions, gives teachers an opportunity to analyze the data they deem important, provides opportunities for engagement rather than isolation, and puts educators in charge of their professional growth and development. Singer adds the additional benefit of sustainability. Action research conducted in inquiry groups is typically easier to sustain and continue than research conducted in isolation. The Southwest Educational Developmental Laboratory provides a brief, useful video entitled *Promoting Teacher Inquiry: A Study Group Approach*. It can be accessed online at no charge at http://www.sedl.org/pubs/catalog/movies/teaching09.mov.

The benefits of collaboration are extensive, and I hope you have discovered in this section ways to make collaboration a part of your action research study. *Researching Teaching: Exploring Teacher Development through Reflexive Inquiry* by Cole and Knowles is a wonderful source of information in this area, and its authors provide sound suggestions for making collaborative efforts successful.

TIME TO REFLECT

In making decisions about the intervention, participants, and ways you might collaborate, consider the following reflection questions—either on your own, in a collaborative group, or with a critical friend. Note reflections in your journal.

- In what ways does the intervention align with your values? What assumptions, preconceived notions, or biases do you have about the intervention?
- How did you choose your participants? Have you chosen or left out participants based on assumptions or biases you have about them? How might these assumptions and biases impact your study and what you are able to learn from your study?
- In what ways might collaboration enhance your study? In what ways might it make your study difficult? What assumptions do you have about collaborating with peers, parents, students, or university faculty? What are the potential risks and benefits of collaborating?

Activity 4.2 provides activities for describing the intervention (if applicable), the study setting and participants, and collaborative activities.

ETHICAL GUIDELINES FOR ACTION RESEARCH STUDIES

Historically, individuals engaging in academic educational research, including higher education faculty, advanced graduate students, and others involved in educational research, have been bound by ethical guidelines that protect the rights of human subjects/participants. These guidelines have been put into place to ensure that participants are not harmed or deceived, that they have been informed regarding what participation entails, that they have agreed to participate, and that they have been assured that the confidentiality of their responses and their participation will be maintained.

There has been a great deal written about whether these ethical guidelines are necessary and/or appropriate for research conducted by practitioners. As Zeni (2009) suggests, guidelines for educational research are based on those established for quantitative and qualitative research conducted by outsiders and thus are not well fitted to the type of research conducted by practitioners, who are insiders. For example, ethical guidelines for educational research require that the researcher explain precisely which types of data will be collected before the study begins. However, as Zeni (2001) explains, the action research process is one that can change along the way as ongoing reflective planning takes place; practitioners who conduct research often decide during the study which types of data should be collected as new questions and new directions emerge.

A number of suggestions have been put forth regarding ethical guidelines for action research, including Zeni's (2009) criteria that the action researcher/ practitioner be responsible and accountable, aware of larger social justice issues that extend beyond a classroom or school, and caring and respectful

ACTIVITY 4.2
Planning the Intervention

1. Describe the intervention you will use in your study. Write in sufficient detail so that a colleague could use your plan in his or her own setting.

Research paper activity: Provide a heading for the intervention (e.g., *Intervention, Research Plan, Innovation,* or something similar), and place this section after the section on participants (next activity). This is not necessary for studies that do not focus on an intervention (e.g., descriptive studies).

Journal activity: Keep a log of unexpected occurrences during the intervention (interruptions, extension or reduction of planned activities, etc.). These anecdotal notes may help explain outcomes as data are collected.

2. Describe the participants in your study. Start by describing your setting (school or district). Include information on the type of school or district, its size and location, and any other information that provides a snapshot of the setting. Next, describe the specific group of participants. Remember that context is important in action research. If you disseminate the findings of your study, it is imperative that you provide a detailed description of your participants to your audience. This will allow others to determine whether they might expect results with their own participants to be similar to your results. Consider including information on achievement or ability level, parental involvement, behavior, motivation, and engagement. When describing your school or district, consider including information on location (rural, suburban, urban), school climate, socioeconomic status, and special programs.

Research paper activity: Provide a heading for the participants (e.g., *Participants, Students, Sample,* or something similar), and place this section after the research questions (Activity 4.1) and before the intervention section.

3. If you are collaborating, describe who will be collaborating with you and the ways in which they will be contributing to your action research study. Explain each collaborator's role and how work will be shared in the collaborative group.

Research paper activity: Place this information in the intervention section. You may wish to use a subheading such as *Collaboration* or *Research Team.*

Journal activity: Keep a record of collaboration efforts. Include information on collaborators, meetings, discussions, ideas generated, and so on.

of participants. However, procedural guidelines for conducting ethical action research have not yet been agreed upon by the professional community. So, for the time being, guidelines for outsider educational research must be observed. You need permission to conduct an action research study if the data you are collecting on human participants will be disseminated (including as research paper for a course, as a presentation at your school or district, as a conference presentation, or through publication). Most school districts require individuals—even teachers and administrators in the district—to obtain permission before conducting any type of research. If you are completing your action research project as part of a university requirement, the university also has its own procedures for approving research involving human participants, which may include directions for faculty sponsorship of the study.

When conducting an action research study in a school or school district (not in a college or university), the first step is to contact the district office and inquire about the approval process for research studies. Obtain necessary paperwork and begin completing it as soon as possible. If completing the study is also a university course requirement *or* if the project will take place in a college or university setting, contact the university's institutional review board (IRB). It is necessary to obtain an IRB application and complete it before formally beginning the study.

There are three levels of IRB review: exempt, non-exempt (full board review), and expedited. All three levels require some type of review of the project—even studies that are *exempt*—but full review, in which an entire IRB committee must come together to review and approve a study, is required only under certain conditions such as when there is potential harm to participants or when protected populations are used (e.g., pregnant women, prisoners, the mentally disabled). Most practitioner studies go through exempt or expedited review because research studies are based on typical educational practices that do not disadvantage a group (comparison studies where one group receives instruction and another does not *would* potentially disadvantage the group receiving no instruction) or that would potentially bring harm to participants. Those interested in the full federal guidelines provided by the U.S. Department of Health and Human Services may access the guidelines at www.hhs.gov/ohrp/.

Although the process of obtaining permissions can be burdensome, it is a necessary and important step of the action research process. Obtaining permissions will protect you, your participants, your school, and your university. If you are a parent, you probably would not want your child's teacher to conduct a research study that involves your child without telling you and obtaining your permission. You also probably would not want the teacher to report information about your child without your written permission. Always extend the courtesy of obtaining permission from the participants in your study, regardless of whether they are children or adults.

All participants must agree in writing to be part of the study. If the study includes individuals younger than 18 years of age, a requirement is to obtain their parents' permission to use data obtained on them in the study. Parental consent can be obtained using an informed consent form. On an informed consent form, it is imperative to explain the purpose of the study, the nature of participation in the study, that confidentiality will be maintained, and that participation is voluntary. Further, a statement must be included that says there will be no penalty for withdrawing from or not participating in the study. Figure 4.2 is an informed consent template for minors that can be adapted for

---

Informed Consent Form

Authorization for a Minor to Serve as a Research Participant

Dear Parents,

I will be conducting a study in our classroom to determine [include purpose here]. I am writing to ask permission to use the data I collect from your child during this process. Participation in this study involves only regular classroom activities. You may contact me at any time regarding your child's participation. My phone number is [include phone number here]. The principal of the school has approved this study.

The purpose of the study is to [briefly describe purpose here]. The study will take place at [name location] and will last for [give time frame]. [Briefly describe the procedures you will follow.] During the study, I will collect various forms of data to determine whether [name of intervention] was successful. Possible types of data I will collect include [list data collection strategies such as samples of student work, surveys/questionnaires, interviews, observations, test scores, etc.]

Benefits of participating in this study include [describe the benefits]. Only [name(s) of researcher and collaborators] will have access to the data collected in this study. Your child's participation in this project is strictly confidential. Only I [and names of collaborators and/or supervising professor if study is part of a university assignment] will have access to your child's identity and to information that can be associated to your child's identity. [If applicable, state when data or documentation will be destroyed].

Use of data from your child is voluntary. You may contact me at any time if you do not wish to have your child's data included in the study.

Please check the appropriate box below and sign the form:

☐ I give permission for my child's data to be used in this study. I understand that I will receive a signed copy of this consent form. I have read this form and understand it.

☐ I do not give permission for my child's data to be included in this project.

_____	_____
Student's name	Signature of parent/guardian

_____
Date

FIGURE 4.2 Informed consent template for minors.

use in most studies. If your study includes adult participants, alter or adapt the form accordingly. Please keep in mind that this form is an example only. Check local, district, or university policy for specific requirements. Each participant and/or parent should sign two copies of the form. One is kept by the participant or parent and the other should be returned to you and filed in a safe place. Minors must also be given the opportunity to agree to be in the study by giving their assent. Figure 4.3 is a student assent template that can be altered for use in your study, if applicable.

If you are a teacher, you may be required by your district or university IRB to have written permission from the school or school district where your study will take place. Check the procedures in your school system and/or university IRB before collecting any data for your project. If a school or school district consent form is required, you may be able to use the consent template authorizing a school to participate in a study, which is included in Figure 4.4 (this form may need to be adapted for your particular setting).

Occasionally, parents will return a consent form on which they have indicated they do not want their child to be part of a research study. When

---

Student Assent Form
Authorization to Serve as a Research Participant

Dear Student,

I will be conducting a study in our classroom to determine [include purpose here]. I am asking permission to use the data I collect from you during this process. Participation in this study involves only regular classroom activities. You may ask me questions at any time about this study. The principal of the school has approved this study.

The purpose of the study is to [briefly describe purpose here]. The study will take place at [name location] and will last for [give time frame]. [Briefly describe the procedures you will follow.] During the study, I will collect various forms of data to determine whether [name of intervention] was successful. Possible types of data I will collect include [list data collection strategies such as samples of student work, surveys/questionnaires, interviews, observations, test scores, etc.]

Benefits of participating in this study include [describe the benefits]. I will not include your name in any report about this study. You have the right to ask me not to include your data in the study or to tell me later if you no longer want your data included.

If you agree to let me use your data in the study, please print and sign your name below.

I give permission for my data to be used in this study.

_____   _____
    Student's Printed Name   Student's Signature

_____
        Date

FIGURE 4.3 Student assent form.

Authorization for a School to Serve in a Research Study

Project: The purpose of this study is to examine the effects of

Researcher:

Employment Affiliation: Phone Number:

Location of the study:

Supervising University Professor (if applicable):

Purpose of the study:

Procedures to be followed:

Time and duration of the study:

Benefits of the study:

Persons who will have access to the records, data, tapes, or other documentation:

When the records, data, tapes, or other documentation will be destroyed (if applicable):

I understand that participation in this project is voluntary, and I understand that a parent or guardian may withdraw his/her child from this study at any time by notifying the researcher.

Statement of confidentiality:

The participation of the students in this project is confidential. Only the researcher, collaborators, and supervising professor [if appropriate] will have access to the students' identities and to information that can be associated with their identities.

Please check the appropriate box below and sign the form:

    ☐ I give permission for my school to participate in this project. I understand that I will
        receive a signed copy of this consent form. I have read this form and understand it.
    ☐ I do not give permission for my school to participate in this project.

_____   _____

    Signature of principal   Date

FIGURE 4.4 Authorization for a school to serve in a research study.

this happens, educators often get confused as to whether this means the child cannot be part of the instructional activities in the action research project. For this reason, make it clear on the consent form that the intervention is part of your normal instructional activities that all students will be a part of and that you are seeking permission only to *use/report* data collected on participants. Follow up with parents who have any questions or concerns about the study. Activity 4.3 provides steps for gaining participants' informed consent. Note that you may need to work through some of the activities in Chapter 5 on strategies for collecting data prior to completing and submitting forms.

TIME TO REFLECT

In thinking about ethical concerns related to your study, consider the following reflection questions based on those by Zeni (2009)—either on your own, in a collaborative group, or with a critical friend. Note reflections in your journal.

- Whose permission should you seek in conducting this study? Do you see this as valuable?
- How might parents, students, colleagues, and so on feel about your study? In what ways does this relate to gaining their consent? How might others' perspectives, biases, or assumptions influence your study?
- Who stands to gain from this research? Will the process be a learning experience for you, for your participants, or for others?

ACTIVITY 4.3
Gaining Informed Consent

1. Contact the review board that oversees research studies. If you are conducting your study in a K–12 school/district setting, contact the school district office to locate the individual or board that reviews research studies. If you are conducting your study as part of a university's requirement (or in a university setting), contact the university's institutional review board (IRB). Contact both the school district IRB *and* the university IRB if your study is both in a K–12 school/district setting and is part of a university requirement. Once you have made contact, request information on the review process(es).
2. Complete and submit paperwork to applicable IRBs.
3. Once the study is approved, distribute informed consent forms to participants. Keep returned forms in a safe place. Be sure to analyze data on only those individuals who have granted consent.

Summary

The purpose of this chapter was to provide information on the steps of the action research process that occur during initial planning—articulation of primary and secondary research questions, choosing participants to be in the action research study, planning the intervention that will be used, considering ways to collaborate throughout the study, and adhering to ethical guidelines for research. Activities were provided to take educators through each of these steps of the process. In Chapters 5 and 6, the remaining steps of planning the study—including increasing validity and credibility of your study, choosing data collection methods, and creating a timeline—will be described.

5

Strategies for Collecting Data

Chapter Goals

- Explain how collecting multiple forms of data increases credibility in action research studies.

- Describe various types of data—artifacts, observational, and inquiry—that can be collected to answer research questions.

- Illustrate ways to align data collection strategies with primary and secondary research questions.

- Demonstrate the ways in which baseline data can be used in action research studies.

- Provide activities to guide practitioners through the process of choosing data collection strategies that are aligned with the focus of their studies.

Before implementing the research plan developed in Chapter 4, you must decide on the data collection strategies you will use in your action research study. This process involves determining the types of data that must be collected to lead to meaningful, accurate, and appropriate conclusions regarding research questions. Multiple data collection strategies must be employed to establish the credibility of research findings. In this chapter, information is provided on ways to increase the credibility of your study through the collection of multiple forms of data and ways to align data collection with research questions. Numerous data collection strategies—organized in this text as artifacts, observational data, and inquiry data—are also included. The activities in this chapter are provided to help you choose the best data collection strategies for your study.

COLLECTING MULTIPLE FORMS OF DATA TO ESTABLISH CREDIBILITY AND VALIDITY

When planning ways to collect data to answer research questions, a researcher must consider how to best ensure that the findings of study are credible and valid. Credibility can be established through **triangulation**, a process in which multiple forms of data are collected and analyzed. As explained by Rossman and Rallis (2012), triangulation "helps ensure that you have not studied only a fraction of the complexity that you seek to understand" (p. 65).

To illustrate the importance of triangulation, consider an action research study conducted by a high school science teacher on increasing academic achievement in a college preparatory biology class by having students work in collaborative study groups. If the teacher reported the use of collaborative groups was successful because some students had higher test scores after participating in the groups than they did before participating in the groups, you would be wise to question the credibility of this finding. There are a number of reasons why test scores might have increased (for example, the unit studied during the intervention might have been easier or more interesting than previous units). If the teacher had collected multiple forms of data that all pointed to higher achievement during the collaborative groups intervention, credibility of the findings would be increased. In this particular example, the teacher could have looked at many forms of student work in addition to test scores, and she could have observed the collaborative groups as they worked together. She might also have interviewed or surveyed students about their perceptions of the strengths and weaknesses of learning in collaborative groups. Analysis of various student work products (tests, papers, projects, etc.), observational notes, and interview or survey data would help the teacher determine the reasons the intervention was successful.

Consider the credibility of the results of the study if triangulation had been used and these were the findings:

- *Students' grades* increased, on average, by 7 points, and students with the lowest averages prior to the collaborative group intervention made the greatest gains.
- *Observations* of students indicated that peers were able to help each other understand difficult concepts, and students asked more questions

---

triangulation: A method in which multiple forms of data are collected and compared to enhance the validity and credibility of a research study.

about unit content during the collaborative group work and during class lectures.

- *Interviews* revealed that students felt they were able to learn from their peers more easily than learning from the book or listening to a lecture, students spent more time preparing for class so that they would be able to participate in their collaborative groups, and students studied for the unit test with their collaborative group outside of class.

Considering the results of these varied data collection strategies helps us feel confident that the collaborative group intervention did indeed lead to higher academic achievement for the participating students. Further, the observations and interviews help us understand *why* the intervention succeeded. In your own study, you may try an intervention that turns out to be unsuccessful. If this happens, looking at your varied data sources will help you figure out the reasons the intervention did not work, which is critical for ongoing reflective planning. Collecting multiple forms of data and triangulating them will help increase the credibility of your findings, and this will ultimately affect the validity of your study.

TIME TO REFLECT

Refer to the research questions you wrote for Activity 4.1. Then, discuss the following reflection questions with a critical friend, collaborator, or colleague. Write about your reflections in your journal.

- What kinds of data could you collect to answer your primary and secondary research questions? Which would help you measure outcomes? Which would help you answer *why* questions?
- What's more important to you—getting the outcomes you hope for or understanding *why* you do or do not get those outcomes? Which is more important to other stakeholders in this study (such as parents, colleagues, supervisors)? How do these considerations affect your study?

METHODS OF DATA COLLECTION: ARTIFACTS, OBSERVATIONAL DATA, AND INQUIRY DATA

In this section, three categories of data will be described: artifacts, observational data, and inquiry data. Artifacts include various types of student work and products created by participants. There are many forms of observational data, including field notes, checklists, and photographs. Inquiry data are collected to elicit opinions, attitudes, and other types of feedback from participants. Surveys, questionnaires, interviews, and focus groups are typically used for collecting inquiry data. Table 5.1 includes the various forms of data collection strategies for the three data types that will be described in this chapter.

TABLE 5.1   Data Collection Strategies

Artifacts	Observational Data	Inquiry Data
Student-generated: • teacher-made tests • standardized tests • written assignments • performances • artwork • projects • journals • self-assessment • peer review *Teacher-generated:* • lesson plans • journals • self-assessment • peer review *Archived:* • computer-generated reports • school records • documents	• field notes/observational records • logs • narratives • checklists • tally sheets • videotapes • photographs • audiotapes • organizational charts/maps • behavioral scales	• interviews • focus groups • conferencing • surveys/questionnaires • attitude scales

Artifacts

There is a variety of ways to use artifacts to answer research questions. Many action research studies conducted by teachers focus on increasing student achievement. If your study focuses on student achievement, you will want to choose student-generated artifacts, such as assignments, projects, tests, or other types of work, as a data source in your study. If you are an administrator and have decided to focus your study on teachers rather than students (for example, investigating the effectiveness of a new teacher mentoring program), there may be teacher-generated artifacts that would be useful sources of data in your study. These include lesson plans, teacher journals, and self-assessments. A third type of artifact—archived sources—may be useful if you wish to use school records in your study. A variety of archived information, such as computer-generated reports, attendance and discipline records, or standardized test scores, can be valuable data sources.

STUDENT-GENERATED ARTIFACTS. Many types of artifacts can be used to measure students' attainment of learning objectives or students' progress toward non-academic goals. Some artifacts can be used for formative assessment, which occurs during the instructional process to monitor the effectiveness of instruction or intervention. **Formative assessment** artifacts include *quizzes* and other written assignments such as *short papers* or *essays, homework*, and *worksheets*. Utilizing these formative assessments can help determine the effectiveness of an intervention continuously throughout the study. This is beneficial in two ways. First, if formative assessments reveal the intervention is not working, reflective planning can occur during the study and the intervention can be altered as necessary. Second, collecting various types of formative assessments provides an opportunity to see changes—in student learning or professional development, for example—over time. **Summative assessment** is used to measure instructional outcomes at the conclusion of an intervention or intervention unit. Artifacts used in summative assessment include *projects, performances, papers*, and *teacher-made tests. Standardized tests,* which can also be considered a type of summative assessment, are not often used in action research studies, but they can be used if appropriate for the purpose of the study (for example, in a schoolwide study that involves utilizing a writing intervention for the purpose of increasing scores on the writing section of a standardized test).

Student *artwork* and student *performances* are often used in studies that take place in art, music, or physical education classes. For example, a band director interested in increasing his percussion students' ability to read music would use student performances as a measure of the effectiveness of his intervention strategy. Artwork can be used to measure both the acquiring of skill (e.g., understanding use of light and dimension in an art class) and changes in affective behavior such as how a student feels about him- or herself. To illustrate this latter use of artwork, consider the example provided in Figure 5.1, which shows two pictures drawn by a first-grade student when he was asked to draw himself at school. In the first picture, which was drawn just prior to the action research study, the child drew his school and drew himself outside the school building. After an intense intervention aimed at helping this child succeed in school, he again was asked to draw himself at school. In the second picture, the boy has drawn himself smiling and inside the school building.

Other forms of student-generated data include student journals, self-assessments, and peer review. Student *journals* can be used for more than just recording feelings and emotions. Students can use journals to record learning struggles, successes, or personal accounts of growth and learning. When using student journals in a study, the first step is to think about the kind of information the journals can provide. Students often need specific guidelines

formative assessment: A method of ongoing assessment used to determine whether progress is being made toward goals.

summative assessment: A method of assessment used at the conclusion of instruction or intervention to determine whether goals have been met.

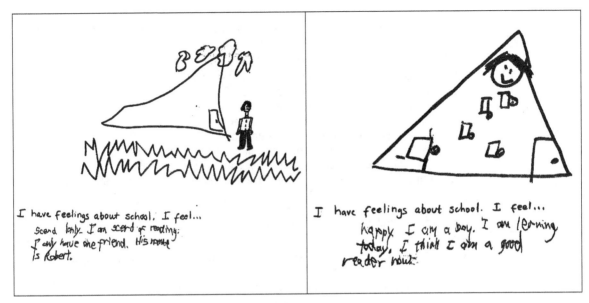

I have feelings about school. I feel...
Scared only. I am scard of reading:
I only have one friend. His name
is Robert.

I have feelings about school. I feel...
happy I am a boy. I am learning
today, I think I am a good
reader now.

FIGURE 5.1 Student artwork example.

or prompts for journal writing, which can increase the chances that information in the journals will be useful. Here is an example: Consider an action research study that focuses on increasing writing achievement in a fifth-grade class. The teacher has decided to utilize student journals for two purposes. First, the teacher will provide journal prompts to gather information about student perceptions of the writing intervention being used. Second, responses in the journals will be analyzed to determine whether writing achievement has improved. Some of the journal prompts used might be

> *The most difficult part of writing for me is . . .*
>
> *Writer's workshop* [the intervention] *has helped me . . .*
>
> *I still struggle with these things when I write . . .*
>
> *Writing makes me feel . . .*

To assess any changes in writing achievement from the journal entries, the teacher would need to use a standard form of assessment, such as a scoring rubric, to evaluate student work. The use of rubrics will be described later in this section.

Self-assessments are completed by students as they evaluate their own work or their progress toward a certain goal, which may be academic, motivational, behavioral, or affective. Self-assessments can be particularly useful as a type of formative assessment because they indicate students' perceptions

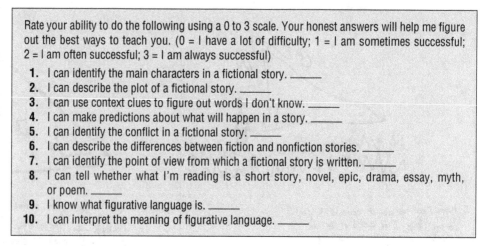

Rate your ability to do the following using a 0 to 3 scale. Your honest answers will help me figure out the best ways to teach you. (0 = I have a lot of difficulty; 1 = I am sometimes successful; 2 = I am often successful; 3 = I am always successful)

1. I can identify the main characters in a fictional story. _____
2. I can describe the plot of a fictional story. _____
3. I can use context clues to figure out words I don't know. _____
4. I can make predictions about what will happen in a story. _____
5. I can identify the conflict in a fictional story. _____
6. I can describe the differences between fiction and nonfiction stories. _____
7. I can identify the point of view from which a fictional story is written. _____
8. I can tell whether what I'm reading is a short story, novel, epic, drama, essay, myth, or poem. _____
9. I know what figurative language is. _____
10. I can interpret the meaning of figurative language. _____

FIGURE 5.2 Academic self-assessment for reading comprehension (7th grade).

of their progress toward learning objectives. If self-assessments reveal that students are struggling, the teacher can engage in reflective planning and make changes to the intervention as necessary. When self-assessments are used, the teacher must make clear to students that honesty and accuracy on the self-assessments are critical so that teaching activities can be planned to increase student learning or growth. This will help reduce the incidence of students providing positive, but inaccurate, self-assessments. Figures 5.2 and 5.3 provide examples of self-assessment. Figure 5.2 is an example of an academic self-assessment.

In Figure 5.3, a behavioral self-assessment is displayed that includes a teacher assessment component. This type of assessment can be useful for providing feedback to students showing how the teacher's assessment is similar to or different from the student's assessment. It also allows the teacher to keep track of differences in student and teacher perceptions of assessment.

Rate how you did in class today following the classroom behavioral objectives. Use this scale:

A = GREAT!; B = pretty good; C = could use some work; D = could use a lot of work; F = TERRIBLE!

STUDENT ASSESSMENT	BEHAVIOR	TEACHER ASSESSMENT
A B C D F	I stayed in my seat.	A B C D F
A B C D F	I raised my hand to speak.	A B C D F
A B C D F	I completed my work.	A B C D F
A B C D F	I paid attention to the lesson.	A B C D F
A B C D F	I did not disturb my classmates.	A B C D F

FIGURE 5.3 Behavioral self-assessment for Johnny Vincent (Mr. Mathis, 4th grade).

Peer review involves having a student evaluate the work of another student, which gives them an opportunity to provide and receive feedback from peers on their work or progress. Peer review can be especially useful when students are allowed to revise their work based on the feedback they get from peers. When peer review is used, standard criteria for assessment in the form of a scoring rubric should be used. Often, the same scoring rubric used by the teacher to grade students' work can be used in the peer review process.

No matter which types of student artifacts are used in the action research study, steps must be taken to ensure artifacts do indeed measure what they are intended to measure, meaning they are valid. For example, if a teacher-made test will be used as a type of summative evaluation in the study, the test must accurately measure what was taught during the intervention. So, in a study focused on teaching students multiplication facts (2 × 9, 3 × 4, etc.), measuring their knowledge of multiplication facts using a word problem test (*Farmer John has three rows of corn with four seeds planted in each row. How many stalks of corn can he expect if all the seeds grow?*) would not accurately measure whether students know multiplication facts. Scrutinize your assessment methods to ensure that they are aligned with instruction. Ask collaborators or a critical friend to look at your assessment methods and help you determine whether the methods are valid for measuring what you want them to measure.

Also, keep in mind that your assessment of student artifacts must somehow be standardized. Simply stated, this means that all work is assessed in the same way. For work that is considered subjective in nature—such as essays, papers, projects, performances, or artwork—you will need to take steps to ensure students are assessed in a standard way. The most efficient way to do this is to create a **scoring rubric**. In creating a scoring rubric, the criteria by which students will be assessed must be determined, and then a decision must be made regarding how different levels of performance on these criteria will translate into an evaluation, score, or grade. If you will be creating a scoring rubric for your own study, there are several books on creating scoring rubrics that may be helpful to you, including the following:

Burke, K. (2010). *From standards to rubrics in six steps* (3rd ed.). Thousand Oaks, CA: SAGE.

Stevens, D. D., & Levi, A. J. (2011). *Introduction to rubrics: An assessment tool to save grading time, convey effective feedback, and promote student learning* (2nd ed.). Sterling, VA: Stylus Publishing.

---

scoring rubric: A guideline for measuring whether objectives have been met based on predetermined performance criteria.

In addition, there are some useful websites for teachers who wish to create scoring rubrics:

- *Kathy Schrock's Guide for Educators—Assessment Rubrics* (available at http://school.discovery.com/schrockguide/assess.Html)
- *Rubrics: Scoring Guidelines for Performance Assessment* by Adele Fiderer (available at http://teacher.scholastic.com/professional/profdev/summerbookclubs/grade46)
- *RubiStar for Problem-Based Learning Activities* (available at http://rubistar.4teachers.org/)

You may wish to conduct your own Internet searches using the keywords *rubric, scoring rubric,* or *grading rubric.* Two examples of scoring rubrics are provided in Figures 5.4 and 5.5. Figure 5.4 is a mathematics scoring rubric, and Figure 5.5 is a public speaking performance scoring rubric.

TEACHER-GENERATED ARTIFACTS. Many of the student-generated artifacts described previously are similar to the types of teacher-generated artifacts that can be used when teachers are the study participants. Journals kept by teachers are a good source of data, and they can be used to evaluate both affective and behavioral information. For example, if a principal or staff development specialist were interested in studying the effect of a mentoring program for first-year teachers, she might ask first-year teachers to keep a daily or weekly journal about meetings with mentors. As described in the previous section, journal prompts could be used to

SOLVING LINEAR EQUATIONS AND INEQUALITIES IN ONE VARIABLE			
	Advanced (4)	Proficient (3)	Basic (2)	Emerging (1)
Solution	Student demonstrates a thorough understanding of the concepts and provides correct solutions for all problems.	Student demonstrates good understanding of concepts and provides correct solutions at least 80 percent of the time.	Incorrect solution provided, but student demonstrates some understanding of concepts.	Student provides incorrect solution.
Procedure	Student uses correct procedures at all times.	Student uses correct procedures at least 80 percent of the time.	Student always or often uses incorrect procedures but demonstrates some understanding of how to use procedures.	Student uses incorrect procedures in an attempt to solve the problem.
Explanation of Solution	Explanation of solutions are correct and are provided for all problems.	Explanation of solutions are correct at least 80 percent of the time.	Explanations of solution are incorrect, but student can explain some procedures correctly.	Explanation of solutions are incorrect.

FIGURE 5.4 Math scoring rubric (Mr. Compton, 8th grade algebra).

	Excellent (4)	Good (3)	Adequate (2)	Poor (1)
Clarity	Speaker clearly enunciates all words.	Speaker clearly enunciates most words.	Speaker enunciates some words.	Speaker does not enunciate.
Eye Contact	Speaker maintains eye contact with audience.	Speaker often makes eye contact with audience.	Speaker makes little eye contact with audience.	Speaker does not make eye contact with audience.
Grammar	Speaker makes no grammatical errors.	Speaker makes few grammatical errors.	Speaker makes some grammatical errors.	Speaker makes numerous grammatical errors.
Information	Speech includes many facts related to topic.	Speech includes some facts related to topic.	Speaker includes few facts related to topic.	Speaker includes no facts related to topic.
Volume	Speaker maintains appropriate volume level throughout speech.	Speaker uses appropriate volume level during most of the speech.	Speaker uses uneven volume throughout the speech.	Speaker uses inappropriate volume level throughout the speech.

FIGURE 5.5 Public speaking performance rubric (Mrs. Hall, beginning speech).

ensure certain types of needed information are included in the journal. Prompts might include

The most useful information my mentor has shared with me was . . .

I wish my mentor would help me with . . .

My mentor has helped me with classroom management by . . .

My mentor has helped me with my instruction by . . .

Self-assessment and peer review are other sources of teacher-generated artifacts. *Self-assessment* can be used to gather teachers' perceptions of their strengths and weaknesses, their understanding of state mandates, or their content knowledge. An example of a teacher self-assessment is provided in Figure 5.6. It should be noted that, with self-report data such as this, respondents might provide answers they think are expected of them or are socially desirable rather than provide an honest and accurate self-assessment. With all types of self-assessments, it is imperative to explain to the respondents that honest responses are desired. Other methods, such as allowing respondents to remain anonymous or informing respondents that there are no risks in providing honest responses (and following through on this policy), may increase the likelihood that responses are honest.

Peer review as a teacher-generated artifact can be used to allow teachers to receive feedback from colleagues on various aspects of their teaching, which could include topics such as teaching effectiveness, participation in curriculum

This self-assessment will be used to determine areas for mentoring during this school year. Our ability to provide the best and most useful mentoring for you relies on your honesty and candor as you complete this assessment.

Please rate your abilities in each of the following areas using the scale:

1 = I need a lot of help in this area
2 = I am making progress in this area, but I need some help
3 = I do not need help in this area

Also list your strengths and weaknesses in each area.

1. Classroom management   1 2 3
    Strengths:
    Weaknesses:

2. Use of class time   1 2 3
    Strengths:
    Weaknesses:

3. Lesson planning   1 2 3
    Strengths:
    Weaknesses:

4. Understanding the content I teach   1 2 3
    Strengths:
    Weaknesses:

5. Working with students who have special needs 1 2 3
    Strengths:
    Weaknesses:

6. Understanding school procedures   1 2 3
    Strengths:
    Weaknesses:

FIGURE 5.6 Teacher self-assessment for first-year teachers at Griffin High School.

planning, communicating with parents, and classroom management. The self-assessment for first-year teachers provided in Figure 5.6 could also be used for peer review. For example, a mentor teacher or administrator could use the assessment to determine areas in which the new teacher needed mentoring.

Lesson plans are another type of teacher-generated artifact that can be useful in action research studies. For example, in an action research study that focused on training teachers to use a new method for teaching reading comprehension, the researcher would be interested in determining whether teachers were utilizing their training and using the new method during instruction. Evaluating lesson plans is one way the researcher can look for evidence that teachers are indeed incorporating the new reading comprehension methods into their lessons.

Archived artifacts.   Archived artifacts, such as computer-generated reports, school records, and school documents can be useful sources of data in some action research studies, particularly studies conducted at the school level. For example, a media specialist I worked with utilized *computer-generated reports* in an action research study she conducted on the use of the Accelerated Reader program at her school. In working with teachers, she observed that some teachers were not implementing the program—which assesses a student's reading level, allows the student to choose books to read on that level, and then assesses the student's success on a reading comprehension test—effectively or with much enthusiasm. The purpose of the media specialist's study was to train the teachers in the effective use of Accelerated Reader with the hope of getting them to buy into the program. One aspect of the Accelerated Reader program is that it generates computer reports for students and classes regarding each student's reading level and his or her rate of success on the reading comprehension tests. The media specialist was able to use these computer-generated reports to determine whether training the teachers to use Accelerated Reader had an effect on students' reading levels and reading comprehension.

School records are another source of archived data that may be useful in an action research study, providing information on attendance, disciplinary actions, retention rates, or standardized achievement scores. Finally, *documents* such as PTA bulletins, committee meeting minutes, and school handbooks can be good sources of data, particularly if the action research study involves analyzing perceptions, goals, school culture, or procedures. For example, analyzing PTA bulletins can reveal issues teachers and parents see as important. Analysis of the school handbook can reveal information on the culture, climate, and rules in a school. Studying committee meeting minutes can indicate how time is spent during meetings, what issues are seen by teachers and administrators as important, and how much progress is made toward achieving goals over time.

TIME TO REFLECT

With your primary and secondary research questions in front of you, consider the following reflection questions—either on your own, in a collaborative group, or with a critical friend. Note in your journal your reflections.

- What types of artifacts could be used to help you answer your research questions? What steps might you take to ensure these artifacts measure what you intend to measure (meaning they are valid)?
- What could you do to ensure your analysis of artifacts is fair and unbiased?
- How can you encourage participants to give you honest, thoughtful responses in journals and self-assessments (if relevant)?
- If your analysis of artifacts reveals something difficult for you (such as ineffective teaching or colleagues who are critical of you), how accepting will you be of that information? How will you create a safe space for participants to provide information or feedback that might be critical or negative?

Observational Data

Observational data can be the most important source of information in an action research study. Whereas artifacts can help you decide whether an intervention has had an impact (for example, evaluating student work to look for gains in achievement), observational data can help determine why an intervention was successful or unsuccessful and how the context of the setting affected the study. To illustrate, consider an action research study conducted by a principal on the use of teacher study groups to improve school climate. The principal could interview or survey teachers to determine whether school climate improved because of the intervention, but knowing only whether there was an improvement would greatly limit the credibility of the study. Observations of teachers as they worked in the study groups could reveal teacher attitudes and perceptions about the issues related to school climate. Continuing to observe the study groups throughout the study would allow the principal to see how attitudes and perceptions change over time, and the ongoing observations could provide the principal with the opportunity to understand how the complex issues dealt with by teachers interact to impact school climate. The deeper level of understanding that comes with good observational data collection leads to effective and ongoing reflective planning.

As you determine the best ways to use observation in your own action research study, you must consider how observational data will be used to inform your action research study, what it is you want to observe, who you want to observe, and what role you wish to play in the observation. First, how will observational data be used in your study? Is the purpose to evaluate how the intervention is working or how participant behavior is affected by the intervention? Deciding on the purpose of your observation will help you establish what it is that you want to observe.

Once you know what you want to observe, you must also determine who you want to observe. If you are conducting a study with a large group of students, it may not be possible to observe each participant. If this is the case in your study, how will you choose who you observe? Will you focus on those students who have struggled the most in the past? Will you choose only the high achievers? Will you randomly select a small number of individuals to observe? Will you systematically choose so that you are able to observe different types of participants? Will you simply make general observations of the setting? Once again, the best rule here is to focus on the purpose of your study and on your primary and secondary research questions. In order for you to answer your questions, who must be observed in your study?

Finally, you must consider the role you wish to play in observation. If you are a teacher studying your classroom, you will be a participant-observer. As a teacher, you cannot simply sit back and watch what goes on in your classroom. Even if you are observing students as they work in collaborative groups, you will still be teacher and facilitator—a participant in the classroom environment. In other types of action research studies, it is possible to be an observer without having to participate in the action. For example, a principal or administrator could observe a teacher study group without actually being a part of that group (although the non-participant status could change if the teachers attempted to bring the administrator into the discussion).

Although it is difficult to be anything but a participant observer in educational action research, the observer can engage in different levels of observation. For example, if it is critical to the purpose of your study that you engage in ongoing observation during your study, you will probably choose to make notes throughout the study, even during the intervention. If, instead, it is critical for you to stay focused on the intervention, it may be necessary to video and/or audio record during your study so that you can concentrate on teaching during the intervention and make observations from the video later. Finally, if it is important in your study to have some type of non-participant observation in order to get a different perspective of what is occurring during your study, you may wish to ask a critical friend or collaborator to make some observations of your research setting. Comparing your observations with another colleague's or critical friend's observations is a method of peer debriefing, and it can be useful for checking biases and getting a second opinion about what the observations indicate.

One method of collecting observational data is through *observational records* or *field notes*. Field notes are kept throughout the study and include detailed information about implementation of the intervention, participant responses, and surprising events. Field notes are best kept in a journal, and they should be entered each day of the study or each day the intervention takes place. Because you may be both a participant and observer in your study, it can be difficult to record detailed information as you are teaching or facilitating. It is more reasonable to jot brief notes as significant or note-worthy events occur, but it is critical to make more detailed notes as soon as possible. Establish a time each day—during planning time, during lunch, or at the end of the day—to expand the notes made earlier. Remember, too, that it is not necessary to write down every event that occurs. Focus on making notes that are relevant to the study.

When you observe something that seems to be vital for describing or understanding aspects of your study, you may wish to write a *narrative* account of the event. A narrative is simply a detailed description of an event used to portray detailed contextual information. Consider this example: A fourth-grade teacher focused his action research study on a severely withdrawn and socially shy child whose withdrawal from peers was negatively affecting his classroom participation, acceptance by peers, and academic achievement. Here is the teacher's narrative account of Juan's activities after fourteen weeks of intervention:

> Juan raised his hand, and when I called on him, he quietly asked me if he could work with Rita to complete his math sheet. Over the past three weeks, Juan has been requesting to work with Rita on some math assignments. Rita is a good math student but is quiet and reserved much like Juan, though she participates in class and has many friends. Each time Juan has worked with Rita, he has gone to her desk, watched her complete some math problems, and waited for her to say the first word. Usually Rita will ask Juan a question such as, "Which one are you stuck on?" or "What problem are you working on now?" Juan then points to the problem or quietly says the number of the problem. Of the several times Juan has worked with Rita, he has rarely said a word to her. Instead, he watches how she completes a problem, listens to her explanation, and then tries a problem himself as Rita shows him how to do it. Today, though, Juan went to Rita's desk and very quietly said, "I don't know how to do this problem [long division, worksheet 5.1, question 4]. I keep getting stuck here [what to do with the remainder]." Rita showed him how to work the problem and then asked him if he understood. This is the first time she has asked him a question like that. It appears she took her cue from Juan. Because he was more vocal today—initiating a conversation—she was too. Juan responded, "I think so," and then attempted to complete the next problem on his own. Rita watched quietly, and when he was done and had successfully calculated the answer, she looked at Juan, smiled, and said, "That's right! You did that really fast." This was the first time she had encouraged Juan in that way. Juan, who rarely looks his peers or me in the eye, looked at Rita, smiled, and said quietly, "Thanks." He then went back to his seat and completed his assignment. When he was done, which was much sooner than the majority of his classmates, Juan raised his hand. When I called on him, he came to my desk and showed me his paper, though students were not required or even asked to do this. I asked Juan if he wanted me to grade his paper then, and he nodded yes. I scored his paper and he missed only one problem, which was one of the most difficult. I showed Juan which answer was incorrect and he said, "What did I do wrong?" I showed him his mistake and explained how to fix it. Juan then went back to his desk with his paper, fixed his mistake, and then sat quietly. Marcus then came to my desk and said he didn't understand what to do. I asked Rita, Juan, and Melinda if any of them would be willing to help Marcus since they were already finished with their assignments. Even Juan said yes. Marcus chose to work with Rita, but when Samantha asked for

help and I told her she could work with Juan or Melinda, she chose to work with Juan. Though he seemed a bit reluctant at first, Juan patiently showed Melinda how to work one of the problems. He spoke very quietly and at one point Melinda said she couldn't hear him. Juan spoke a bit louder then and continued to explain how to do the problem. After several minutes, Melinda said, "Oh! I get it!" She thanked Juan and sat down to complete her assignment. When I asked for volunteers to try some new problems on the board, Juan kept his head down, which is his usual behavior. However, he was attentive as his peers completed their work on the board, and he raised his hand to help Marcus when he was stuck on his problem.

This narrative was written from brief field notes (see Figure 5.7) jotted by a teacher during his action research study. Because it is difficult, if not impossible, to write detailed narratives during an observation, it is necessary to expand field notes soon after the observation to ensure that important details are remembered. Narratives such as these can provide much insight in certain action research studies. In the study focusing on Juan, the narrative account expresses the nuances of Juan's behavior that help us understand exactly how he is changing as a result of the teacher's intervention. The narrative is much more useful in understanding Juan as a person and in understanding the change in his behavior than a brief description such as, "Juan now works well with other children, asks questions in class, and has improved his grades from Ds and Fs to As and Bs." Keep in mind that writing numerous narrative accounts can be a time-consuming enterprise, so carefully choose the events you wish to explain through a narrative.

DATE	TIME	BEHAVIOR
Oct. 16, 2007	0946	Juan asked to work with Rita (math worksheet 5.1)
	0948	Juan initiated conversation with Rita: "I don't know how to do this problem [5.1, #4]. I keep getting stuck here [Remainder]".
	0950	Rita showed Juan how to work the problem and asked if he understood [new behavior/conversation]. Encouraged Juan. Juan made eye contact, said, "thanks."
	1002	Juan asked me to review his problems [new behavior]—only 1 wrong answer. Juan asked me to explain his mistake.
	1005	Juan offered to help Marcus and Samantha [new behavior]. Juan worked with Samantha. Samantha asked Juan to speak up.
	1018	Juan helped Marcus with problem on board.

FIGURE 5.7 Behavioral log for Juan R., 4th grade, Mr. Brindle.

Field notes and narratives are a great way to collect detailed information. However, it may be useful to make less detailed observations, in which case logs, checklists, and tally sheets can be utilized. A *log* is a running record of activities that is used to record events at specified intervals. To keep a log, you must first determine how often you will record events. For example, if you decide to record information every ten minutes, you must carefully observe the time and each ten minutes write down what is occurring. A log is an effective way of keeping track of activities, but it is not always useful to keep track of participant behaviors. Significant behaviors can happen at any time, not just every ten minutes. Figure 5.8 provides an example of a teacher's log.

Logs can also be kept to record behaviors. Behavior logs are especially well suited to studies that focus on increasing appropriate student behaviors. The log can serve as a running record of inappropriate behaviors and when the behaviors occur. For this type of log, behaviors are written down as they occur, and the time of occurrence is noted with each behavior. Behavior logs can also be used to simply record any type of observed behavior, which is illustrated in Figure 5.7. This log was later expanded into a narrative, which was presented previously.

Checklists and tally sheets are used to track types of behavior or events and their frequency. On a *checklist*, the researcher keeps track of behaviors that are exhibited or events that occur. A *tally sheet* is used to keep up with

TIME	EVENTS
0900	Began class with focusing exercise on the amoeba. Assignment was on board: Draw and label all parts of an amoeba.
0910	Discussed collaborative assignment for today: In assigned groups of 5, students design a new single-cell life form.
0920	Students working in groups: reading assignment sheet, asking for clarification, making notes
0930	Students working in groups: Group 1: Students silently reading/skimming textbook Chapter 7. Group 2: Students engaged in debate about food source. Group 3: Group leader has assigned separate tasks to each group member. Group 4: Students discussing shape of their organism. Group 5: Students independently working quietly on sketches and ideas.
0940	Students working in groups: G1: Discussing all necessary elements to describe for project. G2: Discussing reproduction. G3: Still working on separate tasks. G4: Sketching life form. G5: Group members sharing sketches and ideas.
0950	Break for whole-class question/answers.
1000	Each group completes progress sheet to turn in.
1010	Dismissal.

FIGURE 5.8 Teaching log for Jurdell Jackson, Honors Biology, 2nd Period.

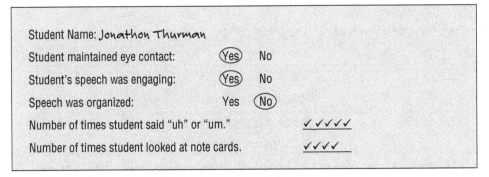

Student Name: Jonathon Thurman

Student maintained eye contact:	(Yes)	No
Student's speech was engaging:	(Yes)	No
Speech was organized:	Yes	(No)
Number of times student said "uh" or "um."		✓ ✓ ✓ ✓
Number of times student looked at note cards.		✓ ✓ ✓

FIGURE 5.9 Checklist and tally sheet for persuasive speech.

the number of times a behavior is exhibited. Both checklists and tally sheets are used to gather information at a point in time such as during a class period, at lunch or recess, during a group activity, or during a performance. Checklists and tally sheets can be combined, as can be seen in Figure 5.9.

Figure 5.10 is an example of a checklist that could be used to monitor activities during collaborative work. An effective and useful checklist should include those behaviors that are deemed important in relation to the intervention or the desired effects of the intervention. Thus, in the example in Figure 5.10, the teacher has listed the desirable traits of effective collaboration (the intervention), and he uses the checklist to monitor which groups exhibit those traits. Analysis of the checklists and other forms of data that may be collected (student work, field notes, surveys) will help the teacher determine the traits that are necessary for collaborative group work to be most effective.

Figure 5.11 shows an example of a tally sheet used to monitor behaviors. In this example, the teacher is studying the effects of a behavioral intervention for a child with autism who is mainstreamed in a regular fourth-grade classroom. Using tally sheets in a study such as this can help the researcher see how behavior changes over time during and after the intervention process. The tally sheet is different from a behavior log. On a behavior log, behaviors are written down as they happen. On a tally sheet,

BEHAVIORS/ACTIVITIES	GROUP 1	GROUP 2	GROUP 3	GROUP 4	GROUP 5
All members actively participate.	✓		✓		✓
Group members are respectful of one another.	✓	✓		✓	✓
Group members attempt to complete work on their own before asking me questions.	✓		✓	✓	
Group stays on task.	✓		✓	✓	
Group completes and turns in progress sheet.	✓	✓	✓		✓

FIGURE 5.10 Collaborative groups checklist, Honors Biology, 2nd Period, Mr. Jackson.

Observed Student: Micah R.   Date: March 15   Time: 0830-0930

Undesired Behaviors		Desired Behaviors	
Tapping pencil:	✓✓✓✓✓	Asking for help with work:	✓✓
Spinning pencil:	✓	Raising hand for attention:	✓
Mumbling:	✓✓✓✓✓✓	Responding when spoken to:	✓✓✓
Talking out in class: ✓✓		Following oral directions:	

Notes: Micah responded three times when spoken to (out of seven opportunities). Micah was given oral directions five times during this period but did not follow directions at any time. Micah was asked three times to stop mumbling, once to stop tapping his pencil, and once to begin his work. He responded once with "Ok" when I asked him to stop mumbling, but he did not stop.

FIGURE 5.11 Tally sheet for Micah R., 4th grade, Mrs. Ellison's class.

common behaviors—particularly those that are focused on in the study—are listed on the sheet before the observation. Marks are made during the observation time to note how many times, if any, the behavior occurred.

Behavioral scales, like tally sheets, checklists, and behavioral logs, are used to provide an assessment or evaluation of behavior. A behavioral scale is used to determine a general assessment of behavior rather than keep track of the number of times a behavior occurs. A number of behavioral scales have been created to allow teachers, counselors, administrators, and other school staff to provide data that can be analyzed to determine whether a student exhibits signs of attention deficit disorder, hyperactivity, characteristics of autism or Asperger's syndrome, developmental delays, behavioral problems, and so on.

Video and *audio recordings* are not observational methods but are tools for observation. Often, as a participant as well as an observer in your study, you will lack the time to make observational notes on the spot. Also, as you teach or facilitate during the intervention phase of your study, it will not be possible to see and hear everything that is occurring. For these reasons, you might wish to consider video and audio recording parts of your study. You and your collaborators—as well as a peer reviewer or critical friend—can make observations from a video. Audio recordings are useful too, but they do not allow the researcher to see what is occurring. Audio recording can be helpful, though, particularly if the intervention involves collaboration on the part of participants. A principal investigating teacher study groups or a teacher studying the effects of collaborative learning cannot observe all groups at once. If each group is audio recorded, however, the principal or teacher can go back and listen to a record of events for each group.

As you determine whether you will use video and/or audio recording in your study, you need to consider several things. First, it is imperative that you have permission from participants, their parents (if participants are minors), and your school before you record participants either by video or audio. You also must decide what you will record and how often you will record. Keep in mind you will need to make observational notes from videos and transcriptions from audio recordings, and both activities are extremely time-consuming. For that reason, take time to think about how recording can help you answer your research questions. It is unlikely you will need to record every event during your entire study in order to get useful information. Come up with a plan that is reasonable and that will provide the kinds of data needed to answer research questions. The last thing you need to consider is choosing recording equipment. Video and audio recording can be frustrating, especially when equipment does not work properly. Make sure to do a test run before using any equipment. If groups of participants will be recording themselves, make sure they practice recording and listening to themselves so that they will know how loudly to speak so that the recordings are clear. Finally, clearly mark all video and audio recordings with dates, times, and participant information. You should plan to look at videos or listen to audio recordings as soon as possible.

Photographs are another tool for data collection. Although photos do not provide the kind of detailed information that a video can provide, they do offer a point-in-time reference, and they can be useful when included in a publication or presentation of an action research study. Burns (2010) provides a number of ways photos can be used in action research, including for illustration of the intervention strategy used, for presenting a lasting visual reference of classroom tasks and activities, and for personalizing the participants in the study. Consider the effectiveness of using photographs in the study about Juan, the shy and withdrawn student who was described earlier in a narrative. Including pictures of Juan before the intervention to compare to pictures during and after the intervention could be a powerful indicator of how Juan's behavior changed over time. Early pictures might show Juan away from others during classroom activities, whereas pictures taken during and after the intervention might show Juan working with other students. Pictures such as these, in addition to the narrative and other sources of data, would be powerful evidence of the change in Juan after the intervention phase.

Photographs can also be useful to show what an intervention looks like or to provide examples of student work. For example, a teacher studying the use of Reader's Workshop could use a series of pictures to show the different types of activities that are part of the intervention. She could also take pictures of student work or student performances (book reports, students engaged in debate about an issue from a book, oral presentations, dioramas relating to a story) to graphically illustrate the type of work and the quality of work that students provide. Photos used in these ways are useful when included in publications or presentations of the action research study. As Yin (2011) explains, "photographs should be well chosen to reflect a central facet of a study and its context" (p. 246). Be sure to secure permission from participants (and their parents if they are minors) before using photographs in your study.

Organizational charts or *maps* are used to provide various types of data related to the layout of an environment (the classroom, media center, playground) and the interactions of individuals in that environment. A media specialist, for example, could use a map of the media center to evaluate its layout. To begin, the media specialist would create a floor plan of the media center. Once the floor plan was created, the media specialist would make several observations of students and teachers as they used the media center, making notes on the floor plan. An example of an organizational map is provided in Figure 5.12.

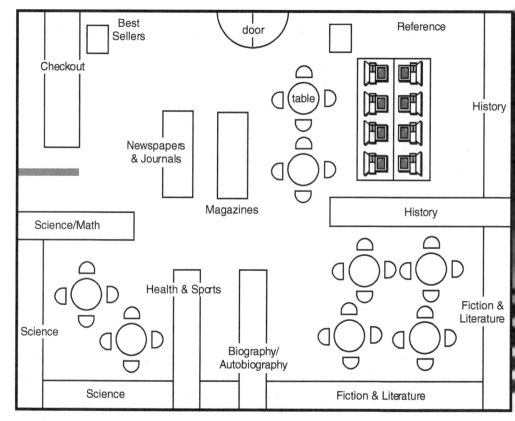

FIGURE 5.12 Media center floor plan for James Madison Middle School.

TIME TO REFLECT

Refer back to your primary and secondary research questions, and then consider the following reflection questions—either on your own, in a collaborative group, or with a critical friend. Note in your journal your reflections.

- What types of observational data could be used to help you answer your research questions?
- How might your assumptions and biases affect your perception of what you observe? How might you keep your biases in check when dealing with observations or observational data?
- How might your presence affect participants' actions? How will you know if what you observe is participants' authentic behavior?

Inquiry Data

Inquiry data are used to gather information from participants about their knowledge, values, beliefs, past experiences, feelings, opinions, attitudes, or perceptions. In action research studies, inquiry data can provide a researcher with participants' perceptions about the effectiveness of an intervention, ways the intervention could be improved, and feedback regarding positive and negative aspects of the intervention. Consider the example provided at the beginning of this chapter about a biology teacher's study of collaborative study groups. Collecting inquiry data in the form of interviewing students revealed to the teacher the students' attitudes about learning in collaborative study groups. Students expressed that it was easier for them to learn from peers than from the textbook or class lecture. Further, students said they spent more time preparing for class because they wanted to contribute to their collaborative group. In the interviews, students also explained that they studied for tests with their collaborative group outside of class, which is something they had not done in the past.

Allowing participants to express their ideas and opinions about various aspects of your study is a good way to add to the richness of your investigation. Inquiry data can help you answer the *why* questions in your study by providing your participants' assessment of the effectiveness of the intervention. This leads to a thorough understanding of reasons the intervention was successful (or unsuccessful). Further, analysis of the inquiry data participants provide is important in the ongoing process of reflective planning.

Inquiry data can be collected verbally in face-to-face meetings with participants through interviewing, holding focus groups, or by conferencing. There are many benefits to collecting these types of verbal data. One benefit is that participants have the opportunity to provide detailed feedback. Another benefit is that the researcher can shift the focus of the inquiry meeting based on participants' comments, and the researcher can ask questions as they arise in conversation with participants. Although verbal inquiry data are a rich source of information, there are negative aspects of collecting this type of data. First, if you wish to interview participants individually, the process of interviewing, transcribing the interviews, and analyzing the interview data can be time-consuming. Also, you must be able to facilitate your meetings with participants so that you maintain some measure of control in the meetings (you don't want it to turn into a free-for-all gripe session) while allowing participants freedom to express what they think is important for you to know. Finally, you must be able to listen to *criticism*—in both ways this term is defined: as a disapproval and as an assessment or analysis—without penalizing, denigrating, or reprimanding the critic. In action research, one of the most difficult aspects of data collection, particularly with inquiry data, is that participants may be reluctant to provide honest responses. Students may find it difficult to tell teachers how they honestly feel about the teacher's instruction or the way the teacher interacts with students. Teachers also may worry about providing their principal or another administrator with honest answers to interview questions. Thus, it is important to make your interviewees feel at ease. You must inform your interview participants that you cannot improve your practices without their honest answers, and you must assure them there will be no penalty for answering honestly. Although it may be hard for you to receive negative feedback, always keep in mind that any information participants provide is useful for helping you understand how to improve your practice. If eliciting honest answers is problematic in your particular study, consider having a colleague or collaborator collect inquiry data for you.

Interviewing participants can occur through a structured or unstructured process. In a *structured interview*, the researcher prepares a list of specific questions before the interview that guides the process. In an *unstructured interview*, the researcher asks broad questions and then lets the interview proceed on its own course. A *semi-structured interview*, which involves asking some planned questions and then allowing participants to speak about related issues that are important to them, can be useful in action research. Using a semi-structured interview is a good way to make sure that questions important to the researcher are answered while providing participants with an opportunity to add other useful information.

If you will use interviewing as a method for collecting inquiry data in your study, there are several steps to take in the planning process. First, determine the purpose of the interview. Think about how interview data will help you answer your primary and/or secondary research questions. Second, you must decide whom you will interview. If you are a teacher conducting a study in your classroom, you may not be able to interview all students because of the time needed. If, instead, you will interview only some participants, how will you decide who the interviewees will be? Will you choose randomly from the entire class? Will you choose systematically—for example, a few high-achieving, average-achieving, and low-achieving students or a few students who responded well to the intervention and some who responded poorly to the intervention—so that you get multiple perspectives? Be sure to carefully choose interviewees, keeping in mind that various perspectives may be important to help you find meaningful and credible answers to your research questions.

The third consideration in planning your interview is to determine whether you will conduct a structured, unstructured, or semi-structured interview. To help you decide, consider the purpose of interviewing in your study. If, for example, you are a teacher who wishes to elicit students' opinions about a new teaching strategy and their perceptions about its effectiveness, a semi-structured interview is a good choice. Specific questions such as, "How did working in the collaborative groups affect your learning?" "Do you prefer learning on your own, listening to class lectures, or working in a collaborative group?" and "In what ways is learning in a collaborative group different than learning in other ways?" could be followed with more open-ended questions, such as, "Tell me why you think learning in collaborative groups was so helpful to you" (following a participant's response that learning in the groups was helpful) and "How could I make the collaborative groups better?" Throughout the semi-structured interview, you should ask follow-up questions based on the participants' responses.

In some cases, an unstructured interview is the best way to gather information. This is particularly true early in the action research process if you are collecting baseline data, if you want to use participant feedback as you plan your intervention, or if you want to know how participants feel the intervention is going. For example, a principal interested in investigating the use of teacher study groups might choose to begin his study by interviewing teachers about their opinions of the study group concept. Information provided would be useful in planning how best to implement the study groups. If most interviewed teachers expressed that teachers should volunteer to be in study groups rather than be forced to participate in them, the principal would be wise to begin the study group intervention phase by asking teachers to participate. Once the volunteer study groups were formed, the principal could use unstructured interviews at the end of early study group sessions, asking a broad question such as, "In what ways, if any, is participation in this study group helping you in your classroom?" Feedback could be used for ongoing reflective planning for future study group sessions.

Structured interviews do not allow for the depth of responses and information that is so useful in action research studies. In fact, an interview that is too structured—one that allows for only yes and no answers, for example—is not much different from a survey. At times, though, a structured interview can be useful. A kindergarten teacher I worked with used a structured interview at the beginning of her study to determine her students' attitudes about writing. In the interview she asked questions such as, "Do you like to write?" "Do you like working in our writing center?" and "Why do people write?" The teacher was able to determine students' attitudes about writing and their perceptions about the uses of writing before the study began. This provided her with baseline data, which was later used to compare students' attitudes about writing after the intervention had been utilized. It also provided her with information about students' perceptions of the purposes of writing, which guided the initial reflective planning as she prepared the intervention.

If you plan to interview participants in your action research study, consider these interviewing strategies provided by Seidman (2006):

- **Listen more and talk less.** Listen to what the interviewee is saying and make sure you understand it.
- **Follow up on what the interviewee says.** When you ask questions in an unstructured interview, make sure the questions are related to what the participant has said. Ask for clarification on points you do not understand, and ask the interviewee to provide a story or example to illustrate his or her point.
- **Avoid asking leading questions.** Don't use words or tones that imply the correct response. For example, don't say, "Why are study groups more fun than studying by yourself?" Instead say, "Tell me about working in the study group."
- **Keep interviewees focused and ask for specific details.** If an interviewee gets off the topic, guide him or her back to it. Ask for specific, concrete details about experiences ("Describe the activities you engaged in during the collaborative group exercises").
- **Do not reinforce interviewees' responses.** Agreeing or disagreeing with an interviewee's response implies that there are correct and incorrect answers to your questions, which may impact the way he or she answers subsequent questions.

Rossman and Rallis (2012) suggest asking questions that provide participants opportunities to elaborate their answers such as, "Would you tell me more about that?" and "Could you go over that again?" (p. 184). Follow-up questions to participant responses can be used to gather additional information, clarify the interviewee's meaning, and get specific details that can aid in contextual understanding (Rossman & Rallis).

Focus groups are used for interviewing groups of participants. There are several advantages of using focus groups. One advantage is that focus groups allow for interviewing many participants at one time. As Fontana and Frey (2005) explain, focus groups provide a flexible environment that can help encourage participants' recall of events and that can produce "rich data that are cumulative and elaborative" (p. 128). In a focus group interview, responses of one participant can help other participants recall important information that they wish to share. Members of the focus group respond not only to the researcher, who moderates the discussion, but also to other individuals in the focus group. Thus, responses to questions build on others' responses, which can result in much richer data than that collected in individual interviews.

Moderating a focus group discussion involves more work on the part of the researcher than conducting individual interviews. Fontana and Frey (2005) provide several useful suggestions for moderating focus groups:

- Do not allow a person or a small group of people to dominate the discussion.
- Encourage participation from silent focus group members.
- Obtain responses from all members of the focus group.
- Balance the task of moderating the group and asking structured questions with allowing for evolving questions and interactions.

Also, follow the guidelines for interviewing listed earlier. Make sure to ask questions and guide the focus group discussion to elicit responses that will help answer primary and secondary research questions. Listen more than you talk. Ask for clarification. Emphasize the importance of honest responses.

Conferencing involves in-depth conversation between the researcher and a participant relating to some aspect of the action research study. Often, conferencing is used by a teacher in conjunction with a student work product. For example, a teacher studying ways to improve writing achievement could conference with a student about an essay written for class. The point of the conference would be to obtain information about the process of writing the essay. Questions such as, "How did you choose your essay topic?" "What strategies did you use to organize your paper?" and "How did you come up with the thesis for your paper?" are a few examples of the kinds of questions that could be asked during the conferencing session. Conferencing used in this way can be instructional because it allows for conversation and discussion of the elements of writing, and it can be informational because it provides the teacher with data regarding the strategies the student used during the writing process.

A teacher I recently worked with conducted an action research study on the effectiveness of her mentoring of a first-year teacher. Throughout the study, the mentor teacher used conferencing to discuss with the new teacher the effectiveness of various strategies the mentor had shared (classroom management techniques, instructional strategies). The conferencing sessions provided the mentor with a rich source of data: The mentored teacher gave feedback on the effectiveness of the mentor's strategies and her perceptions of why they did or did not work. The mentored teacher also shared information about difficulties she was still encountering in the classroom and asked for assistance in some of those areas, which provided the mentor with data for ongoing reflective planning. Finally, the mentor teacher was able to analyze the exchanges made during the conferences with the mentored teacher, which provided an illustration of the relationship between the two teachers.

If you decide to collect verbal inquiry data, either in the form of interviews, focus groups, or conferencing, be sure to audio record all sessions. This will allow you the freedom to actively listen during conversations with interviewees without having to take detailed notes. Follow the suggestions for audio recording provided in the section on observations. Remember that you may need to transcribe the audio recordings before analyzing the verbal inquiry data, which can be a time-consuming task. If a large amount of audio is to be transcribed, consider hiring a professional transcriber.

Inquiry data, in addition to being collected through conversations with participants, can be collected in written form using surveys/questionnaires or attitude scales. The benefit of these methods is that information can be collected from many participants at one time. It can take hours or even days to interview all students in a class, but a questionnaire can be given to that same class and completed in just a few minutes. Analyzing written inquiry data also takes less time than analyzing verbal inquiry data. The disadvantage of written inquiry data is that it does not allow for the depth of response that verbal inquiry data allows. Further, it is much easier to get participants to verbally answer questions and provide detailed responses than it is to get participants to provide detailed written information on open-ended questions.

Surveys or *questionnaires* are a good alternative to the structured interview. Questions asked during a structured interview can instead be written on a survey and distributed to participants—providing that participants are able to read the survey. In the earlier example of the kindergarten teacher's structured interview, it would not be wise to use a survey instead of an interview because children would not be able to read the survey. Keep in mind that if you use a survey in your action research study, your participants' reading ability must be high enough so that they can understand written questions. Ensure that the reading level of your survey matches the reading level of your participants.

Surveys and questionnaires are good alternatives to interviews and focus groups when time constraints are such that interviewing is impossible or when the researcher is seeking responses to a predetermined set of questions. In some cases, participants may feel more comfortable providing honest answers to an anonymous survey than being subjected to an interview in which their identity is known. Consider, though, that sometimes it is necessary that names are included on surveys. For example, you may want to compare multiple sources of data for each individual participant to determine whether a participant's work, your observations of the participant, and the participant's answers on a survey are related. If this is the case in your study, you should have participants include their names on surveys.

If matching different types of data is not important in your study, using an anonymous survey is fine.

If you plan to use a survey in your action research study, first consider how data from the survey will help you answer your primary and/or secondary research questions. Refer to your research questions as you plan questions for your survey. Consider this example: A middle school language arts teacher is interested in studying the effectiveness of literature circles for increasing student achievement and interest in reading. His primary research questions are "Does the use of literature circles increase students' reading achievement?" and "Does the use of literature circles increase students' interest in reading?" Secondary questions relate to *why* questions: "Why are literature circles effective (or ineffective) for increasing achievement and interest in reading?" and "In what ways does participating in literature circles change students' attitudes about reading?" The teacher could use a survey to measure students' perceptions of literature circles. An example is included in Figure 5.13.

Students, please complete this survey on literature circles. Answer each question, and provide as much information as you can on the open-ended questions. It is important to be honest in your answers because I will use the information you provide to help me plan future language arts lessons. You do not have to put your name on this survey. Thanks for helping me with this important project. Mr. K.

1. What have you learned about reading as a result of participating in your literature circle?

2. After participating in your literature circle, do you feel you are a better reader, a worse reader, or about the same kind of reader you were before working in the literature circle? (circle one)   Better   Worse   Same

   Why?

3. Has participating in the literature circle changed the way you feel about reading for school?(circle one)   Yes   No

   If yes, how has it changed the way you feel about reading for school?

4. Has participating in the literature circle changed the way you feel about reading for fun? (circle one)   Yes   No

   If yes, how has it changed the way you feel about reading for fun?

5. What activities during the literature circle have been most helpful to you?

6. What activities during the literature circle have been least helpful to you?

7. How can we improve the literature circle activities?

8. Is there anything else you would like to say about literature circles? If so, please write your comments here.

FIGURE 5.13 Student survey on literature circles (Mr. Kaston, 7th grade).

The literature circle survey provided in Figure 5.13 is aligned with the teacher's research questions. Survey question 2 relates to students' perceptions of how their reading achievement has changed because of participating in literature circles. Question 1 provides students with an opportunity to explain how literature circles have helped them develop reading skills. Questions 3 and 4 are concerned with students' attitudes about reading and how the literature circles have affected those attitudes. The remaining questions allow students to express ways the literature circles have been effective and ineffective and provide students with an opportunity to give feedback on ways to improve the literature circle activities. Notice, too, that the survey begins with a request to provide detailed information. The teacher has also explained the importance of providing honest responses and has increased his chances to get honest responses by telling students they do not have to write their names on the survey.

Surveys have a variety of uses in action research studies. They can be used with different types of participants—students, teachers, parents, school staff, administrators—and they are a simple way to collect data on large groups of participants. Here are several suggestions for those interested in using surveys or questionnaires in action research studies:

- **Ensure that survey questions are aligned with research questions** (Burns, 2010). It is critical that you create your survey so that it will provide the kinds of information you need to answer your research questions, meaning that it is valid for measuring what you want it to measure. Refer to your primary and secondary research questions often as you work on your survey items.
- **Pilot test the survey before administering it to participants** (Burns, 2010). Pilot testing the survey with a small group of participants or having colleagues, collaborators, or a critical friend evaluate the survey before it is administered are good ways to identify any problems with it and increase confidence that the survey is valid for the purposes of your study. The pilot test and/or collaborator review can help identify reading level problems, ambiguous questions, redundancies, instructions that are unclear, and unnecessary questions.
- **Keep your survey brief and to the point.** The longer your survey, the less likely your participants will complete it. Participants generally will not provide in-depth responses to open-ended questions on a long survey.
- **Do not ask questions that are unrelated to your primary or secondary research questions.** Often researchers will include questions on their surveys because they think responses will be interesting. For example, the language arts teacher who created the literature circle survey in Figure 5.13 may be interested in whether students' parents read at home and in fact may hypothesize that his best readers come from homes where reading is valued. However, including a question

on parents' reading habits will in no way help the teacher answer his research questions. Avoid including questions in your survey about gender, race, or other demographic variables unless they are specifically related to your research questions. Avoid any other questions that are only tangentially related to your study.

In certain circumstances, you may wish to use an online survey, which can have several benefits. When participants complete online surveys, their responses are automatically placed in a data or spreadsheet file, which saves time analyzing data. Online surveys can also be useful when surveying certain groups, such as parents or teachers. Online surveys can even be used with students as long as they have Internet access. Before using an online survey, ensure participants have access to and are comfortable using an online format. A number of survey tools are available to use, such as Survey Monkey (www.surveymonkey.com), SurveyTool (www.surveytool.com), and Zoomerang (www.zoomerang.com), which allow you to build surveys using existing templates. Some companies offer free software trials or allow users free access for small-scale surveys.

Attitude scales are surveys that focus on the way participants feel about certain topics. They are useful to researchers in a variety of ways: to measure students' attitudes about school, their abilities, or their self-concept; to measure teachers' attitudes about school policies, school climate, mentoring activities, or professional development activities; and to measure parents' attitudes about school rules or availability of teachers, staff, and administrators (to name just a few). Attitude scales typically contain close-ended questions to which participants choose a response—such as "I am confident in my ability to multiply fractions: strongly agree, agree, disagree, strongly disagree"—however, open-ended items are also occasionally included.

The guidelines for creating an attitude scale are similar to the survey guidelines listed previously. In addition, a number of attitude scales have been published in the literature that may be useful in your study. These include the School Achievement Motivation Scale (Chiu, 1997), the Teacher Rating of Academic Achievement Motivation (Stinnett, Oehler-Stinnett, & Stout, 1991), the Reader Self-Perception Scale (Henk & Melnick, 1995), the Writer Self-Perception Scale (Bottomley, Henk, & Melnick, 1998), the scale for Teacher-Perceived Student Behaviors: Disrespect, Sociability, and Attentiveness (Friedman, 1994), the Motivated Strategies for Learning Questionnaire (Pintrich & deGroot, 1990), and the Early Adolescent Self-Esteem Scale (DuBois, Felner, Brand, Phillips, & Lease, 1996). A number of other attitude scales are also available, and they can be found in academic journals and teacher magazines. Conduct an online search and library search to locate scales in your area of research. Also, review scale descriptions available on the Character Education Partnership website, which provides a number of scales at various levels (www.character.org/assessment).

If you use an established or published attitude scale, make sure the reading level is appropriate for your participants. You may need to make changes to the scale so that items align with the purpose of your action research study. If you plan to create your own attitude scale, make sure the response choices on the scale are appropriate for the questions. For example, appropriate response choices to the prompt "I am confident in my ability to multiply fractions" are *strongly agree, agree, disagree,* and *strongly disagree.* It would not be appropriate to use response choices such as *always, frequently, sometimes,* and *never* for the prompt unless the purpose of the study is to measure *how often* students are confident in their ability to multiply fractions. Be sure to pilot test the scale or have a collaborator or critical friend review it before administering the scale. An attitude scale for math is included in Figure 5.14. This attitude scale could be used in a study by a teacher who wishes to determine students' confidence in completing certain math tasks before and after implementing an intervention.

Students, please complete this attitude scale. Please write your name on this sheet because I will use it to plan activities to help you improve your achievement in math. It is important that you are honest in your responses. Your honesty will help me plan the best instructional activities for you.

Rate your confidence in completing each activity by circling one of the choices (very confident, somewhat confident, not confident at all).

1. I am confident in my ability to add fractions that have the same denominator.

    very confident   somewhat confident   not at all confident

2. I am confident in my ability to add fractions that have different denominators.

    very confident   somewhat confident   not at all confident

3. I am confident in my ability to multiply simple fractions (such as $\frac{1}{2} \times \frac{1}{4}$).

    very confident   somewhat confident   not at all confident

4. I am confident in my ability to multiply complex fractions (such as $2\frac{1}{2} \times 3\frac{1}{4}$).

    very confident   somewhat confident   not at all confident

5. I am confident in my ability to divide simple fractions (such as $\frac{1}{2} \div \frac{1}{4}$).

    very confident   somewhat confident   not at all confident

6. I am confident in my ability to divide complex fractions (such as $8\frac{1}{2} \div 2\frac{1}{4}$).

    very confident   somewhat confident   not at all confident

---

FIGURE 5.14 Mathematics attitude scale (Mrs. Cho, 5th grade).

TIME TO REFLECT

Refer to your research questions as you work through the following reflection questions—either on your own, in a collaborative group, or with a critical friend. Note reflections in your journal.

- What types of inquiry data could be used to help you answer your research questions?
- How will you feel if inquiry data you collect is critical, negative, or difficult to hear?
- What steps might you take to make your participants feel safe in providing open, honest inquiry data? Will your presence (such as serving as the interviewer) prevent participants from providing honest responses? If so, how might you deal with that?
- What assumptions, biases, and preconceived notions will you enter the inquiry data collection process with, and how might they affect your study?

THE IMPORTANCE OF COLLECTING BASELINE DATA

The preceding section introduced a number of ways to collect data in your action research study: through artifacts, observations, and inquiry. As you decide the best ways to collect data to answer your research questions, you may need to think about collecting baseline data before beginning your intervention. Baseline data are collected before the implementation of an intervention, and they are used to make comparisons of participants before and after the intervention occurs. If you are a teacher interested in examining the ways a strategy for teaching the writing process impacts students' writing achievement, it would be a good idea to collect writing samples from students before implementing the strategy intervention. Collecting writing samples during and after the intervention would allow you to determine the ways in which students' writing improved. If, instead, you measured student writing only after the completion of the intervention, it would be impossible for you to determine the ways student writing was impacted by the intervention.

As you plan ways to collect data to answer your research questions, think about whether baseline data are important in your study. If you wish to determine ways in which an intervention affects achievement or attitudes, you will need to measure these constructs before beginning the implementation phase of your study. Artifacts created by participants before intervention implementation are one source of baseline data. You may be able to use existing artifacts, or you may need to have participants create certain artifacts to produce baseline data. You can also make baseline observations, conduct baseline interviews, or collect baseline surveys prior to implementing your intervention.

ALIGNING DATA COLLECTION STRATEGIES WITH RESEARCH QUESTIONS

Aligning data collection strategies with research questions has been stressed throughout this chapter, and it will be repeated here one last time. It is essential that you refer to your primary and secondary research questions as you determine the best ways to collect data for your study. Ask yourself these questions:

- What types of data should I collect to answer my research questions?
- What types of data should I collect to help answer the *why* questions in my study?

Work with a critical friend or collaborator as you work through this important step of determining ways to collect data to answer your research questions. Here are some suggestions for making sure data collection strategies match research questions:

- Refer to your primary and secondary research questions as a first step in choosing data collection strategies.
- If the purpose of your study is to increase student achievement, be sure to choose several types of student-generated artifacts to examine as one data source.
- If the purpose of your study is to examine changes in attitudes, feelings, or opinions, use verbal and/or written inquiry data as one data source.
- Regardless of the purpose of your study, it is critical to utilize observational data. In rare instances, observational data are not useful, but in most action research studies, utilizing observational data is essential for understanding the reasons an intervention was successful or unsuccessful, or understanding the context of a research setting or site.
- Choose multiple data collection strategies so that you will be able to triangulate data.
- Work with a collaborator or critical friend in the data collection development process.

In Activity 5.1, you will complete several activities that will assist you in creating your data collection plan and ensuring that the chosen data collection strategies are aligned with your primary and secondary research questions.

ACTIVITY 5.1
Choosing Data Collection Strategies

1. Write your primary and secondary research questions. Leave several lines of open space between questions.

2. Under each question, write at least three (but no more than five) data collection strategies that can help you answer the research question. Provide examples of the specific kinds of information you plan to obtain (e.g., instead of writing, *I will use student-generated artifacts*, write something more specific, such as, *I will have students complete persuasive essays as a form of student-generated artifact*).

3. Determine whether baseline data are important in your study. Write a justification for your determination. If you do plan to collect baseline data, explain which data collection strategies you plan to use and provide examples of the specific types of baseline data you plan to obtain.

4. In a sentence or two, write an explanation of how the data collection strategies (including baseline strategies, if appropriate) will provide you with the data you need to answer your research questions.

5. If you haven't already done so in the Time to Reflect activities in this chapter, share your data collection ideas with a critical friend or collaborator. Obtain feedback and suggestions on ways to improve your data collection plan. Write down feedback provided.

Research paper activity: Based on collaborator/critical friend assistance and your reflections on your answers to the previous questions in this activity, write a data collection plan for your study. For each research question, write a detailed explanation of the types of data you will collect (including baseline data, if appropriate) and a timeline for collecting data. Provide a justification for your data collection plan that explains how your plan will help you answer your research questions. Place this information under a heading such as *Data Collection Plan* or *Data Collection Strategies* and have it follow the section on the intervention.

Journal activity: Use your journal as a place to make or keep observational records. Make a commitment to write in your journal each day during the intervention and/or data collection phase of your study. Make notes on the way you are implementing your intervention as well as the way participants respond to the intervention.

Summary

This chapter explained the importance of triangulating data sources to increase credibility in action research studies. It also focused on describing multiple ways to collect artifacts, conduct observations, and acquire inquiry data, and an explanation of how to collect baseline data was provided. Finally, methods for ensuring data collection strategies aligned with research questions were described. Activity 5.1 led you through the steps of creating a data collection plan. Once your plan is in place, you will be ready to complete the final steps of research planning and then begin implementation of the intervention phase of your study. Chapter 6 focuses on these final steps of the planning process—increasing validity of the study, engaging in continuous reflective and reflexive planning, and establishing a timeline for the research project.

6

Final Planning Before Implementation of the Study

Chapter Goals

- Explain ways to define validity in action research and suggest ways to align methods of increasing validity with the nature and purpose of the study.
- Illustrate the process of ongoing and continuous reflective planning.

- Demonstrate ways to create time lines for action research projects.
- Provide activities to guide practitioners through the processes of increasing validity, creating a project timeline, and engaging in action planning.

Chapters 4 and 5 provided guidelines for planning the study and collecting data to understand the research problem or determine the effectiveness of the intervention. Prior to collecting data, however, it is necessary to finalize the research plan, which includes planning ways to increase validity of the research results, creating a timeline for the completion of the action research project, and engaging in continuous reflective planning throughout the study. This chapter provides information in each of these areas and includes activities that will guide these final planning activities.

DEFINITIONS OF VALIDITY

As explained in Chapter 5, practitioners engaged in action research must consider both the credibility and validity of their research studies. Credibility can be increased by collecting multiple forms of data and triangulating data sources. The term *validity* has a number of meanings in educational research. In quantitative research, validity can refer to the degree to which results are true for the participants (*internal validity*), the degree to which the results can be generalized beyond the participants in the study (*external validity*), or the degree to which a test or assessment measures what it is supposed to measure (*test validity*). Different types of validity that are appropriate for qualitative studies have been described by a number of qualitative researchers, including Maxwell (1992) and Eisner (1991).

Perhaps the most widely referenced validity criteria in qualitative research are the four trustworthiness criteria described by Lincoln and Guba (1985), who explain that the validity of a qualitative study can be increased by (1) establishing the verisimilitude of the research findings for the context that was studied (*truth-value validity*), (2) determining the extent to which results of a research study are applicable to other contexts and other individuals (*applicability/transferability*), (3) establishing whether research results would replicate with the same or similar participants and/or contexts (*consistency/dependability*), and (4) showing that results are an accurate representation of what occurred rather than the result of the researcher's bias, motivation, or interest (*neutrality/confirmability*).

Among proponents of action research, there has not been much discussion about how to best define validity in action research. However, Anderson, Herr, and Nihlen (1994, 2007) have suggested five distinct criteria for assessing validity/trustworthiness in action research and some action research theorists have supported these criteria. According to Anderson and colleagues (2007), *democratic validity* is the extent to which stakeholders have collaborated in the research process and/or the extent to which the researcher has taken into account their various points of view. *Outcome validity* is the degree to which there has been a successful resolution to the research problem. Successful resolution does not necessarily mean coming to the end of the study but instead may mean beginning a new round of action planning based on initial results. *Process validity* refers to the use of appropriate processes for studying the research questions. Process validity relies on the researcher's commitment to carry out the study in a way that allows the researcher to engage "in a way that develops a depth of understanding or change" (Anderson et al., 2007, p. 150) rather than superficially studying the research problem. A fourth type of validity, *catalytic validity* (from Lather, 1991), is the extent to which the research transforms or changes the researcher's views and/or practices. Anderson and colleagues (2007) explain, "Catalytic validity/trustworthiness

TABLE 6.1   Rosario's Study and Validity Questions/Considerations

Type of Validity	Rosario's Questions
Truth-value validity	In what ways can I ensure my results are accurate and truthful?
Applicability/transferability	How might my results be useful beyond my particular classroom and with other students?
Consistency/dependability	Would I get the same results with other students similar to mine?
Neutrality/confirmability	How do I show results are indicative of what actually occurred during the study and do not reflect my personal desires or biases?
Democratic validity	Which stakeholders should collaborate or have a voice in the study? In what ways should I involve them?
Outcome validity	How will I use results for continued planning, ongoing reflection, and deepening my personal understanding?
Process validity	What do I need to do to ensure I have looked deeply at the problem so I understand the ways context and processes have impacted results?
Catalytic validity	In what ways will processes and outcomes change my practice?
Dialogic validity	Do I need a critical friend to discuss my study and results with so I can determine whether my planning and interpretations are on track?

asks researchers to address how understanding has deepened and changed over time" (p. 151). Finally, *dialogic validity* is the extent to which research processes and outcomes are aligned and make sense to others. To increase dialogic validity, the researcher explains processes and results to others (e.g., stakeholders, collaborators, critical friends), which can lead to refinement of processes as well as to new ways of interpreting data.

To illustrate these types of validity within the context of a research study, recall Rosario, the third-grade teacher introduced in Chapter 4 who wished to improve students' writing achievement and, after her review of the literature, decided to create writing rubrics with students. Table 6.1 provides questions Rosario may ask herself as she considers ways to increase her study's credibility.

DETERMINING WAYS TO INCREASE VALIDITY

Thus far, nine types of validity for qualitative or action research studies have been presented, and, incredibly, even more types of validity have been proposed for qualitative research (for other validity terms, see Lather, 1993; LeCompte & Goetz, 1982; Wolcott, 1994). As illustrated in the discussion of reflection (Chapter 2), the process of action research often involves making decisions (e.g., *How do I align my values and actions?*) that are based on the purpose of the study. In determining ways to increase validity in your action research study, you will need to consider your values, the nature of the study, its purpose, and the audience with which you will share your results. Criteria for validity may be established for you if the study is intended for a particular audience. Whereas colleagues may expect information regarding truth-value validity, transferability, and outcome validity, a professional organization or a journal's review board may expect Lincoln and Guba's trustworthiness criteria to be followed. If the purpose of the study is purely to inform your own educational practice, you may wish to focus on truth-value validity, outcome validity, and catalytic validity. Collaborative research should include democratic validity as one way to establish the study's credibility.

As you determine ways to increase validity in your own study, think back to your goal when you began to conceptualize the study. Did you wish to conduct a study of your own practice, did you wish to conduct a collaborative study within an educational community, or did you wish to be part of a study that focused on issues of social justice? As you answer this question, consider the various forms of validity presented, and choose methods for increasing validity that are aligned with your initial goal. For example, in considering validity issues, Rosario may determine that at this stage in her investigation, she is not concerned with the transferability of her results to other students. That may be a concern after her initial research cycle—particularly if other teachers become interested in her use of rubrics and wish to try the intervention in their classrooms—but it is not a present, pressing issue. Instead, she may wish to focus on democratic validity because involving students in the rubric planning and giving them a voice is aligned with her values. She may also decide she needs to reduce her bias and be open to other interpretations of results (thus increasing neutrality and dialogic validity) to ensure accuracy and increase understanding. She might further wish to understand the ways setting and context impact results (e.g., Does creating/using rubrics work better with some students? If so, which students most benefit? How might the activity be changed to better work with other students?) and would therefore be concerned with process validity.

Once you have determined which validity conditions are necessary for your study, the next step is to choose specific methods for increasing validity. Strategies for increasing the different forms of validity are described here. In Table 6.2, these strategies are graphically aligned with the various forms of validity described in this section.

Steps for increasing validity:

- *Utilize peer debriefing* (Lincoln & Guba, 1985; Rossman & Rallis, 2012). Peer debriefing involves discussing your study with a colleague, peer, or critical friend who is not invested in the study (not a

TABLE 6.2   Strategies for Increasing Validity

Type of Validity	Focus	Strategies
• Truth-value validity • Process validity	Accuracy of facts and findings; correct interpretations made and correct conclusions reached	• Persistent and prolonged observation • Triangulation • Accurate data recording • Member checks • Peer debriefing • Negative case analysis • Biases made clear
• Outcome validity • Catalytic validity	Ability of study to increase understanding, resolve problems, and transform practices	• Presentation of results • Continuous, ongoing reflective planning
• Applicability/transferability • Consistency/dependability	Usefulness of the results in different settings and contexts and with different individuals	• Thick description of setting, study, and participants • Ongoing investigation with different participants
• Neutrality/confirmability	Evidence that results are accurate and are not a result of researcher bias	• Peer debriefing • Accurate data recording • Member checks • Triangulation • Biases made clear • Audit trail
• Democratic validity	Evidence that stakeholders collaborated and/or were given a voice in the research process	• Peer debriefing • Member checks • Audit trail
• Dialogic validity	Sharing or disseminating research findings, seeking feedback about the accuracy of interpretations and conclusions	• Peer debriefing • Member checks • Presentation of results

collaborator). During the debriefing session, you discuss with your peer your interpretations of collected data. The peer debriefer can provide alternative interpretations, help point out your biases and the way your values may be coloring your interpretations, and assist you in formulating new directions for ongoing study.

• ***Engage in persistent and prolonged observations*** (Lincoln & Guba, 1985; Rossman & Rallis, 2012). The longer you are able to collect data, the more likely you are to see the true effects of your intervention. Prolonged observation will help you determine whether the intervention is effective after the newness of it wears off. Persistent observation will allow you to gather enough data to add to the credibility of your study and help answer the *why* questions.

- **Be sure to record data accurately** (Maxwell, 2009). Accurate recording during your action research study is critical. You must plan for ways to record as much information as possible when important events occur. Sufficient detail should be included in observational records, field notes, and notes from interviews. It can be helpful to record parts of your study, using either audio or video, so that you can revisit events and conversations, and record them accurately.

- **Use member checks** (Lincoln & Guba, 1985; Rossman & Rallis, 2012). Member checks are a useful way to reduce bias and increase credibility in your study. Member checks involve discussing your interpretations of data with the participants of your study. This allows you to determine whether your findings accurately represent participants' actions and responses. Also know as *respondent validation*, member checks can serve as a test of "fairness of observations" by giving participants a say in whether their responses and experiences have been accurately, truthfully, and fairly captured (Simons, 2009, p. 131).

- **Triangulate data sources** (Anderson, Herr, & Nihlen, 2007; Rossman & Rallis, 2012). As described in Chapter 5, collecting multiple sources of data is a necessary step in action research. When a researcher uses multiple sources to corroborate findings (for example, *teachers' self-reports* indicated that they implemented a new policy for ensuring discipline procedures consistently for all students, *percentages of discipline referrals* for each ethnic group were similar, and *conferences* with teachers at each grade level revealed that teachers believed the new discipline policy was fair and necessary, and they were committed to following it), the credibility of the findings is increased.

- **Provide thick description of the setting and study** (Lincoln & Guba, 1985; Maxwell, 2009). Providing thick description means describing in detail the setting, participants, intervention, and research methods employed in the study (completed in Chapter 4 activities). Portraying the setting and study in this way provides an audience or readers with the information needed to determine whether the study is generalizable, transferable, or useful in their settings. When the research setting shares characteristics with the audiences' or readers' setting, generalizability is increased.

- **Employ techniques in negative case analysis** (Lincoln & Guba, 1985; Maxwell, 2009). Negative case analysis involves qualifying research findings by analyzing data that are not supported or corroborated by other sources of data. Data that do not "agree" with the majority of the other data collected are considered the negative case. In the example just cited about the new discipline program aimed at ensuring equitable treatment of students in different racial groups, the three sources of evidence—teachers' self-reports, percentages of discipline referrals, and conferences with teachers—corroborated the finding that the new policy was in place and working effectively. If, however, there were a negative case, such as an area in which the policy did not seem to be working well, the case would need to be analyzed to determine why the policy was not working. Then the results could be refined to explain that, overall, the policy was effective, but under certain conditions (which would be described) the policy was less effective.

- ***Make clear any researcher bias*** (Merriam, 2009). It is important as you plan your study that you consider any biases you have at the outset. Engaging in reflection at the beginning of the research process is one way to clarify any initial biases. As you have completed the *Time to Reflect* activities in earlier chapters, you have continued to consider your biases and the ways they may affect your decisions. Remember that bias is defined as any preconceived ideas about the participants, setting, intervention, or the research process itself. Although the word *bias* has many negative connotations, in the case of research you can be biased if you believe with certainty that your intervention will be successful. As Rossman and Rallis (2012) suggest, "Try not to let this opinion . . . prevent you from seeing clearly and widely" (p. 49). As you begin the intervention phase of your study, review the biases, assumptions, and preconceived ideas you've written about in your journal. Referring to these biases as you collect and analyze data will help keep biases in check. In addition, include information on biases—and how you dealt with them—in the research report.

- ***Make available an audit trail*** (Lincoln & Guba, 1985; Richards, 2005). An audit trail is simply a record of data analyzed in the study. This may include analyzed artifacts, video or audio recordings, transcribed notes from observations or interviews, field notes, records of ways data were analyzed and interpreted, the timeline of the study, and the researcher's journal. When the audit trail is made available, it is possible for the audience and/or stakeholders to look at both the researcher's results and the actual data to see if results and interpretations are accurate. Making audit trails available is particularly important in larger studies that involve policy, program, or curricular decisions. As Richards (2005) explains, the audit trail demonstrates a "researcher's ability to show convincingly how they got [their results and] how they built confidence that this was the best account possible" (p. 143). It is important to note that data in which participants can be identified (e.g., video) should not be shared unless participants' identities are not revealed.

- ***Present results to key audiences*** (Anderson, Herr, & Nihlen, 1994, 2007). Anderson and colleagues suggest engaging in dialogue with peers as a way to increase dialogic validity. In sharing results with others, peers are able to review each others' work and provide feedback on the soundness of both the research process and the researcher's conclusions. Key audiences can include colleagues as well as stakeholders in the process (e.g., parents, students, teachers, administrators).

• ***Engage in continuous, ongoing reflective planning.*** In the process of action research, a researcher continually reflects on what is occurring during the study and makes changes to the research plan as necessary. For example, a principal engaged in a project on teacher study groups may determine to alter the intervention plan if sources of data indicate that changes are warranted. If the principal's observations lead her to believe the groups need more than one week to prepare for their study group meetings, she would be wise to alter the intervention plan to allow for a longer period of preparation time between meetings. Ongoing reflective planning also allows a researcher to change data collection strategies based on experiences during the data collection phase. If the principal investigating study groups determines that observing the study groups for the first fifteen minutes of each group session is not resulting in useful observation data, she could plan to spend longer periods of time observing the groups. Later in this chapter, additional information is provided on ways to engage in continuous reflection throughout the remainder of the action research cycle.

TIME TO REFLECT

Think about the goals you have for your study and ways you plan to collect data to answer your research questions. Then, discuss the following reflection questions with a critical friend, collaborator, or colleague. Journal about your reflections.

- How important is it that your results are accurate and aren't a result of your biases? That you've made the right conclusions? That your results can transform your practice or the practice of others? That you collaborated with stakeholders? That you share results with others?
- Consider what is most important *to you* from the preceding prompt and align what you value with validity types. What strategies will you need to engage in to increase validity in your study?
- What are the challenges of the strategies you have chosen (for example, what might you do if your member checks or peer debriefing reveals a bias in your interpretations)?
- How confident are you that you have clearly described the assumptions, biases, and preconceived notions you have about your topic and the research process itself?

Activity 6.1 provides steps for creating a plan to increase the validity of your study.

ACTIVITY 6.1
Creating a Plan for Increasing Validity

1. Refer to your response to Activity 2.2 to determine your initial goals in conducting your action research study.
2. Determine the types of validity that are applicable in your study. Consider your values, the purpose of your study, the nature of your reflective activities in planning the study (look back at your written reflections to the *Time to Reflect* activities), and your audience.
3. Create a plan for increasing validity that is aligned with the types of validity you deemed applicable for your action research study.

Journal activity: Include in your journal issues related to validity in your study. Your journal is a place to record information from peer debriefing and member checks. You can also refer to previous journal entries related to bias, descriptions of the setting and events that have occurred, and negative cases. The journal is one potential source of data that can be part of the audit trail. In addition, reflections written in the journal—on the intervention, data, and the progress of the study—can be used for ongoing reflective planning.

Research paper activity: Under the heading *Plan for Increasing Validity* (or a similar heading such as *Validity Issues* or *Validity of the Study*), write a section that explains the types of validity chosen for your study, a justification for choosing those types of validity (with a link to values, the purpose, nature of reflection, and audience of the study), and the methods used for increasing those types of validity. It may be necessary to complete this section of the paper after the conclusion of the study so that the methods used and the results of using those methods can be described in detail. This section should follow the section on data collection strategies employed (see Activity 5.1).

ENGAGING IN CONTINUOUS, ONGOING REFLECTIVE PLANNING THROUGHOUT THE STUDY

A key element in the action research process is reflecting throughout the process. This act of reflection goes beyond simply revisiting or thinking about what is occurring during the intervention. Reflection in action research means considering actions taken throughout the study and changing those actions as necessary. This may mean altering an intervention plan so that it better aligns with values, changing data collection strategies as the study progresses, or modifying the project timeline. You may already have made changes based on the continuous reflective and reflexive inquiry you engaged in as you completed the *Time to Reflect* activities in the earlier chapters. Changes like these are a normal part of the action research cycle as practitioners reflect on their goals and values, consider biases and assumptions, and negotiate the dynamic and ever-changing world of school or educational settings.

To understand the way reflective planning will continue to be used throughout the remainder of your study, consider, for example, a career counselor studying an intervention focused on working with ninth-grade students to establish academic and personal goals for structuring high school activities (courses taken, extracurricular participation, community service) aligned with students' postsecondary goals. If, in the third week of her intervention, the counselor determined that many participating students had clear career aspirations but did not understand the realities of their chosen professions, she would probably want to provide time for instruction, discussion, and research on the day-to-day activities of the professions of interest to the students. She might determine that adding a "shadow day" in which participating students spend a day with an individual from the community in the student's chosen profession could help students understand what certain professions are really about.

Additional intervention activities similar to the shadow day would need to be planned and implemented as the counselor collected formal and informal data to determine what was and was not working in her intervention. Altering the plan would help the counselor make steady progress toward her goal of helping students prepare for life beyond high school. Making changes to the intervention would alter the timeline (additional time would need to be added to the intervention), and it might mean adding data collection strategies. In this case, the counselor could choose to collect data on the new intervention phase, focusing on *observations* of students researching and discussing chosen professions, *journal entries* about students' shadow days, and *student conferences* about what was learned in researching a chosen profession and spending a day with someone in that profession.

Remember as you begin your action research study that ongoing reflection is an important element of your project. As the study begins and you start to look at the various sources of data collected, reflect on what is working and what isn't working. When a certain strategy isn't effective, use the different sources of data you are collecting to determine why the strategy isn't working, and then alter the intervention plan using your best judgment (based on the data and what was previously learned in reviewing the literature) about how to make the strategy more effective. Gather feedback from collaborators, peer debriefers, or a critical friend.

Collect additional data on changes, analyze the data, and keep working to make the intervention as effective as possible. This may mean making drastic changes such as restructuring the entire intervention. More often, though, it will mean making small changes along the way, such as adding strategies to help a few struggling students or changing/adding data collection strategies.

Remember to be reflexive in your inquiry, challenging yourself to keep thinking about assumptions, biases, and preconceived notions and how these might be affecting your ongoing planning as well as your interpretations of data. Engage your critical friend in that process. Be sure to record all changes and reflective/reflexive inquiry in your journal. If you are writing up your results (for a paper, presentation, or publication, for example), you will be able to use the record in your journal to write about what actually occurred in the study rather than simply what was planned at the beginning of the study.

CREATING A TIMELINE FOR THE PROJECT

Once an intervention plan has been created and data collection strategies have been decided upon, the next step is to create a timeline for the action research project. Creating a timeline will help you sketch a plan for when activities and the intervention will take place, when data will be collected and analyzed, and when you will begin writing results. The timeline will help you maintain your research focus and will give you some indication of how much time should be planned for each phase of the research process.

Provided here are two types of timelines. Both timelines show activities for a research project on using student contracts. Figure 6.1 displays the timeline in list form, providing activities for each date listed. Figure 6.2 displays the timeline in a Gantt chart, which is a method borrowed from the business world to graphically display activities for certain dates. You may wish to use both types of timelines. Using a list-form timeline will enable you to include detailed information about what will happen on each date or time period during the study. This should be written like a lesson plan and include enough information to help ensure that you complete each planned step of the intervention. Supplementing a list-form timeline with a Gantt chart can provide you with a visual depiction of events for each phase of the study. This type of display works well in keeping you on track regarding upcoming intervention steps, data collection stages, and dates for analysis and writing. Activity 6.2 will take you through the steps of creating a timeline.

September 2–September 9: Initial reflection.

September 9–September 30: Review of literature.

October 1–October 8: Contact principal, school district, and university Institutional Review Board to secure permissions for study.

October 1–October 25: Gather baseline data (student work samples, observational notes) Conference with students on October 23rd.

October 7–October 31: Phone parents to discuss action research study. Send home permission forms. Collect permission forms. Follow-up phone calls to parents if necessary.

November 1–November 29: First contract phase.

    November 1: Discuss contract procedure with students.

    November 4: Conference with students to establish first contracts.

    November 5–6: Work with students to create rubrics for contract grading.

    November 14–15: Contact parents to discuss student progress on contracts.

    November 27–28: Student presentations (videotaped).

    November 29: Conference with students to discuss accomplishment toward contract goals.

January 16–February 14: Second contract phase.

    January 17: Conference with students to establish contracts.

    January 19–20: Creation of rubrics for contract grading.

    January 31: Contact parents to discuss student progress on contracts.

    February 12–13: Student presentations (videotaped).

    February 14: Conference with students to discuss accomplishment toward goals.

February 17–March 14: Third contract phase.

    February 17: Conference with students to establish contracts.

    February 18–19: Creation of rubrics for contract grading.

    March 3: Contact parents to discuss student progress on contracts.

    March 12–13: Student presentations (videotaped).

    March 14: Conference with students to discuss accomplishment toward goals.

March 17–April 1: Data analysis (observation notes in journal, videotapes, transcripts from student and parent conferences, rubrics, artifacts).

April 2–April 15: Writing results and putting the action research report/paper together.

April 16–April 30: Revisions of the paper.

FIGURE 6.1 List-form timeline for student contract project.

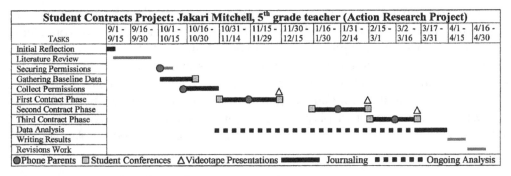

TASKS	9/1 - 9/15	9/16 - 9/30	10/1 - 10/15	10/16 - 10/30	10/31 - 11/14	11/15 - 11/29	11/30 - 12/15	1/16 - 1/30	1/31 - 2/14	2/15 - 3/1	3/2 - 3/16	3/17 - 3/31	4/1 - 4/15	4/16 - 4/30

Student Contracts Project: Jakari Mitchell, 5th grade teacher (Action Research Project)

Tasks: Initial Reflection, Literature Review, Securing Permissions, Gathering Baseline Data, Collect Permissions, First Contract Phase, Second Contract Phase, Third Contract Phase, Data Analysis, Writing Results, Revisions Work

Legend: ● Phone Parents □ Student Conferences △ Videotape Presentations ▬▬ Journaling ■ ■ ■ ■ ■ ■ Ongoing Analysis

FIGURE 6.2 Gantt chart for student contract project.

ACTIVITY 6.2
Ongoing Reflective Planning and Creating a Timeline

1. Create either a list-form timeline *or* a Gantt chart for your action research study. Include a detailed plan for implementation of your intervention and the dates the intervention will take place. The plan should also include information on when data will be collected and when (if at all) meetings with collaborators will take place. Include when analysis of the data will occur.
2. Share your timeline with a collaborator or critical friend and seek feedback on the feasibility of your plan. Make changes to the timeline as necessary.
3. Begin the intervention phase of the study.

Journal activity: In your journal, keep track of changes to the research plan. Describe how ongoing reflection shapes changes to the research plan.

Research paper activity: Make changes to previously written sections of the paper if/when ongoing reflective planning leads to changes in the project. If the intervention changes, reflect these changes in the intervention plan (see Activity 2.2). If the data collection plan changes, add these changes to the data collection strategies section of the paper (see Activity 5.1).

Summary

This chapter described the final steps of planning an action research study (increasing validity of the study, engaging in continuous reflective planning, and creating a timeline) before implementation of the intervention research study. Several types of validity relevant in action research studies were described, and methods for choosing ways to describe validity—based on the nature and purpose of a particular study—were presented. In addition, the importance of engaging in ongoing reflective planning to increase the effectiveness of interventions was illustrated. Finally, both a list-form timeline and a Gantt chart were provided as methods for displaying a study timeline.

As you complete this chapter, it is time to begin the implementation phase of your study. In Chapter 7, methods for analyzing data are presented. It is important to begin reading this chapter as the intervention begins so that you can analyze data throughout the study. This ongoing analysis will make it possible to engage in continuous, ongoing reflective planning.

7

Strategies for Data Analysis

Chapter Goals

- Explain the process of interim analysis and its importance in action research.

- Demonstrate ways to analyze, report, and display results for quantitative data.

- Illustrate ways to analyze results for qualitative data using thematic analysis.

- Describe the process of triangulating data sources.

- Illustrate ways to draw conclusions from data.

- Provide activities on the processes of data analysis, triangulation, and making conclusions about the results of the study.

INTERIM DATA ANALYSIS

In Chapter 5, a number of strategies were presented for collecting data during your action research study. At this point in the action research cycle, you should be implementing your intervention and collecting multiple forms of data to answer your research questions. You need to begin making sense of data *as you collect the data*. The analysis of data is an ongoing process that should occur throughout the study rather than at the end of it. Huberman and Miles (1998) define the collection and analysis of data during the study as **interim analysis**. Johnson and Christensen (2012) explain that the purpose of interim analysis is "to develop a successively deeper understanding of [the] research topic and to guide each round of data collection" (p. 517). This process allows for changes in data collection strategies when problems or questions arise based on ongoing data analysis. Thus, interim analysis is part of the continuous, ongoing reflective planning described in Chapter 6.

You may be thinking it would be much easier to analyze all the data from your study after they have all been collected. But waiting until the end of your action research study—remember, in this cycle there really is no end—lessens your ability to gather the information you need to make your study credible and valid. Consider, for example, an action research study conducted by a teacher studying the impact of using student learning contracts. During the teacher's first interview with a student, the teacher concludes the semi-structured interview by asking the student if there is anything else she would like to say about learning contracts, to which the student replies, "Some of the smart kids think it's unfair that some of us who don't get such good grades have raised our averages now that we have the contracts." This comment, though based on only one student's interview, may deserve to be further investigated as a negative consequence of or negative attitude toward using learning contracts. In future observations of students as they work on their learning contracts and discuss them with each other, the teacher may choose to look for evidence of this negative attitude. Further, during future interviews, the teacher could ask structured questions such as, "Have you heard any positive or negative comments from other students about using learning contracts?" and "Do you feel that using learning contracts is a fair way to evaluate all students?" These added interview questions, in addition to formal observations related to students' attitudes about the learning contracts, could result in data that are important for understanding reasons the learning contract intervention is successful or unsuccessful. If the teacher had not engaged in interim analysis and reflective inquiry based on that analysis, she would have missed the opportunity to collect information critical to the study.

Interim analysis is an informal process of ongoing data analysis and reflective planning, which means all that is required is looking at and thinking about data as it is collected and then making changes or additions to strategies, if necessary. The more structured and formal data analysis process will indeed occur once all data have been collected. At that point, the process of data analysis is one of reducing data, interpreting it, and drawing conclusions. Strategies for data reduction of quantitative forms of data, which include reporting, comparing, and displaying information, are much

---

interim analysis: Analyzing data throughout the research study for the purpose of enhancing data collection strategies based on emerging problems or questions.

different from the strategies used to reduce qualitative forms of data, which involves studying the data to find patterns and themes.

In this chapter, data analysis strategies for quantitative and qualitative data are presented. Keep in mind that the techniques explained in this chapter are organized differently than the way data collection strategies were organized in Chapter 5. The methods used to analyze artifacts are not separate or distinct from the methods used to analyze observational data. To clarify, some artifacts are analyzed using quantitative techniques, whereas other types of artifacts are analyzed using qualitative techniques. The same holds true for observational data and inquiry data.

Also presented in this chapter are methods used for drawing conclusions from data, which involve triangulating data sources to determine valid and credible answers to research questions. Ways to verify findings and increase validity of the study will be described as well. Activities that will help you analyze your data are presented in this chapter.

USING SOFTWARE PACKAGES TO ANALYZE LARGE AMOUNTS OF DATA

Although it is beyond the scope of this book to describe the ways in which software can be used to analyze quantitative and qualitative data, you should be aware that several software packages are available. For individuals interested in statistical analysis of quantitative data, SPSS, SAS, Minitab, and Excel can be used to determine statistical differences or relationships in data. For those interested in using qualitative software to analyze large amounts of qualitative data, NVivo (www.qsrinternational.com) and ATLAS.ti (www.atlasti.com) are some of the most popular software packages available. Learn more about how these different types of software can be used to analyze data by visiting the web pages listed here. Other useful links include:

- *Electronic Statistics Textbook:*
  www.statsoft.com/textbook/stathome.html

- *VassarStats:*
  http://faculty.vassar.edu/lowry/VassarStats.html

- *Audience Dialogue—Qualitative Software:*
  www.audiencedialogue.net/soft-qual.html

And for help using Excel to enter and analyze data, check out these online tutorials:

- *Internet for Classrooms—Using Excel to Analyze Classroom Data:*
  www.internet4classrooms.com/excel_task.htm

- *Microsoft—Create Data Sets with Excel 2007:*

  www.microsoft.com/education/en-us/teachers/how-to/Pages/data-sets.aspx

- *Microsoft—Survey Design and Analysis Using Excel 2007 Tutorial:*

  www.microsoft.com/education/en-us/teachers/how-to/Pages/survey.aspx

There are also number of video tutorials available online through YouTube on using Excel to analyze data. Table 7.12 at the end of this chapter provides additional links to software packages for analyzing quantitative and qualitative data.

ANALYSIS OF QUANTITATIVE DATA: REPORTING, COMPARING, AND DISPLAYING

Quantitative data can be generated from test scores, rubric-scored work (written assignments, performances, artwork, projects), closed-ended self-assessment items, computer-generated reports, school records, checklists, tally sheets, behavioral scales, attitude scales, and closed-ended survey items. Specific data from some of these data-gathering tools, however, are not quantitative in nature, although the data can be analyzed quantitatively. For example, in Table 7.1, items from self-assessments, peer reviews, rating scales, and surveys are provided. Although the *responses* to these items are not quantitative, the data can be described by counting or averaging the number of responses for each item. For example, analyzing a closed-ended self-assessment item in which students indicated whether they were strong, average, or weak readers would involve counting the number of students who chose *strong*, the number who chose *average*, and the number who chose *weak* (e.g., in Mr. Phillips's class, five students said they were strong readers, three students said they were average readers, and two students said they were weak readers). Numbers of responses could also be counted for the closed-ended peer review items, the attitude scale items, and the closed-ended survey items.

For the behavioral scale item, which includes numerical responses, the actual number chosen for each item could be tallied, as in the previous example, but numbers could also be averaged to describe results. For example, a teacher of a self-contained class for students with behavior problems could look at her five students' average number of physical outbursts (Jim = 2, Sherian = 1, Paul = 1, Beth = 0, Trey = 1) and report that, on average, students exhibited one physical outburst per day. This was determined by calculating the average ([2 + 1 + 1 + 0 + 1] ÷ 5 = 1) and then looking back at the scale to determine what the average (1) means.

The steps of analysis for quantitative forms of data include reporting, comparing, and displaying data. The first step in the analysis process is to look at various data sources and determine which can be analyzed quantitatively.

TABLE 7.1 Examples of Quantitative Items for Self-Assessments, Peer Reviews, Rating Scales, and Surveys

Closed-ended self-assessment item	*Circle your response:* 1. The type of reader I am: **Strong Average Weak** 2. The type of writer I am: **Strong Average Weak**
Closed-ended peer review item	*Evaluate your mentor teacher in the following areas:* E = excellent, G = good, A = average, P = poor 1. Assisting with instructional planning: **E G A P** 2. Assisting with classroom management: **E G A P**
Behavioral scale items	*Evaluate the frequency of the following behaviors.* 0 = never, 1 = up to 2 times per day, 2 = three + times per day 1. Defying authority: **0 1 2** 2. Physical outburst: **0 1 2**
Attitude scale item	*Circle your response:* SA = strongly agree, A = agree, D = disagree, SD = strongly disagree 1. I'd rather read than watch TV. **SA A D SD** 2. I am a good reader. **SA A D SD**
Closed-ended survey item	*Circle your response:* SA = strongly agree, A = agree, D = disagree, SD = strongly disagree 1. I like deciding how my work will be evaluated. **SA A D SD** 2. Learning contracts are a fair way to evaluate students. **SA A D SD**

Next, follow the guidelines given in the following subsections for *tests, closed-ended items, checklists and tally sheets,* and *computer-generated reports and school records.* These guidelines suggest ways to organize data, report in written form what the data indicate, and graphically illustrate results.

Tests

A number of different test formats can be analyzed quantitatively. First, follow guidelines for the recording of data based on whether the test was teacher-made, a standardized test, or some type of work scored using a rubric:

- ***Teacher-made tests:*** Score tests and record scores for each student. Consider looking for patterns of errors, which can indicate what students know and can do as well as any areas where they may be lacking.
- ***Standardized tests:*** Use score reports to record scores for each participant. Record a standard score such as normal curve equivalent (NCE) score, percentile rank, or stanine. If scores are broken into subcategories (e.g., the reading section includes a vocabulary subsection and a reading

comprehension subsection), record subsection scores as well. If you are conducting a schoolwide action research study with a large number of participants, you may want to look at scores for classes or grade levels rather than for individual students.

• ***Rubric-scored work*** (written assignments, performances, artwork, and projects): Using the rubric, score each student's work. Record a score for each student. If the rubric contains subsections (e.g., a writing rubric that includes a separate score for thesis development, transitions, audience, and mechanics), record a score for each subsection.

Record scores in a grade book or in your research journal. If you are familiar with spreadsheet programs such as Excel, you can input grades on a spreadsheet and then generate graphical displays of the data from the spreadsheet program. Other software programs that are used for statistical data analysis, such as SAS or SPSS, can also be used if you are familiar with the programs and have access to them. Keep in mind, though, that unless you are analyzing a large amount of data (such as in a schoolwide study), inputting information on a spreadsheet or in a statistical program is not necessary. In fact, in action research studies that involve a small number of participants, using software can be more work than making calculations by hand.

Whether you record data by hand or use a computer, you should record the data so that each row contains data for one student, the same way grades are recorded in a grade book. Also, using numbers as codes for responses (e.g., 1 = *emerging*, 2 = *basic*, 3 = *proficient*, 4 = *advanced* or 1 = *strongly disagree*, 2 = *disagree*, 3 = *agree*, 4 = *strongly agree*) will allow you to find averages for responses and create charts with computer software. Averaging can produce strange results, such as a score that is between points. This is true for ordered data that is not quantitative. For example, averaging an essay score for a student could result in a score of 2.75, which is a point not represented on the 4-point rubric described previously. However, the score can be interpreted as between the basic and proficient level. An example of how to record data is provided in Table 7.2.

Once data have been recorded, you can report, display, and/or compare data. Reporting the data simply means providing an explanation of what is found. For example, average total scores for each of the four essays in Table 7.2 could be reported in this way: *The average score on the persuasive essay was 6.4 points. On the Hero essay, the average score was 7 points; on the My Perfect World essay, the average score was 8.1; and on the My Worst Day essay, the average score was 9.5.* These averages were calculated by adding Total Scores for each essay and dividing by the number of scores. For example, the average for the persuasive essay was determined by adding the ten students' scores (6 + 6 + 6 + 7 + 6 + 8 + 4 + 9 + 3 + 9), which equaled 64, then dividing by the number of scores (10 students' scores) to arrive at

TABLE 7.2 Rubric Scores for Writer's Workshop Study

	Persuasive Essay (Baseline)				Hero Essay				My Perfect World Essay				The Worst Day Essay			
	C	M	T	TS	C	M	T	TS	C	M	T	TS	C	M	T	TS
Abdullah, Momar	3	2	1	6	3	2	2	7	3	2	3	8	3	3	4	10
Adams, Jason	2	3	1	6	3	3	1	7	3	2	2	7	3	3	3	9
Crenshaw, Mandi	2	2	2	6	3	2	2	7	3	2	3	8	4	3	3	10
Davidson, Bakari	3	3	1	7	3	3	2	8	3	3	3	9	4	3	4	11
Gonzales, Jorge	3	2	1	6	2	2	2	6	3	2	2	7	3	3	2	8
Huynh, Sarah	4	2	2	8	3	2	3	8	3	3	3	9	4	3	3	10
Timmons, Freda	2	1	1	4	3	1	1	5	3	2	2	7	3	2	2	7
Vinson, Cyndi	3	4	2	9	2	4	2	8	3	4	3	10	4	4	4	12
Warren, Robert	1	1	1	3	2	1	1	4	2	2	2	6	2	3	2	7
Whaley, Donetta	3	3	3	9	3	3	4	10	2	4	4	10	3	4	4	11

Key: C = Content, M = Mechanics, T = Transitions, TS = Total Score, 1 = emerging, 2 = basic, 3 = proficient, 4 = advanced

an average score of 6.4. Data from Table 7.2 could also be graphically displayed in a chart form. An example is provided in Figure 7.1. This chart was created in Excel.

Another way to report data is to make comparisons across different data points. For example, the data provided in Figure 7.1 could be compared in this way: *The average total score on the persuasive essay, which students wrote before we began the Writer's Workshop intervention, was 6.4. Scores increased throughout the intervention phase of the study. On the second essay, average total scores rose to 7 points, and on the third essay,*

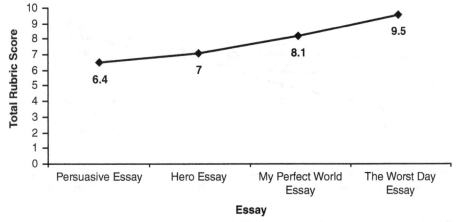

FIGURE 7.1 Average essay score based on total rubric score.

total scores rose once again to 8.1. On the final essay, students' average total score was 9.5—just over a 3-point gain compared to the baseline data.

If you are analyzing test scores or rubric-scored work in your action research study, begin by recording the data, averaging scores when appropriate, and thinking about ways to display data. Choose strategies that will help you learn as much as you can about your data and that will help you explain your results to others in a way that is simple and understandable. Look back at Table 7.2. There is much more data displayed than what has been described in the previous examples of reporting, displaying, and comparing data. The teacher who collected these data may also be interested in seeing how students' writing skills increased in the three areas measured on each essay— content, mechanics, and transitions. This deeper level of analysis can help the teacher determine whether the Writer's Workshop intervention is more helpful to students in some areas but not others, which is critical for ongoing reflective planning. Figure 7.2, which was created using Excel, contains a chart display of average scores on the four essays for each subsection of the rubric.

This chart is useful for seeing where students made the greatest gains. A teacher reading this chart could report and compare data in this way: *Throughout the Writer's Workshop intervention, students improved in content, mechanics, and transitions. Their greatest gains, however, were in the area of transitions. Baseline data indicated that the average score for students in this area was 1.5, which was just below the basic level. Students' scores gradually increased during the intervention, and on the last essay, students' average score on transitions rose to 3.1, which is at the proficient level.*

Closed-Ended Items

When analyzing closed-ended items from self-assessments, peer reviews, behavioral scales, attitude scales, or surveys, first record data by participant for each close-ended item in a grade book or journal, or use a spreadsheet

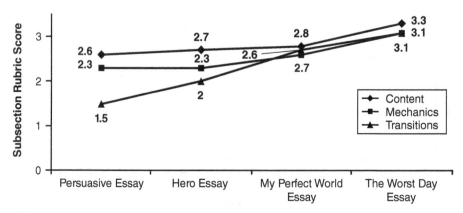

FIGURE 7.2 Subsection rubric scores for essays.

TABLE 7.3   Student Survey Data for Writer's Workshop Study

	I know how to use correct grammar when writing essays.		I know how to use transitions in my writing.		I like to write.		I am a good writer.		Writer's Workshop has helped me become a better writer.	
	B	F	B	F	B	F	B	F	B	F
Abdullah, Momar	4	4	3	4	3	4	4	4	na	4
Adams, Jason	1	3	2	3	2	2	2	1	na	2
Crenshaw, Mandi	1	3	1	2	2	3	2	3	na	4
Davidson, Bakari	2	3	1	3	1	3	2	3	na	3
Gonzales, Jorge	2	3	2	3	2	3	3	4	na	3
Huynh, Sarah	1	3	2	3	3	3	2	3	na	2
Timmons, Freda	2	3	1	2	1	3	2	2	na	3
Vinson, Cyndi	2	4	3	4	1	3	3	3	na	4
Warren, Robert	2	2	2	2	1	1	2	3	na	1
Whaley, Donetta	1	3	2	3	1	2	3	2	na	3

Key: B = Baseline Survey, F = Final Survey, 1 = strongly disagree, 2 = disagree, 3 = agree, 4 = strongly agree

or statistical software package. An example of how to record data for closed-ended survey items is provided in Table 7.3.

Once data have been recorded, think about the best ways to report, display, and compare the data. As you look at your data, remember that you want to explain results in a way that helps you answer your research questions. You also want to explain the data in a way that is understandable so that others can learn from the outcomes of your study. There are several ways to report, display, and compare the data presented in Table 7.3. In fact, the table itself is a display of the data. Other graphical displays could be created from the data as well. The chart provided in Figure 7.3 is one way to display the data.

Figure 7.3 displays data from the closed-ended items on the Writer's Workshop survey, and because results are included from the baseline survey and the final survey, it is easy to compare differences between the two. The researcher displaying this chart could explain it in this way: *Student responses to the survey items were averaged, and comparisons were made between responses on the baseline survey and responses on the final survey. For each of the four closed-ended survey items, students' confidence in their writing abilities and attitudes toward writing improved. On the baseline survey, most students strongly disagreed or disagreed that they knew how to use correct grammar and transitions when writing essays. On the final survey, most students agreed or strongly agreed that they could use correct grammar*

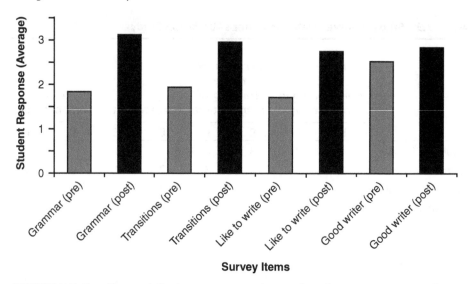

FIGURE 7.3 Baseline and final survey comparisons of students' responses to the survey on Writer's Workshop.

and transitions when writing. There was also a change in students' attitude toward writing. On the baseline survey, the average response to the prompt I like to write *was between* strongly disagree *and* disagree. *On the final survey, more students agreed that they like to write. Although students' confidence in their writing abilities and their attitudes about writing increased, there was little change in students' responses to the prompt* I am a good writer. *On both the baseline and final surveys, the average student response was between* disagree *and* agree.

Another way to display the data shown in Table 7.3 is to record changes in survey responses for each student. This would be appropriate in a study in which the teacher wished to analyze changes in achievement, attitudes, and confidence in writing for individual students. Table 7.4 displays changes in survey responses for each student.

Displaying data in this manner provides the teacher with information regarding individual students. Looking at data this way, it is clear that Robert's confidence using correct grammar and transitions has not been affected by his participation in Writer's Workshop. His negative attitude toward writing also has not changed. Notice that Momar's survey responses show he hasn't changed much either, but his writing confidence and attitude toward writing were good prior to the Writer's Workshop intervention. The teacher might conclude from these data—especially if confirmed by other sources of triangulated data—that Momar should continue participating in the Writer's Workshop, but different strategies should be used with Robert.

TABLE 7.4 Changes in Students' Self-Assessment of Writing

	I know how to use correct grammar . . .			*I know how to use transitions . . .*			*I like to write*			*I am a good writer*		
	B	**F**	**C**	**B**	**F**	**C**	**B**	**F**	**C**	**B**	**F**	**C**
Abdullah, Momar	4	4	0	3	4	+1	3	4	+1	4	4	0
Adams, Jason	1	3	+2	2	3	+1	2	2	0	2	1	−1
Crenshaw, Mandi	1	3	+2	1	2	+1	2	3	+1	2	3	+1
Davidson, Bakari	2	3	+1	1	3	+2	1	3	+2	2	3	+1
Gonzales, Jorge	2	3	+1	2	3	+1	2	3	+1	3	4	+1
Huynh, Sarah	1	3	+2	2	3	+1	3	3	0	2	3	+1
Timmons, Freda	2	3	+1	1	2	+1	1	3	+2	2	2	0
Vinson, Cyndi	2	4	+2	3	4	+1	1	3	+2	3	3	0
Warren, Robert	2	2	0	2	2	0	1	1	0	2	3	+1
Whaley, Donetta	1	4	+3	2	3	+1	1	2	+1	3	2	−1

Key: B = Baseline Survey, F = Final Survey, C = Change

1 = strongly disagree, 2 = disagree, 3 = agree, 4 = strongly agree

Checklists and Tally Sheets

When analyzing data from checklists and tally sheets, the first step is to record behaviors or events and, for checklists, the number of times they occur. An example of one way to record data from a checklist is provided in Table 7.5.

This record is a useful display of the behaviors and activities for each group during the three collaborative group activities. Based on this record, the teacher could identify several important pieces of information:

- Group 2 did not work well together and made no improvement between the first collaborative activity and the last collaborative activity.
- Groups 1 and 3 worked well together consistently from the first activity through the third activity.
- Groups 4 and 5 improved their collaboration between the first and third activities.
- More emphasis must be placed on all group members participating in the collaborative activity and completing activities on their own.

This information, particularly when considered with other data sources, can provide useful information about differences in increased achievement between and among groups. For example, if there are no changes in achievement in Group 2, a possible explanation is that, because the group did not work well together and were not collaborative, there was little opportunity for learning. When data can be used to help understand reasons an intervention

TABLE 7.5 Collaborative Groups Checklist, Honors Biology, Mr. Jackson

Behaviors/Activities	First Activity					Second Activity					Third Activity				
GROUP NUMBER —>	1	2	3	4	5	1	2	3	4	5	1	2	3	4	5
All members actively participate.			✔		✔			✔		✔	✔		✔		✔
Group members are respectful of one another.	✔	✔		✔	✔	✔	✔	✔	✔	✔			✔	✔	✔
Group members attempt to complete work on their own before asking me questions.	✔		✔	✔		✔	✔	✔	✔	✔				✔	✔
Group stays on task.	✔		✔	✔		✔		✔	✔		✔		✔	✔	✔
Group completes and turns in progress sheet.	✔	✔	✔			✔	✔	✔	✔	✔	✔	✔	✔	✔	✔

is unsuccessful, there is an opportunity to look for ways to improve the intervention. This is an example of the ongoing planning that can take place as interim analysis of data is followed by reflective and reflexive inquiry focusing on reasons for the interim results.

A method for recording tally sheet information is provided in Table 7.6. These data represent a behavioral tally sheet for one student over several days. The recorded data on the tally sheet could be displayed a number of ways, which is illustrated in Figures 7.4 and 7.5. Figure 7.4 displays the number of occurrences for mumbling and talking out between February 1 and February 19. In Figure 7.5, the number of occurrences of desired behaviors between February 1 and February 19 are displayed.

TABLE 7.6 Tally Sheet for Micah R., 4th Grade, Mrs. Ellison

DATE:	2/1	2/2	2/3	2/4	2/5	2/8	2/9	2/10	2/11	2/12	2/15	2/16	2/17	2/18	2/19
UNDESIRED BEHAVIORS															
Tapping pencil	5	6	4	6	4	7	4	5	3	3	4	3	2	1	3
Spinning pencil	1	4	3	3	4	6	2	3	4	2	3	1	0	2	1
Mumbling	7	9	5	4	4	8	4	4	3	2	5	2	2	3	2
Talking out	2	2	0	3	3	4	2	2	1	1	3	0	1	1	1
DESIRED BEHAVIORS															
Asking for help	2	0	1	2	3	1	2	2	3	4	2	4	4	5	3
Raising hand	1	0	0	2	2	0	1	1	2	3	0	3	2	3	4
Responding	3	3	5	4	5	3	5	5	6	5	4	5	6	6	5
Following directions	0	0	1	0	0	0	1	1	3	2	1	3	3	2	4

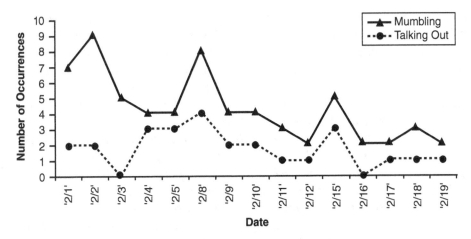

FIGURE 7.4 Behavioral chart for Micah R. (undesired behaviors).

These figures, which were created in Microsoft Excel, do not display all recorded data because the charts were difficult to read when I attempted to display four behaviors on each one. As you determine the best ways to display the data in your study, always attempt to create graphical displays that can be easily read and understood, even if it means creating a number of separate charts to display the data.

Displayed data such as those provided in Figures 7.4 and 7.5 are easier than recorded data (Table 7.6) to understand and describe. The data in Figures 7.4 and 7.5 could be described this way: *There was a decrease in Micah's mumbling over the three-week intervention period. In the first week, Micah mumbled an average of 5.8 times per day, which decreased to 4.2 times per day the second week and 2.8 times per day the third week. During*

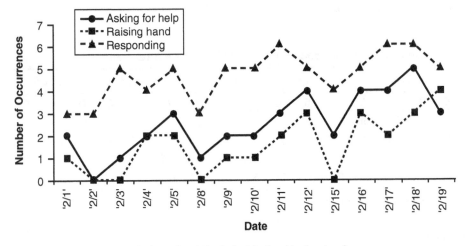

FIGURE 7.5 Behavioral chart for Micah R. (desired behaviors).

the second and third weeks, Micah's mumbling was greater on Monday and tended to decrease throughout the week. Micah's talking-out behavior did not decrease as much as his mumbling. In the first and second weeks, Micah talked out an average of 2 times per day, which decreased to 1.2 times per day the third week. During the second and third weeks, Micah talked out more often on Mondays than on other days. As the second and third weeks progressed, Micah's talking-out behavior decreased.

Desired behaviors increased over the three-week intervention period. The first week, Micah asked for help an average of 1.6 times per day, which increased to 2.4 times per day the second week and 3.6 times per day the third week. There was less of an increase in raising his hand for attention and responding when spoken to, however. The first week, Micah raised his hand for attention once per day, on average, which increased to 1.4 times per day the second week and 2.4 times per day the third week. Micah responded when spoken to an average of 4 times per day the first week, 4.8 times per day the second week, and 5.2 times per day the third week. (NOTE: Only some data have been described here, based on the displays in Figures 7.4 and 7.5. Other information on pencil tapping, pencil spinning, and following oral directions should be provided to give a complete explanation on how behaviors changed during the intervention.)

Computer-Generated Reports and School Records

When analyzing data from computer-generated reports and school records, first record information relevant to your action research project as you review reported/recorded data. Consider the best way to record the information, whether it is by student, grade level, teacher, year, or another method. Computer-generated reports, as well as some school records such as discipline reports, retention rates, and attendance, can be displayed, reported, and compared in much the same way as checklist and tally sheet data are.

An example of a data record from a computer-generated report is provided in Table 7.7. The record includes the number of books read, the average

TABLE 7.7   Data from Computer-Generated Reading Report for Third-Grade Teachers

TEACHER	Week 1			Week 2			Week 3			Week 4			Week 5			Week 6		
	N	R	C	N	R	C	N	R	C	N	R	C	N	R	C	N	R	C
Jimenez	0.5	2.3	70	1.0	2.5	68	1.3	2.1	72	1.7	2.4	73	2.1	2.2	75	2.8	2.0	80
Southe	1.5	3.1	70	2.5	3.0	75	5.8	3.2	70	6.2	3.4	76	5.5	3.8	80	6.1	3.8	82
Reynolds	1.2	2.8	68	1.2	2.7	72	1.5	2.5	74	3.0	2.2	76	3.2	2.8	82	3.8	3.1	80
Johnson	4.1	3.1	80	3.8	3.4	82	5.2	3.6	84	6.2	3.5	82	6.5	3.7	83	6.3	3.8	85

Key: N = Average number of books read per student

R = Average reading level

C = Average reading comprehension score

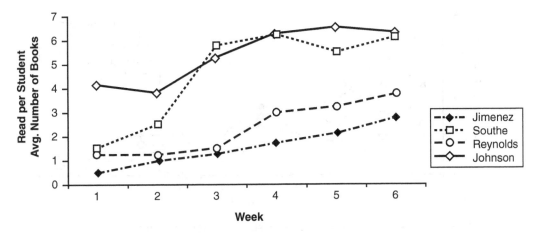

FIGURE 7.6 Average number of books read per student each week.

reading level of the books read, and the average reading comprehension score for each of four third-grade classes over a six-week period.

There are several ways these data can be reported, displayed, and compared. For example, the average number of books read per student per week could be displayed on a chart like the one shown in Figure 7.6. This graphical display shows that there were increases in the number of books read per student each week for each of the four teachers' classes. Figure 7.6 can be used to explain the gains made by students in each class, and it can be used to compare gains between classes. Other graphical displays could be created for the computer-generated data to show differences and gains in reading levels of books and reading comprehension scores.

To use information from school records, first record the data by hand or input the data into a spreadsheet or statistical software package. An example of how to record data is provided in Table 7.8. These data are from school records on discipline referrals, and they have been recorded for five sixth-grade teachers over a 10-week period.

TABLE 7.8 Number of Discipline Referrals for Sixth-Grade Classes

					Week					
	1	2	3	4	5	6	7	8	9	10
Bridges (6A)	4	2	3	4	5	3	4	4	3	2
Reinhardt (6B)	9	12	8	6	7	4	3	3	1	0
Gregory (6C)	15	9	6	8	6	3	0	1	2	1
A. Lewis (6D)	5	4	5	6	3	1	2	3	1	2
J. Lewis (6E)	7	6	9	5	5	4	3	2	0	0

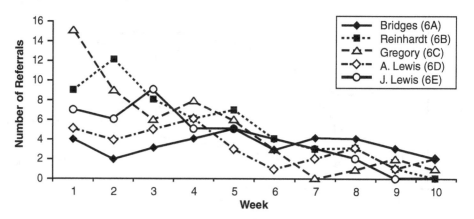

FIGURE 7.7 Sixth-grade discipline referrals during ten-week intervention.

A description of these data can be made from the recorded information provided in the table, but they can also be displayed to show whether there were changes in the number of discipline referrals over the 10-week period. Displaying the data makes the job of making comparisons a much easier task. An example of one way to display the data is provided in Figure 7.7.

Figure 7.7 displays a large amount of data, and it is a bit hard to read printed in black and white. However, it is clear from the graph that the number of discipline referrals decreased in each of the sixth-grade classes over the ten-week period. The largest decrease occurred in Mrs. Gregory's class, and the smallest decrease occurred in Mr. Bridges's class. A graphical display such as this one is helpful for reporting changes in the number of discipline referrals and comparing changes among the five classes.

In this section, several examples were provided on ways to record, report, and display quantitative data. Explanations and examples were also included on methods for making comparisons with data. The examples provided show just a few of the many ways to explain and display results of your research study when quantitative data are used to answer research questions. As you begin the process of organizing and analyzing your quantitative data, follow these steps:

1. ***Gather together quantitative data sources and record information.*** Record data in a grade book, journal, or computer spreadsheet. Double-check information as you record it to prevent data recording mistakes.
2. ***Create graphical displays of data.*** Work with a collaborator or peer to brainstorm ways to display data. Display data using several methods, if possible, to ascertain the display method that is easiest to understand.
3. ***Examine displayed data to determine the best ways to explain results.*** Study displayed data and then verbally describe important points. Reread your written explanations while looking at your records

and graphical displays to ensure that you have accurately described data and data comparisons.

4. ***Share your analyses and graphical displays with collaborators, peers, or a critical friend.*** Colleagues can help you determine whether your analyses, charts, figures, and graphs make sense.

5. ***Make notes in your journal about how your analyses can be used to answer research questions.*** Often, researchers become so involved in experimenting with different ways to make sense of their data that they lose sight of the research questions they are trying to answer. As you work on your data analysis, refer often to your primary and secondary research questions. Make sure to analyze your data in ways that can help you answer your research questions. Once that is accomplished, analyze the data in different ways, based on the questions that have arisen as your study has progressed, so that you can try to answer your *why* questions.

TIME TO REFLECT

Review your interim analysis of the quantitative data in your study. Then, discuss the following reflection questions with a critical friend, collaborator, or colleague. Write reflections in your journal.

- As you have engaged in interim analysis of your quantiative data, what have you learned? Did you find what you expected? What do you still want to know? What new questions do you have?
- Have results from interim analysis of your quantitative data challenged your assumptions or preconceived notions about your topic? Has the analysis made clear any biases or made you think about them?
- Has interim analysis revealed any issues or generated new questions for you that require you to alter your research plan? What ongoing reflective planning have you done (or do you plan to do) because of interim analysis?

Activity 7.1 is provided to take you through the steps of analyzing quantitative data.

ANALYSIS OF QUALITATIVE DATA: LOOKING FOR THEMES AND PATTERNS

The analysis of qualitative data is a process of making meaning from data sources that can be interpreted in a number of ways. Qualitative data sources—which in this text include field notes, logs, interviews, focus groups, conferences, documents, journals, and open-ended items from surveys, scales, self-assessments, and peer reviews—can be explained and used to answer research questions only after they have been interpreted. This process requires deeper analysis of data than those processes used to explain quantitative data sources.

ACTIVITY 7.1
Analysis of Quantitative Data

1. Write your primary and secondary research questions. Keep them in sight as you work through the analysis of your quantitative forms of data.
2. Gather all quantitative data sources that will be analyzed in your study. Match each quantitative data source to the primary or secondary research question it will be used to answer. NOTE: Remember that some data sources will be used to answer more than one question.
3. Create records for each data source. Use a computer spreadsheet if you would like to create computer-generated figures or charts.
4. Display results for each data source. Share your displayed data with a collaborator or critical friend and ask for feedback on the appropriateness and understandability of the displays. Rework displays based on provided feedback.
5. Produce a written description to explain displayed data. Share descriptions and graphical displays with a collaborator or critical friend. Rework explanations based on provided feedback.
6. Answer any research questions that can be answered with your quantitative data sources. For example: *My primary research question was Will students' achievement in writing increase as a result of the* Writer's Workshop *intervention? Based on analysis of student essays, writing achievement did improve throughout the intervention. The average total score on the persuasive essay, which students wrote before we began the Writer's Workshop intervention, was 6.4. Scores increased throughout the intervention phase of the study. On the second essay, average total scores rose to 7 points, and on the third essay, total scores rose once again to 8.1. On the final essay, students' average total score was 9.5—just over a 3-point gain compared to the baseline data. Students improved in each of the three areas we tackled during the intervention: content, mechanics, and transitions. The greatest gains were in the area of transitions. Baseline data indicated that the average score for students in this area was 1.5, which was just below the basic level. Students' scores gradually increased during the intervention, and on the last essay, students' average score on transitions rose to 3.1, which is at the proficient level.*

What if I don't find what I expect? As you begin analyzing your data, you may discover that your results are not what you expected. This is a normal part of the research process. Remember this: No matter what you find, your results will help inform and improve your practice and will make you a better educator. Often, beginning action researchers are frustrated when they discover their intervention has not produced the results that were expected. But even when this occurs, using data to answer the *why* questions can help the researcher reach conclusions about ways to improve the intervention to attain desired outcomes.

Journal activity: As you analyze quantitative data sources, make notes in your journal about results that are unexpected. Your analysis of data is likely to bring about new research questions (e.g., "Why does the intervention seem to work better for some kids but not others?"), so keep track of new questions as they arise.

Berg and Lune (2012) explain that the interpretation of qualitative forms of data involves analyzing action and activity as if they were text. What this means is that in order to understand data based on observations, interviews, or conversations, we must first convert the data to text. Obviously, some forms of qualitative data are already in textual form (journals, responses to open-ended survey items), but other forms of data must be recorded as text form to make them ready for analysis. Once qualitative data have been recorded in text form, the text is analyzed to search for categories and themes in the data. Shank (2002) calls this process, which involves building general themes from specific examples in the data, **thematic analysis**. Although a number of qualitative researchers and theorists have explained that themes emerge from data, Shank's explanation of emerging themes is closer to what actually happens in the analysis process:

> . . . themes do not really emerge from data. What emerges, after much hard work and creative thought, is an awareness in the mind of the researcher that there are patterns of order that seem to cut across various aspects of the data. When these patterns become organizationized [*sic*], and when they characterize different segments of data, then we can call them "themes." (p. 129)

The process presented in this text for analyzing qualitative forms of data follows the iterative and sequential process of becoming immersed in the data, analyzing the data, and interpreting the data (Rossman & Rallis, 2012). The five-phased cycle presented by Yin (2011) that aligns with this iterative process involves the following phases:

Phase 1. Compiling: All qualitative data are compiled and sorted. Data that are not in textual form are written so that they are recorded as text. This means that audio recordings of interviews, focus groups, and conferencing sessions must be transcribed either word for word or by transcribing the most salient pieces of data. Data that are already in textual form (from lesson plans, journals, self-assessments, peer reviews, documents, observational or field notes, logs, narratives, organizational charts, scales, and open-ended survey items) should be assembled or gathered together. Video recorded observations must be described in written form or transcribed.

Phase 2. Disassembling: Data must be broken down into smaller pieces or categories through a coding process that occurs as patterns in the data are observed.

Phase 3. Reassembling: Coded data are reassembled into themes by looking at ways categories are related to one another.

---

thematic analysis: Analyzing specific examples in qualitative data to discover general themes.

Phase 4. Interpreting: Reassembled data are described in such a way as to tell the story revealed in the data.

Phase 5. Concluding: Conclusions are drawn from the interpretation of the data.

These phases are described in greater detail in the remainder of this chapter.

Bogdan and Bilken (2007) provide a number of coding category examples, including the following:

- *Setting/context:* Provides descriptive information on aspects of the research setting
- *Participants' perspectives:* Describes what participants think about certain issues
- *Definition of situation:* Illustrates participants' understanding of setting and context
- *Ways of thinking:* Describes participants' understanding of self and/ or others
- *Processes:* Explains patterns of behavior over time
- *Activities:* Illustrates recurring, typical behaviors
- *Events:* Describes specific or particular nonrecurring, meaningful events
- *Strategies:* Describes methods used by participants to accomplish certain tasks
- *Relationships:* Defines social roles and typical behavioral patterns among or between people

This list is not meant to be exhaustive. You may find many of these categories in your own data, but categories not listed may be relevant as well.

Several examples of coded textual data will be presented in this section. Keep in mind that the examples are based on excerpts from much larger textual documents. They are provided to show the ways in which categories and codes are constructed and themes are established from codes.

Interviews, Focus Groups, and Conferences

Data should be audio-recorded and then transcribed. There are several ways to transcribe data, and one example is provided in Table 7.9, which displays an excerpt from an interview transcription from a principal's action research study about teacher study groups. On the left side of the table, the interview has been transcribed word for word. In the column to the right of the transcribed interview, the researcher has disassembled the data and coded the interview.

As you read the transcript and reviewer's codes in Table 7.9, you may determine other ways the interview could be coded. This is what makes the

TABLE 7.9   Coded Interview Transcription for Teacher Study Groups Project

March 6, 2012. Interview with Ms. Aronson. [interview begins 2:45]	Researcher Notes and Codes

Principal: *After participating in your study group with other teachers for the last six weeks, do you think that the study group has benefited you in any way?*

Mrs. A: Yes. In our group we have all sixth-grade language arts teachers, and it's been great to be able to talk about the kinds of problems we have. Like the transition period the kids go through when they first get here. Their first few weeks of middle school . . . it's just tough. They have no idea what the expectations are. We talked about that the first couple of times the study group met. It was great just to get a chance to talk about the frustrations. I think that some of the teachers in the study group like having a place just to vent their frustrations. But for me, I liked brainstorming ways to make the transition time easier. Some of the other teachers had really good ideas, like giving students written information about procedures for class work and homework. Georgetta, who is also my mentor teacher, said that she makes each student keep an agenda. She checks it every day. The kids know what's due and when. They have to have their agendas signed by their parents every week. Her kids understand the expectations right from the start, so it seems that they have an easier transition.

[study group behavior: *discussing similar problems*] **positive***

[topic discussed: *transitioning for sixth-grade students*]

[study group behavior: *sharing frustrations*] **positive***

[study group behavior: *venting*] **negative***

[study group behavior: *brainstorming*] **positive***

[ideas from colleagues: *written procedures* and *using agendas*]

Principal: *So the study group has been beneficial to you because you get to exchange ideas with other teachers?*

Mrs. A: Yep, that's a big part of it. It's beneficial, I think, just to get a chance to gripe sometimes. And it's good to talk to your colleagues and find out that most people are in the same boat. Another thing is that, when we talk in our study group, I get to learn stuff about the other teachers.

[benefits: *a place to gripe, not alone, getting to know colleagues*]

Principal: *Can you give me an example of the kind of stuff you learn about from other teachers?*

Mrs. A: Yeah, I mean when I listen to the others talk, I can see who's got classroom management down, who has good ideas for group work, who I just really want to avoid because they're negative about everything. I guess part of the study group is having the opportunity to identify who can help you with different things. Like I now know to go to Jerry about special ed because he knows all about working with IEPs and the legal stuff. Plus, he has some really good ideas about what kinds of activities work well with inclusion kids.

[benefits: *learning from colleagues with special knowledge. Learning who to avoid.*]

[study group behavior: *negative colleagues*] **negative***

[ideas from colleagues: *classroom management, group work, working with students who receive special education services*]

Principal: *Are there negative aspects of being in the study group?*

(continued)

TABLE 7.9 *(continued)*

March 6, 2012. Interview with Ms. Aronson. [interview begins 2:45]	Researcher Notes and Codes
Mrs. A: Some, I guess. For one thing, I hate to hear people go on and on about their problems and never once say anything about how to fix the problem. And I don't want my time wasted by people who want to talk about their personal problems. I mean, that's for the teacher's lounge, not for the study group. And sometimes it's hard to find the time to prepare for our study group meeting, especially when we're supposed to read before we go.	[study group behavior: *colleagues who go on and on about problems, wasting time, talking about personal problems*] **negative*** [barriers to study group participation: *preparing, reading*]
Principal: *What can you tell me about the reading your group has done?*	[benefits: *reading topics are chosen by participants*]
Mrs. A: Well, it's all been good. Based on topics that we've decided we want to know more about—like transitioning. Our study group leader finds some articles or book chapters for us to read on the topic. We usually have a week or so to do the reading. It's not a lot of reading really, but sometimes it's hard to find the time.	[procedures: *group chooses topic, leader finds reading materials*] [barriers to study group participation: *finding time to read*]
Principal: *Is the reading helpful?*	
Mrs. A: Yeah, most of it is. Sometimes when I haven't had time to do the reading, I've gone to the study group and then decided I had to do the reading. Like when the reading was on using cooperative groups. I didn't do that reading, but when I went to the group, the people who had read were talking about all these ideas from one of the book chapters, and they were really excited. So that made me want to read what I'd missed. And I did read it that night. There were some really good suggestions in that reading.	[study group behavior: *colleagues excited about reading, excitement is inspiring*] **positive*** [benefits: *reading topics are useful*]
Principal: *Is there anything else you'd like to tell me about the study groups?*	
Mrs. A: Well, in our group last week we talked about the idea of getting professional development credits for our study group work. I mean, what we're doing is really working on professional development, so it would be nice to get credit for it. A lot of us feel like it would be more helpful to get credit for what we're doing than to go to those staff development things at the district office that really don't help us. Maybe if we got credit for it and people could choose whether they wanted to be in a study group or go to a staff development thing . . . I mean, maybe that would be best. Then those of us who like the study group could continue and get credit. And the others who don't like the study group could quit the group and just do staff development stuff. It's just an idea.	[improving study groups: *give professional development credit for participation, let colleagues who don't like the study group go to staff development*] [benefits: *study group is more useful than staff development activities*] [study group behavior: *negative colleagues*] **negative***
Principal: *Thanks for the information you have provided. I appreciate your time.* **[Interview ends 2:56 p.m.]**	

analysis of interview data a subjective process. One person's disassembly (and understanding) of these data may be much different from another person's. Notice in the example that several codes, based on the patterns that emerged in the interview, have been developed: *study group behavior, topics discussed, ideas from colleagues, benefits of study groups,* and *barriers to study group participation*. As other interviews are analyzed, these codes would be applied to the transcripts, and new codes would be added as the researcher identifies areas where additional codes are needed. Part of this process is one of negotiation. As you become more familiar with your data, some codes will be combined into a new code, some codes will be deleted, and new codes will emerge.

Ryan and Bernard (2000) suggest that a researcher develop a codebook once all texts have been analyzed. In the teacher study groups example, this would occur after all interviews had been transcribed and analyzed, and codes had been applied. Include in your codebook an explanation of each code and any quotes or examples that powerfully illustrate the code. An entry in the codebook might look like this:

Code	Description	Quote/Example
SGB	Study group behavior [ways study group members interact]	I've gone to the study group and then decided I had to do the reading. Like when the reading was on using cooperative groups. I didn't do that reading, but when I went to the group, the people who had read were talking about all these ideas from one of the book chapters, and they were really excited. So that made me want to read what I missed.

Once you have created a codebook, review your codes, descriptions, and examples. The next step is to reassemble the data by organizing the codes—based on patterns you see—into larger categories or themes to determine what has been revealed in the qualitative data that can be used to answer research questions. For example, if the principal investigating study groups is interested in answering the question "How does participation in a study group improve or change teachers' practices?" The information provided in the interviews might lead to several themes related to changing teachers' practices: Teachers can share ideas, they are able to brainstorm solutions to problems, they learn from each others' areas of expertise, and they learn from reading and discussing books and articles about teaching. Within those themes may be smaller chunks of information that also help answer the research question. For example, there may be several ways teachers share ideas in study groups (e.g., by bringing in example lessons or by sharing assessment strategies), and they may be learning from their colleagues' areas of expertise in content, classroom management, or some other area.

Observational Records and Field Notes

Analysis of observational records and field notes is identical to the process described for interview data. If the observation has been video or audio recorded, it should be transcribed so that the text can be analyzed. If observations are in the form of field notes, then the text is ready for analysis. In Chapter 5, the importance of expanding each day's field notes was described. As a reminder, this means that at the end of each day of observation, you read the comments you were able to jot down that day and then expand them while the day's events are fresh in your mind. Expanding field notes is critical for gathering useful observational data that can help answer research questions. Remember to analyze your *expanded* field notes. Table 7.10 includes an example of a method for recording and coding observational data. The technique used here is identical to the method used for recording and coding interview data illustrated in Table 7.9. On the left side of the table are the written observational notes made by the teacher as she watched students working in collaborative groups. The teacher has written notes and codes on the right side of the table.

Once observational data have been coded in this way, codes and notes should be added to your codebook. It is important to review your codes as you analyze more sources of data. This ongoing analysis and review will help you figure out how to organize the themes that emerge and to determine how best to explain what was learned from the data in answering research questions. During the process, you will probably collapse some codes as you realize there is overlap. New codes and categories will emerge, whereas others may be dropped. As you build the categories and codes, you will see themes and patterns in the data. These themes will help you answer your research questions, and they will provide you with the information you need to answer the *why* questions in your study.

Documents and Journals

Because documents and journals are in text form, no recording is necessary. The text sources should be compiled, and if multiple sources will be analyzed (e.g., several students' journals or sets of meeting minutes from different groups), all sources should be analyzed together. To clarify, if you are analyzing the journals of all students in your class, you need to be able to look at them together—even with several journals open at once as you look through them. This strategy will help you see patterns in the data. As categories or codes emerge, make notes in your journal or codebook. Be sure to make notes about where in the data to find the codes. For example, next to a code, you may want to write where to find a data example (*Julie's journal, page 3, first paragraph*). It may be helpful to make copies of certain documents so that you can write codes on the copies or highlight

TABLE 7.10   Recorded and Coded Observational Records (Collaborative Groups)

Observational notes made on 10/18/2012, 4th period. Observation began 1:20 p.m.

Group 1: (members—Sam, David, Joanna, Takesha, and Leigh). After I passed out the group assignment, each member of this group spent about a minute looking over the assignment. Takesha spoke first, asking if everyone understood what was supposed to be done. David said he didn't get the part about cell division, and Takesha asked him if he had done last night's reading. David said no and Joanna replied, "You have to do the reading, David, especially when you know we're going to have a group assignment. If you don't do it, it hurts all of us." David said he'd had football practice and had to study for a hard test in trigonometry. Leigh replied, "Well, I had band practice and I had to study for that test, but I did the reading. It didn't take that long."

I am observing Group 1 today. This is my first formal observation of the group. Informally, I have noticed that this group works pretty well together.

Group Dynamics: Takesha takes the lead in getting the group members ready to work . . . speaks almost like a teacher. Directs others.

Group Dynamics: Expectations are clear: Everyone does the reading and comes prepared. No excuses.

At this point, Sam said they all needed to do the reading, but that they were wasting time continuing to talk about the problem. Leigh said she would explain cell division to David after they decided how to do the activity.

Group Dynamics: Sam gets the group to move on (gender playing a role here?).

Group Dynamics: Leigh offers to help David catch up.

Takesha looked at the assignment and said that there were four areas the assignment covered and asked if they should do the assignment by the "divide and conquer" method. Sam said he felt sure he could answer the first problem, and Joanna said she could do the second one. Leigh suggested that she and David take the problem on cell division if Takesha could do the third problem. There were some nonverbal affirmations of this plan. . . nods by Leigh and David while Sam and Joanna opened their books to start working. Leigh and David got up to find another place to work [perhaps so they wouldn't disturb the others]. Before they left, Takesha said, "I think we should all just make some notes but not answer the questions all the way." She suggested that they come back as a group and talk about their answers and then work together to write answers to the questions.

Group Dynamics: Takesha leading again. Offering way to tackle the assignment.

Division of Labor: All members equally contribute, volunteer to tackle certain problems.

Group Dynamics: Each member begins work. No prodding.

Group Dynamics: Takesha leading.

Division of Labor: All will come back and share information, then group will work together to answer problems.

Takesha, Sam, and Joanna each worked quietly at the table. Takesha and Joanna used their notes and the textbook and jotted notes. Sam used his textbook only.

Problem-Solving Strategies: Use textbook and notes.

David and Leigh: Working in a corner with two desks pulled together. Leigh is reading the question and looking in her notes as David quickly skims the textbook section on cell division. When he's done, he tells Leigh he thinks he has it. She asked him how he would answer the activity question. He read the question and said he wasn't sure. He looked through the textbook section on cell division again and he seemed to be reading more carefully. David then looked at Leigh with a confused look on his face. Leigh said, "The answer isn't in the book. That's the whole point. We have to use what we know about meiosis and mitosis to answer this problem. It's like a brain teaser."

Group Dynamics: Leigh seems to be leading here. . . she leads David in the same way that Takesha leads the group.

Problem-Solving Strategies: Don't rely on the book. Problem is like a "brain teaser."

(continued)

TABLE 7.10 (continued)	
Observational notes made on 10/18/2012, 4th period. Observation began 1:20 p.m.	

Observation shifting back to Takesha, Sam, and Joanna. Sam said that he couldn't find the answer in his book. Takesha said he should look at his notes and think about what's in the book and then "get creative." Takesha and Joanna both write notes in their notebooks for a minute or so. Sam says, "I still don't get it." Joanna shows Sam the question she is answering. She explains that the answer isn't in the book or notes, but that the answer can be figured out from what's in the book and notes. Joanna: "See, there are things I know about asexual reproduction. I have to think about what I know about that. Then I write all that down. When I look at the question, it's like I have to guess how to answer it based on what I know. See?"

Problem-Solving Strategy: Use book and notes and "get creative."

Group Dynamics/Problem Solving: Joanna models how to solve the problem. Using what is known to solve what is unknown.

Sam makes notes in his notebook for a minute or two. David and Leigh come back to the group. David says they figured out how to answer their question. Takesha suggests that they take turns talking about each question. Sam read the first question and then began to explain his answer.

Group Dynamics: Takesha in leadership role.

At this point, Group 2 called me over for help. I was helping other groups for about 15 minutes and then went back to observing Group 1.

Takesha has written responses to questions 1, 2, and 4. The group is working on question 3 now. Sam, David, Joanna, and Leigh have each written notes in their notebooks. I looked at Joanna's notes and saw that they contained detailed answers to the activity questions. They appear to be word-for-word what Takesha has written on the group sheet. [**Question 3 is about differences in chromosomal mutations during mitosis and meiosis.**]

Group Dynamics: Takesha takes responsibility to recording group's answers. Joanna keeps her own record in her notebook.

David is speaking, "Well, we know about how meiosis and mitosis work, and that must be important, right?"

Problem-Solving Strategy: David uses strategy Leigh explained earlier. Group members take turns explaining what they think is important.

Joanna: "Yeah, I think so. The question is about mutations in meiosis and mitosis. It has those two words, so that must be part of the puzzle."

"Part of the puzzle": Leigh, Joanna, and Takesha appear to think of the activities as puzzlers or brain teasers.

David asked Leigh what she thought. He said she seemed to understand mitosis and meiosis pretty well, so she might have some ideas.

Group Dynamics: David suggests to Leigh that she offer some input because she understood the concepts [smoothing things over?].

Leigh looked through her notes again and began describing the differences between mitosis and meiosis to the group. When she said that meiosis only happened in cells that form gametes, Joanna and Sam both began talking at the same time, indicating that they had found the important information. Joanna told Sam to go on. He explained that the chromosomal mutations that happen in meiosis affect the gametes so they appear in the offspring. Joanna agreed with this answer saying, "That's exactly right!"

Problem-Solving Strategy: Leigh looks through notes, verbalizes what she knows, Joanna and Sam have an "aha" moment simultaneously.

Group Dynamics: Joanna defers to Sam. Don't know why. Joanna is usually very verbal. Perhaps to give him a chance to contribute?

TABLE 7.10 (*continued*)

Observational notes made on 10/18/2012, 4th period. Observation began 1:20 p.m.

Takesha wrote down an answer for question 3, and then she read it to the group. Sam changed some of the wording to "be more precise." Takesha then read aloud each question and the group's answers. The group members seemed pleased with the responses. Joanna copied down the answer to number 3 in her notebook, and then she compared her notes on the other answers with the group's sheet. Takesha handed me the assignment and then asked if there was a reading assignment for tomorrow. I said they were to read the next section in the chapter. As I left the group to go to Group 2, I heard Leigh say to David, "Did you write that down?" [in reference to the reading assignment].	Group Dynamics: Sam's suggestion for precision is interesting. He often misses points on assignments for his lack of providing enough information. He seemed pretty proud when he offered the solution to question 3, especially when Joanna reinforced his answer. Group Dynamics: Still hounding David about the reading.
As I collected papers from the rest of the groups, I heard Takesha, Joanna, and Leigh talking about getting together to study for the unit test, which is a week from today. Joanna said she would bring copies of the notes she'd taken today. David and Sam asked for copies of the notes, but did not indicate that they would study with the rest of the group.	I don't know how to code this yet, but there seems to be a positive benefit of this particular grouping—students getting together to study outside of class. Very uncommon for students to study together at this competitive school.

information, which will help you find it easily. An example of coding document sources is provided in Figure 7.8. The figure includes data from the Study Groups project. The documents analyzed are three sets of minutes from one study group's meetings.

Open-Ended Items (Surveys, Scales, Self-Assessments, Peer Reviews)

The first step in analyzing open-ended items is to record responses from all participants. This involves compiling the data sources (e.g., a set of surveys) and recording responses on the open-ended questions. Responses are counted or tallied, and these responses are reviewed and studied to identify codes and themes. As responses are counted, notes should be made of quotes that illustrate the coded response. An example based on student responses to a survey on cooperative group activities is provided in Table 7.11. The question is listed first, and then responses and the number of times each response was made is listed. Quotes taken directly from surveys are included. If surveys are anonymous, they should be identified by a number to make it easier to find recorded quotes.

In this section, methods were presented for analyzing qualitative data. This process involves compiling data, disassembling the data, and then reassembling the data. Once these steps have been completed, you must interpret your data and then write up your results in relation to the answers they provide to your research questions. Further, you should include any additional information that can inform your practice as an educator, even if the information is only tangentially related to your research questions.

**Study Group Meeting
Minutes Feb. 2**

Members Present: Aronson, Mitchell, Stevens, and Little (Young absent)

Discussed transitioning for 6th grade. All agreed it's a big problem for our kids.

Mitchell (group leader) agreed to find some articles on transitioning for the group to read.

Stevens suggested we try to come up with a transitioning program to use next school year. All agreed it's a good idea.

**Study Group Meeting
Minutes March 2**

Members Present: Aronson, Mitchell, Stevens, Little, and Young

Discussed transitioning articles and brainstormed how we might create a program. All agreed it's something we need. Little suggested we develop a plan like the one in the article by McKenna. Consensus reached. Mitchell suggested we put together the plan and share it with the entire 6th grade team at our April faculty meeting. Aronson, Mitchell, Stevens, and Little will work on plan.

**Study Group Meeting
Minutes April 19**

Members Present: Aronson, Mitchell, Stevens, and Little (Young absent)

Discussed presentation made to 6th grade team last week. Consensus reached by group to rework plan based on suggestion from team and principal. Worked through transitioning plan and made requested changes. Plan to be presented to all faculty next week. Little suggested we ask whether meeting with 5th graders at Kerry Elementary can occur in May. If so, who is on the team?

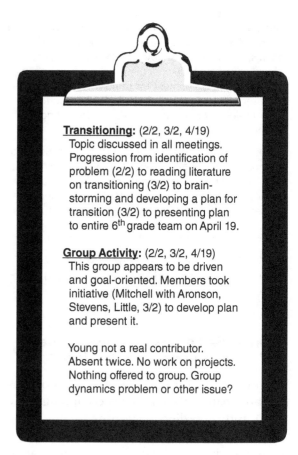

Transitioning: (2/2, 3/2, 4/19)
Topic discussed in all meetings. Progression from identification of problem (2/2) to reading literature on transitioning (3/2) to brainstorming and developing a plan for transition (3/2) to presenting plan to entire 6th grade team on April 19.

Group Activity: (2/2, 3/2, 4/19)
This group appears to be driven and goal-oriented. Members took initiative (Mitchell with Aronson, Stevens, Little, 3/2) to develop plan and present it.

Young not a real contributor. Absent twice. No work on projects. Nothing offered to group. Group dynamics problem or other issue?

FIGURE 7.8 Document analysis from teachers' Study Groups project.

TABLE 7.11   Responses to Open-Ended Survey Items—Cooperative Groups Study

Survey Question 10: *What are the benefits of working with your cooperative group?*

- **People in my group explain things in a way that I can understand** (10 students responded this way). Quote from David: "I don't always get it in class, even when I ask a question. But the people in my group can explain things so I get it. It's like they talk in my language."

- **Solving problems together** (5 students responded this way). Quote from Chantal: "Sometimes it's hard to understand the concepts when I'm just listening to a lecture. I'm trying to take notes, and I have no time to think. But in my group, when I have a question, I just ask, and there's usually someone who knows the answer. And if no one does, we talk it out until we get it. We get to all use what we know to solve the problems together."

- **It makes me study more because I have to prepare** (4 students responded this way). Quote from Takesha: "I know that when I have a group assignment the next day, I have to prepare before I go. I don't want to look dumb. I study more and my grades are higher." Quote from Darren: "My average is higher since I'm doing the reading at home."

Survey Question 11: *What are the negative aspects of working with your cooperative group?*

- **Sometimes people don't participate** (8 students responded this way).

- **I have to read more than I used to** (6 students responded this way). Quote from Michelle: "I liked just coming to class, taking notes, and studying. I did better. There's too much reading now."

- **I don't like people (or a person) in my group** (4 students responded this way). Quote from Maria: "There's one boy in my group who teases me all the time. I hate saying anything in my group."

Writing results, especially results based on qualitative data, can be a difficult task. You may feel like you have so much information that there is no way to coherently explain it all. This is why it is critical that you stay focused on your primary and secondary research questions as you analyze data. Make note of important information that is only peripherally related, but stay focused on the information that provides answers to your research questions.

One strategy that I ask the beginning researchers I work with to use is to begin by writing the research question and then to provide the answer to that question based on analysis of all the data sources appropriate for answering that question. An example is provided here:

> The primary research question in my study was *In what ways will the use of cooperative group activities increase achievement in my fourth period advanced biology class?* Analysis of student work indicated achievement did improve during the 8-week intervention. Baseline data recorded one week before the implementation of the intervention showed that the average test grade was 78, the average quiz grade was 75, and the average lab grade was 85. Scores steadily increased over the 8-week period, and at the end of the data collection

period test averages rose to 85, average quiz grades rose to 95, and average lab grades rose to 91. Interviews conducted with students in the seventh week revealed that most students believed they were learning more and doing better in class because of participation in the cooperative group activities. Eighteen of the twenty-five students said improvement in their work was a direct result of working in the cooperative groups. Benefits of the intervention went beyond simply completing class activities with peers. Half of the students said they were studying more in order to prepare for their group work, and responses on student surveys corroborated this. On one survey, a student wrote, "I know that when I have a group assignment the next day, I have to prepare before I go. I don't want to look dumb. I study more and my grades are higher." This attitude was typical of the students who said they were preparing more for class. When asked why they were preparing more, most students said it was because they didn't want to look dumb in front of their group. Additionally, about half of the students said during the interviews that they were studying for tests and completing assignments outside of class with people from their cooperative groups, although only two students said they had worked with classmates before the cooperative group intervention. In my observations, I did note that students in some groups frequently made plans to get together to study for tests. I had not witnessed this behavior before the intervention.

This example, which is just a short selection of a much more detailed answer to a research question, is provided to illustrate one way to answer research questions based on analysis of data. In the example, results from analysis of both quantitative (test scores and assignment scores) and qualitative (observations, interviews, open-ended survey responses) forms of data are included. The quantitative data—test scores, quiz scores, scores on lab assignments—provide a direct answer to the question, "In what ways will the use of cooperative group activities increase achievement in my fourth period advanced biology class?" Qualitative forms of data help to explain the increases in student achievement. The analysis of the qualitative data—interviews, observations, open-ended survey question responses—helps answer the *why* questions. The intervention was successful, but *why* was it successful? In this example, it appears that the cooperative group intervention was successful because students prepared more for class and studied together outside of class. Notice, too, that in the example there is evidence of triangulation. Data sources have been used to corroborate one another. For example, students reported that they were studying together outside of class, and the teacher observed students planning to get together to study outside of class for a test.

TIME TO REFLECT

Review your interim analysis of the qualitative data in your study. Then, discuss the following reflection questions with a critical friend, collaborator, or colleague. Write your reflections in your journal.

- As you have engaged in interim analysis of your qualitative data, what categories and themes emerged? In what ways did this information help to answer your research questions?
- Through the processes of disassembling, reassembling, and interpreting your qualitative data, did you find what you expected? What do you still want or need to know? What new questions do you have?
- Has the process of analyzing your qualitative data challenged your assumptions or preconceived notions about your topic? Has it made clear any biases or made you think about them?
- Has the qualitative analysis revealed any issues or generated new questions for you that require you to alter your research plan? What ongoing reflective planning have you done or do you plan to do based on what you are finding?

Activity 7.2 is provided to help you complete the steps for analyzing qualitative data. After quantitative and qualitative data sources have been analyzed, the next step is to evaluate both forms of data together

ACTIVITY 7.2
Analysis of Qualitative Data

1. Write your primary and secondary research questions. Refer to these questions often as you go through the process of qualitative data analysis.
2. Compile qualitative data sources. Transcribe any data from audio or video recordings.
3. Read text sources several times and over several days. Disassemble and code data (use examples provided in Tables 7.9, 7.10, and 7.11, and in Figure 7.8).
4. Create a codebook. Define codes and illustrate them with quotes or examples from text sources.
5. Look for themes as you reassemble data. Interpret results and write up major findings. Describe the patterns and themes specifically related to your research questions.
6. Refer to your responses to Activity 7.1. Look for ways that the results of the different types of data you have collected (artifacts, observations, and inquiry data) support each other.

Journal activity: Use your journal as a place to write about the process of qualitative data analysis. You may also maintain your codebook in your journal. Make notes about ways to triangulate your data sources.

to determine answers to research questions. Data should be triangulated during this process. More information on triangulation and drawing valid conclusions is presented in the final section of this chapter.

TRIANGULATING DATA SOURCES AND DRAWING CONCLUSIONS FROM DATA

Recall from Chapters 5 and 6 the importance triangulating or corroborating multiple sources of data, which increases various types of validity related to the accuracy of the results of a study. Corroborating data sources simply means supporting results from one data source with results from another data source. For example, in the cooperative groups study described previously, the actual gain in scores was corroborated by students' reports of increased achievement. Further, reasons for the increased achievement—more preparation for class and studying with peers outside of class—were provided. Students' responses in interviews regarding studying more were supported with survey data that indicated more study time. Interview data in which students indicated they studied with peers outside of class was corroborated by observations of students making plans to get together to study. When multiple data sources are triangulated and point to the same result, confidence about the accuracy of the results of the study is increased.

As you begin the triangulation process, determine whether data sources corroborate one another. For example, if you have analyzed student artifacts such as tests, quizzes, and written assignments and have noted an increase in achievement, look at other data sources to see whether there is other supporting evidence that achievement did increase as a result of the intervention. If observations reveal an increase in students' motivation, a higher completion rate on class work, and greater student participation, these behaviors support or corroborate the improvement in achievement. If inquiry data were collected, say in the form of interviews, and most students said they felt better about their learning, were more interested in the lessons, and were working harder than they had before, this would also support the other data sources. Triangulating data in this example would allow a teacher to say, *Student achievement increased, which was evident when looking at their tests, quizzes, and written assignments. This increase in achievement is supported by observations that revealed higher student motivation, students working harder to complete classwork, and an increase in classroom participation during lessons. Further, students said that because of the new teaching strategy they felt they understood the lessons better, were more interested in the information we were studying, and were spending more time working on assignments and studying for the class.*

As data sources are triangulated and answers to research questions are postulated, conclusions are made about what was learned in the study. In action research studies, conclusions are used for ongoing and continuous reflective planning. Based on the conclusions you reach (Was the intervention effective? Why or why not? What would you do differently?), you need to make future plans regarding how you intend to use the results and conclusions of your study to inform your practice. During the reflective planning stage, the researcher steps back and says, *How can I use what I learned in my study [my results and conclusions] to inform my practice as an educator?* For example, in the collaborative group study described previously, the teacher could plan to continue using collaborative groups but structure each group so that there is strong leadership and more time on task in each group.

Reaching valid conclusions in your study is a critical step in the action research cycle. Conclusions must be reasonable in light of the results obtained. It would be unreasonable, for example, to state, *Although the writing intervention resulted in a decline in students' writing achievement, it is still a good method for teaching writing and I will continue to use it.* This is an extreme example, but it is included as a caution. Very often beginning researchers reach conclusions that are beyond what can be supported by the data. When this occurs, results can inform practice in a detrimental way. One way to prevent that from happening is to focus on increasing the validity of the study and the results of the study by following the guidelines presented in Chapter 6. As a reminder, those strategies include the following:

- Peer debriefing
- Persistent and prolonged observations
- Accurately recording data
- Member checks
- Triangulating data sources
- Providing thick description of the setting and study
- Negative case analysis
- Making biases clear and keeping them in check as data are analyzed
- Constructing an audit trail
- Presenting results to key audiences and eliciting their feedback
- Continuous, ongoing reflective planning

TIME TO REFLECT

Once you have analyzed data and know the results of your study (have answers to your research questions), discuss the following reflection questions with a critical friend, collaborator, or colleague. Use your journal to capture your reflections.

- How did your results align with the expectations or hopes you had when you started your study? What was affirming? What was frustrating?
- How can you use your results to generate new questions to continue your study? How important is it to you to continue the study?
- How do your conclusions fit with the assumptions you had at the beginning of your study? In what ways did your biases come into play as you drew your final conclusions?
- What have you concluded about yourself as a practitioner researcher? In what ways have your values been challenged or changed as a result of this process?

Activity 7.3 is provided to take you through the steps of pulling together the results of data analyses, writing results, and reaching conclusions.

ACTIVITY 7.3
Answering Research Questions and Reaching Conclusions

1. Write your primary research question. Look at all data sources, both quantitative and qualitative, that will be used to answer the question (refer to your responses to Activities 7.1 and 7.2).
2. Triangulate data sources, interpret results, and then construct a written answer to your research question. Support the answer with data. Use graphical displays, examples (of interview comments, answers to surveys, etc.), and quotes to help illustrate and describe results.
3. Repeat steps 1 and 2 with secondary questions.
4. After research questions have been answered, describe any peripherally related information that you think may be important.

Research paper activity: Under the heading *Results of the Study* (or another appropriate heading, such as *Results* or *Findings*), write a section that provides answers to your primary and secondary research questions. Use responses to steps 2 through 4 in the preceding list to complete this section. Include graphical displays, examples, and quotes as applicable. This section should follow the section on increasing validity (Activity 6.1).

5. Refer to the answers to your research questions, and then describe the conclusions you have reached about your study.

6. Conclude with a paragraph about how your results and conclusions will be used to inform your practice (reflective planning).

Research paper activity: Under the heading *Conclusions* (or a similar heading), write a section that provides your conclusions and your future goals based on your engagement in reflective planning. Use responses to steps 5 and 6 in the preceding list to complete this section. This section is the last section of the research paper.

What if triangulation results in data sources that do not corroborate each other? If you find that data sources reveal conflicting information (e.g., in the study on cooperative study groups, the teacher finds that student achievement decreases during the intervention, but other sources of data, such as observations and conferences, reveal that students' interest in and understanding of the content has increased), *collect more data.* As more data are collected, you will be able to determine the reasons that data sources provide conflicting information, you will be able to answer your *why* questions, and you will increase the likelihood that results are valid, credible, and meaningful.

Summary

The purpose of the chapter was to explain the process of analyzing data. The importance of engaging in interim analysis was described, and various ways to analyze, report, and display results for quantitative data were provided. The process of analysis of qualitative data was illustrated through a number of educational examples. The method of triangulating data sources to corroborate sources of evidence was explained, and drawing valid conclusions from results was emphasized.

The next stage of the action research process is one of renewing or beginning again. At this point, each step of the process, from reflecting on practice to identify a problem to determining the effectiveness of an intervention to deal with that problem, has been completed. Now the process begins anew as you reflect on what you have learned and use that information for ongoing reflective planning.

The final chapter of this text is a supplemental chapter for individuals interested in writing and disseminating their results. In Chapter 8, methods are described for completing the written report, which involves compiling the research paper activities provided in Chapters 2 through 7. The written report can serve as documentation of your action research experience to be placed in your professional portfolio. It can also be submitted to an educational journal or teaching magazine for publication or for presentation at a conference. In Chapter 8, specific guidelines for writing your report will be provided.

TABLE 7.12   Software for Quantitative and Qualitative Data Analysis

Software	Uses	Information Available at
SPSS	Quantitative data analysis; descriptive,	www.spss.com
SAS	inferential, and non-parametric statistics	www.sas.com
Minitab		www.minitab.com
NVivo	Coding and analysis of textual data as well as graphical models patterns and relationships	www.qsrinternational.com
XSight	Analysis of data using concept mapping graphics; rapid analysis of interview and other textual data	www.qsrinternational.com/products_xsight.aspx
ATLAS.ti	Analysis of textual, graphical, audio, and video data; feature for automatic coding of data	www.atlasti.com

Writing and Disseminating the Action Research Report

- Explain how to assemble a written report of an action research study.

- Illustrate ways to properly format the written report using APA (6th edition) guidelines.

- Describe methods for dissemination of research results

through presentation and/or publication.

- Provide examples of other methods that may be used to describe research projects.

This is a supplemental chapter for individuals who wish to prepare a written report of their action research studies. The previous chapters of this textbook provided information and activities to help you complete each step of your action research study—from initial reflection on a problem to reaching conclusions about the effectiveness of an intervention for dealing with that problem. You can now take your written responses to the activities in Chapters 2 through 7 (particularly the Research Paper Activities provided with the chapter activities) and assemble them to complete a final written report of your study. This chapter suggests ways to organize the paper, provides examples of how to use proper publication formatting (using APA 6th edition guidelines), and explains the process of disseminating the paper through presentation or publication. At the end of this chapter, alternative methods for reporting research are also provided.

GUIDELINES FOR WRITING THE FINAL ACTION RESEARCH REPORT

The *formatting* guidelines presented here are based on those provided in the *Publication Manual of the American Psychological Association* (APA; 6th edition), and the *content* guidelines presented are based on the suggestions provided in this text for conducting the action research study. A brief explanation is provided about how to format your paper, which is followed by a description the kind of information to include in each section of the final report. A checklist that can be used to evaluate your final paper is also provided.

Paper Format

The paper format guidelines provided here follow the suggestions in the APA Manual (6th edition). Your paper should be typed on standard-size paper. Use a 12-point Times New Roman font. Double-space the entire paper, but do not put an extra line space between paragraphs or before or after headings. Margins should be set at one inch on all sides, and left justification for line spacing (*not* justified so that all lines are of equal length) should be used. The first line of every paragraph should be indented ½ inch. Each page should be numbered, beginning with the title page. All pages of the manuscript should also have the running head in the page header. All headings, the title of the paper, author information, and text should be typed in both uppercase and lowercase letters. Do not use all uppercase letters anywhere in the paper. Use headings to delineate sections and subsections of the paper. For action research studies, two levels of headings are probably sufficient. Center the first level of headings using a **bold** typeface (for major sections of the paper such as the reflection, setting and participants, intervention, etc.), and for the second level of headings use a flush-left, **bold** typeface. Include the following in the written report:

- A title page that includes a running head, the title of the paper, the author's (or authors') name(s) and affiliation(s), and the primary author's contact information. The title page is page 1. Figure 8.1 illustrates how the title page should look.
- An abstract, which is included on page 2. Include in the abstract a sentence on the purpose of the study, a brief description of the setting and participants, a short explanation of the intervention or innovation studied, results of the study, and the conclusions made. Abstracts are typically 250 words or less.
- The action research report, which begins on page 3.
- The reference list, which follows the research report and begins on a separate page. APA format calls for double-spacing references, although additional spaces should not be included between references. Simply maintain double spacing throughout the reference list. The reference list should be titled (at the center) *References*.

Teacher Study Groups   1

Running Head: The Effect of Teacher Study Groups

The Effect of Teacher Study Groups
on Integration of Research-Based
Teaching Practices in the Classroom

Pat Jackson

Shady Grove Middle School
151 Shady Grove Lane
Shady Grove, GA 30117
pjackson@shadygrovems.org.

FIGURE 8.1 Title page example with header.

• Any appendices, which should be placed after the references, beginning on a separate page.

References must be written in APA format, and some general guidelines and examples are provided here. Consult the APA manual for additional information. Also, review Chapter 3 of this textbook for examples of use of headings, citing secondary sources, use of *et al.,* and so on. References should be arranged in alphabetical order by last name. If two or more works by the same author are in the reference list, the earliest publication should be listed first. If there is more than one publication for an author in the same year, use lowercase, italicized letters, beginning with *a* to identify the articles (e.g., Hendricks, 1999*a;* Hendricks, 1999*b*). References are arranged using a hanging indent. Examples of ways to cite various reference types are included here. Pay close attention to the use of commas, italics, and capitalization. New in the most recent edition of the APA manual is the *digital document identifier,* also known as the DOI. Articles or sources that are available online are given a DOI number, and articles with a DOI typically print the number on the first page of the article.

- *Journal articles* (author, date, article title, journal title, volume number, page numbers):

  Sparks-Langer, G. M., & Colton, A. B. (1991). Synthesis of research on teachers' reflective thinking. *Educational Leadership, 48,* 37–44.

  Stenhouse, L. (1981). What counts as research? *British Journal of Educational Studies, 29,* 103–113.

- *Journal articles with DOI* (author, date, article title, journal title, volume number, page numbers, DOI):

  Baskerville, D., & Goldblatt, H. (2009). Learning to be a critical friend: From professional indifference through challenge to unguarded conversations. *Cambridge Journal of Education, 39*(2), 205–221. doi:10.1080/03057640902902260

- *Journal articles available online with no DOI* (author, date, article title, journal title, volume number, page numbers [if applicable], URL of journal homepage):

  Peterson, C. H., & Peterson, N. A. (2011). Impact of peer evaluation confidentiality on student marks. *International Journal for the Scholarship of Teaching and Learning, 5*(2). Retrieved from http://www.georgiasouthern.edu/ijsotl

- *Books* (author, date, title of book, location of publication, publisher):

  Burns, A. (2010). *Doing action research in English language teaching: A guide for practitioners.* New York: Routledge.

  Cole, A. L., & Knowles, J. G. (2009). *Researching teaching: Exploring teacher development through reflexive inquiry.* Nova Scotia: Backalong Books.

- *Electronic version of a book* (author, date, title of book, location of publication, publisher, DOI):

  Duignan, P. (2007). *Educational leadership: Key challenges and ethical tensions.* New York: Cambridge University Press. doi:10.2277/0521685125

- *Chapters in edited books* (author, date, title of chapter, editor, title of book, page numbers of chapter, location of publication, publisher):

  Kemmis, S., & McTaggart, R. (2000). Participatory action research. In N. K. Denzin & Y. S. Lincoln (Eds.), *Handbook of qualitative research* (2nd ed., pp. 567–605). Thousand Oaks, CA: Sage.

  Kemmis, S., & Wilkinson, M. (1997). Participatory action research and the study of practice. In B. Atweh, S. Kemmis, & P. Weeks (Eds.), *Action research in practice: Partnerships for social justice in education* (pp. 21–36). London: Routledge.

- *Technical and research reports* (author, date, report title, report number, location of publication, publisher, URL if retrieved online):

  Anderman, L. H., & Midgley, C. (1998). *Motivation and middle school students* (Report No. EDO-PS-98-5). Washington, DC: Office of Educational Research and Improvement. Retrieved from http://www.eric.ed.gov/ERICWebPortal/contentdelivery/servlet/ERICServlet?accno=ED421281

  Brophy, J. (1998). *Failure syndrome students* (Report No. EDO-PS-98-2). Washington, DC: Office of Educational Research and Improvement. (ED419625)

Note: Additional examples for citing sources in APA (6th edition) are available at the Purdue Writing Lab website (http://owl.english.purdue.edu/owl/section/2/10/).

Content Format

Your paper should include the following: (1) the reflection that led to the identification of your area of focus, including research questions, (2) review of the literature, (3) a description of the participants and setting of the study, (4) an explanation of the intervention or research method used, (5) a description of the data collection strategies used, (6) information related to how you increased validity in your study, (7) a description of the results based on your analysis of the data, and (8) conclusions you made—including your reflective planning—based on those results. The paper needs to logically flow from one section to the next, showing the ways in which the reflection, literature review, research questions, and intervention or study are connected. The reflection and all sections after the literature review should be written in past tense. This means you may need to change the verb tense in the research paper activities you completed in Chapters 2 through 7. The checklist provided in Table 8.1 suggests the information that should be included in each section of the paper.

TABLE 8.1   Checklist for Action Research Report

REFLECTION (see Activity 2.2, Research Paper Activity)

_____ Is the reflection written in first person?

_____ Are reasons clearly stated describing why the issue is important to you?

_____ Are initial actions you planned to take provided?

_____ Have you provided an explanation of the outcomes you desired as a result of your study?

_____ Does the reflection contain a brief description of your educational role and your setting (grade level, subject, etc.)?

_____ Does your reflection illustrate the reflective process(es) you used and their relationship to your core educational values?

LITERATURE REVIEW (see Activity 3.1, Research Paper Activity)

_____ Does the literature review relate to the focus of your reflection?

_____ Is your literature review a *synthesis* of the information you reviewed?

_____ Are reviewed sources clearly relevant to the purpose of your study?

_____ Does a logical transition exist between the reflection section of your paper and the literature review?

PURPOSE (see Activity 4.1, Research Paper Activity)

_____ Have you clearly articulated the purpose of the study, focusing on the intervention or research method used and the outcomes desired?

_____ Is the purpose tied to the reflection?

_____ Does the purpose logically follow the literature review?

_____ Have you clearly articulated the primary *and* secondary research questions?

_____ Are the research questions aligned with your purpose statement?

SETTING/PARTICIPANTS/COLLABORATION (see Activity 4.2, Research Paper Activities)

_____ Have you described the setting and participants in sufficient detail so the context of your educational environment can be understood?

_____ If your study involved collaborators, did you explain the nature of the collaboration and the collaborators' roles in the study?

INTERVENTION/INNOVATION (see Activity 4.2, Research Paper Activities)

_____ Is the intervention based on what was learned in the review of literature?

_____ Have you described the intervention or innovation you used in enough detail so that a colleague could implement the intervention?

METHODS OF DATA COLLECTION (see Activity 5.1, Research Paper Activity)

_____ Did you use multiple forms of data collection to answer your research questions?

_____ Did you provide a justification for the connection between your data collection strategies and research questions?

_____ Did you describe the data collection methods you used in sufficient detail so they could be replicated by a colleague?

_____ Did you include surveys, questionnaires, interview questions, or other data collection instruments in this section or in an appendix?

_____ If baseline data were used, did you describe how baseline data were collected?

TABLE 8.1 *(continued)*

PLAN FOR INCREASING VALIDITY (see Activity 6.1, Research Paper Activity)

_____ Did you describe the types of validity you chose to focus on in your study?

_____ Did you provide a justification for the types of validity chosen and link them to the purpose of the study?

_____ Did you explain the methods used to increase these various types of validity?

RESULTS OF THE STUDY (see Activity 7.3, Research Paper Activity)

_____ Have you provided results, based on multiple sources of data, for each research question?

_____ Have you presented results in appropriate forms (tables, graphs, percentages, examples of work samples, narratives, tally sheets, quotes, etc.)?

_____ Have you given an explanation about how you triangulated data sources?

CONCLUSIONS (see Activity 7.3, Research Paper Activity)

_____ Have you described the conclusions you reached about the effectiveness of the intervention?

_____ Can the conclusions be supported by the results provided in the *Results of the Study* section?

_____ Have you provided future plans (reflective planning) based on your results and conclusions?

GENERAL

_____ Is your paper free of spelling and grammatical errors?

_____ Have you used APA format correctly throughout your paper, including in the reference section?

_____ Is your paper typed in 12-point Times New Roman or Courier font?

_____ Did you use margins of 1" on all sides?

_____ Did you double-space your paper?

_____ Have you included a header with page numbers?

_____ Does your paper have a title page that includes a running head, title of your report, and information about you?

_____ Does your paper contain an abstract of no more than 250 words?

_____ Is the abstract a concise account of the purpose and results of your study?

_____ Have you used headings (and subheadings, if appropriate) in your paper?

DISSEMINATING ACTION RESEARCH FINDINGS

Dissemination of your research findings is an important part of the action research process. There are many ways to disseminate your study, and there are a number of audiences with whom to share your findings. First, I urge you to share results with your participants. Researchers often forget to discuss results with participants, but it is important to let your participants, whether they are students, teachers, parents, or administrators, know what you concluded. Sharing results with participants is a thoughtful way to provide them with a sense of closure to the research project.

After you have shared your findings with participants, consider disseminating the results of your study to a wider audience. You can share results with those in your school community—teachers, administrators, parents—and it may be beneficial to explain your findings to more than one audience. For example, a teacher who finds that increasing students' organizational skills improves their achievement may wish to send a letter home to parents describing the intervention used, the ways it improved students' organization, and the impact it had on students' achievement. The teacher could also share the results of the study, perhaps at a schoolwide or districtwide workshop, with colleagues who might wish to try the intervention in their own classes.

Another way to disseminate the results of your study is to present the work at a professional conference. Professional organizations such as the American Association of School Administrators, the Association for Supervision and Curriculum Development, the International Reading Association, the National Council for Social Studies, the National Council of Teachers of English, the National Council of Teachers of Mathematics, and the National Science Teacher Association are just a few professional organizations that sponsor conferences. Many of these national organizations include affiliated regional groups that sponsor smaller conferences at the state or regional level. You can check an organization's website to find upcoming conferences, conference themes, conference locations, and submission dates and guidelines. Table 8.2 provides links to a few selected organizations' conferences. If you present your study at a conference, you may need to take copies of your paper to give to the audience. Your presentation will need to meet the established time limit (usually between 10 and 25 minutes). In addition, if projectors or computers will be available to presenters, you may wish to prepare overheads or a PowerPoint presentation.

Professional organizations such as the ones mentioned previously also generally support one or more professional journals or magazines, which are other options for disseminating your study. Publishing your work is the best way to disseminate your findings to the largest audience possible. Although it may seem to be an overwhelming project to take on, if you completed the research paper activities provided in this book in Chapters 2 through 7, and if you followed the guidelines presented in the previous section of this chapter for writing the final report, it is likely that your final paper will be of publishable quality. You need only to find a suitable journal or magazine and submit your work for consideration.

To find a place to publish your study, search the websites of the professional organizations that seem best suited to your topic. For example, if your study focused on increasing students' reading achievement, you would focus on the International Reading Association and the National Council of Teachers of English. Once you have found the websites for the professional organization(s), look for a list of journals and magazines that publish action research. Read the description for each journal or magazine to determine which solicit research by educators or administrators. Make sure to read the guidelines to authors for the journal or magazine you select so that you will know exactly how to submit your study for publication consideration. Table 8.2 provides links to journals associated with professional organizations that publish practitioner studies.

TABLE 8.2 Links to Professional Organizations' Conference and Journal Sites

Professional Organization	Conference and Journal Websites
American Alliance for Health Physical Education, Recreation, and Dance	**Conference:** www.aahperd.org/whatwedo/convention/ **Journals:** *Journal of Physical Education, Recreation, and Dance; Strategies: A Journal for Physical and Sport Educators; American Journal of Health Education*: http://www.aahperd.org/publications/journals/
American Association of School Administrators	**Conference:** http://nce.aasa.org/ **Journals:** *The School Administrator*: http://www.aasa.org/SchoolAdministrator.aspx *AASA Journal of Scholarship & Practice*: http://www.aasa.org/jsp.aspx
American Association of School Librarian	**Conference:** http://www.ala.org/ala/mgrps/divs/aasl/conferencesandevents/aaslconferences.cfm **Journals:** *Knowledge Quest, School Library Media Research* http://www.ala.org/ala/mgrps/divs/aasl/conferencesandevents/aaslconferences.cfm
American Counseling Association	**Conference:** www.counseling.org/Convention **Journals:** *Journal of Counseling and Development; The Career Development Quarterly; Journal of Multicultural Counseling and Development*: http://www.counseling.org/Publications/Journals.aspx
American Speech-Language-Hearing Association	**Conference:** http://www.asha.org/events/ **Journals:** *American Journal of Speech-Language Pathology; Contemporary Issues in Communication Science and Disorders; Language, Speech, and Hearing Services in Schools*: http://www.asha.org/publications/
Association for Supervision and Curriculum Development	**Conferences:** http://www.ascd.org/conferences.aspx **Journals:** *Educational Leadership*: http://www.ascd.org/publications/educational-leadership.aspx *International Journal of Education Policy and Leadership*: http://www.ascd.org/Publications/IJEPL.aspx
Council for Exceptional Children	**Conference:** www.cec.sped.org **Journal:** *Teaching Exceptional Children*: http://www.cec.sped.org/Content/NavigationMenu/Publications2/TEACHINGExceptionalChildren/default.htm

(continued)

TABLE 8.2 *(continued)*	
Professional Organization	**Conference and Journal Websites**
International Reading Association	**Conference:** http://www.reading.org/General/Conferences.aspx **Journals:** *The Reading Teacher; Journal of Adolescent and Adult Literacy; Thinking Classroom; Reading Online:* http://www.reading.org/General/Publications.aspx
International Society for Technology in Education	**Conference:** http://www.iste.org/conference/ **Journals:** *Journal for Computing Teachers:* http://www.iste.org/learn/publications/journals.aspx
National Art Education Association	**Conference:** http://www.arteducators.org/news/national-convention/national-convention **Journals:** *Art Education Journal:* http://www.arteducators.org/research/art-education
National Association for the Education of Young Children	**Conference:** http://www.naeyc.org/events **Journals:** *Young Children; Beyond the Journal; Early Childhood Research Quarterly:* http://www.naeyc.org/publications
National Association for Music Education	**Conference:** http://www.menc.org/events/ **Journals:** *Music Educators Journal, Teaching Music:* http://www.menc.org/resources/view/nafme-journals
National Council for Social Studies	**Conference:** www.socialstudies.org/conference **Journals:** *Social Education; Middle Level Learning; Social Studies and the Young Learner:* http://www.socialstudies.org/publications
National Council of Teachers of English	**Conference:** http://www.ncte.org/annual **Journals:** *Language Arts; Primary Voices: K-6; Voices from the Middle; English Journal:* http://www.ncte.org/journals
National Council of Teachers of Mathematics	**Conference:** www.nctm.org/meetings **Journals:** *Teaching Children Mathematics; Mathematics Teaching in the Middle School; Mathematics Teacher; Online Journal for School Mathematics; Journal for Research in Mathematics Education:* http://www.nctm.org/publications/
National Science Teacher Association	**Conference:** http://nsta.org/conferences **Journals:** *Science and Children; Science Scope; The Science Teacher:* http://nsta.org/publications/journals.aspx?lid=tnav

Most educational journals require that the paper is written in APA format, but a few journals require writing in other formats, such as MLA. Make sure your paper is in the format required by the journal to which you will submit your work. Be mindful of other requirements, such as the maximum length of the paper and whether your name and the names of any co-authors should appear on the paper. Often, one copy of the paper will include a title page with the author's or authors' names, and other copies will include a title page with no authors' names. This is so that papers can be blind reviewed by the journal reviewers, which means they do not know who wrote the paper. Many of these same guidelines are often followed when papers are reviewed for presentation at a conference.

You should include with your paper a cover letter to the journal editor explaining that you are submitting your paper for publication. The letter should contain the title of the manuscript and a brief description of the study (no longer than one or two sentences). You must make clear that the study has not been published elsewhere, and if you have presented the paper, you need to report where the paper was presented. Finally, include a statement that explains that you followed acceptable ethical standards through gaining approval to conduct the study (either through a university institutional review board, school district review board, or other reviewing agency) and by gaining informed consent from participants and their parents if the participants were minors. Also, be sure to include contact information such as mailing address, telephone and fax numbers, and an email address. An example cover letter is included in Figure 8.2.

Once the journal editor receives your paper, he or she will determine whether its contents are suitable for the journal. The editor will then send the paper out for review, usually to two or three reviewers. At that point, the editor will contact you to let you know that the paper is under review and to tell you approximately how long the review process will take. Once the editor receives comments from the reviewers, a determination will be made based on those comments whether to accept the manuscript as it is, to accept it but require some revisions, or to reject the manuscript. The editor will then send you a letter or email about the status of the paper with the reviewers' comments. If the article is accepted as it is, which is rare, then you have no more work to do. If the article is accepted with revisions, you must make those revisions in a timely manner and send the revised paper back to the editor. Remember that if the editor asks for revisions, it means the journal is interested in publishing the work, but revisions must be made before it can be published. If the article is rejected, a good strategy is to carefully read the reviewers' comments, make the suggested changes, and submit the article to another journal. Although a rejection is painful, a lot can be learned by reading reviewers' comments and working to strengthen the manuscript. From experience, I have learned that often, with work and perseverance, a rejected manuscript can be revised and eventually published.

Terry G. Smith, Editor
The Journal of Exceptional Teacher Research
June 15, 2012

Dear Dr. Smith,

I have attached a submission to *The Journal of Exceptional Teacher Research* entitled "The Effect of Teacher Study Groups on Integration of Research-Based Teaching Practices in the Classroom." I submit this for consideration as a full-length article.

In this study, I investigated three teacher study groups at the middle school level. Each study group met weekly for an entire academic year for the sole purpose of learning how to use research-based interventions with struggling students. Results indicated the teachers' use of research-based teaching strategies increased, and student achievement data revealed that the teaching strategies had a positive effect on student learning.

This article is not under review elsewhere nor has it been previously published. The Institutional Review Board in my school district granted permission for me to conduct this study, and all participants gave their informed consent to participate.

I hope you find this article suitable for publication in *The Journal of Exceptional Teacher Research*. If you have any questions or concerns, please contact me.

Sincerely,
Pat Jackson
Shady Grove Middle School
151 Shady Grove Lane
Shady Grove, GA 30117
pjackson@shadygrovems.org

FIGURE 8.2 Sample cover letter.

OTHER WAYS TO WRITE UP RESEARCH

There are a number of ways—beyond preparing an article for publication—to write up action research studies. As described in Stringer (2007), action research efforts can be portrayed through drama, poetry, narratives, and memoirs. In fact, sometimes illustrating research through drama or poetry can connect others to the research in ways traditional reports cannot. Macklin Finley (2003) portrayed his action research study with homeless youth in New Orleans during the 1990s through poetry. He explains,

> I constructed poetry from recordings and transcripts of my conversations with street youths and then staged performances of the poems . . . on Bourbon Street for a varied audience of street youths, tourists, business people—anyone who was interested to stop and listen. In these performance poems, I described the lives of

homeless street youths and posed questions to research participants about their lifestyles, political beliefs, and attitudes toward
life, school, and work. The performances generated continuing dialogues with the youths who were featured in the poems, and they
opened up new dialogues about homelessness and street life. . . .
(p. 603)

Another way to write up research is through narrative, or descriptive,
accounts of the study. Stringer (2007) describes narratives as "richly detailed,
thickly described accounts that enable readers to empathetically understand
the lived reality of research participants" (p. 180). He suggests that narratives
should include a description of the project and participants, an interpretation of what happened during the study, and a description of actions taken
during the study. The benefit of using narrative accounts is their power
to portray the contextual specificity inherent in each action research study
(Greenwood & Levin, 2007). Anderson and Herr (2009) further explain that
practitioners who write narrative accounts of their research, rather than
a formal research report, shift "the notion of research as contributing to
an academic knowledge base to sharing professional wisdom" (p. 161).
McNiff and Whitehead (2006) describe four volumes of narratives, *Passion
in Professional Practice*, that illustrate action researchers' improved practice through narrative accounts. These are available online at http://schools.
gedsb.net/ar/passion/pppii/index.html.

Portrait writing is yet another method for reporting action research.
Portrait writing, much like narrative, involves writing descriptive accounts of
the research project, but in story form (Bogdan & Bilken, 2003). Elements
of storytelling are used to illustrate complexities and describe context in
detail. Portrait writing was used in the book *A Gallery of Portraits in Service
Learning: Action Research in Teacher Education* (Duckenfield & Swift, 2002)
to describe service-learning action research projects. The full text is available
online at www.eric.ed.gov (search for ED 470734).

CONCLUDING COMMENTS

Congratulations on completing your action research study. I hope the experience has influenced your work as an educator and has allowed you to see how
you can use the action research process to guide your ongoing professional
development and impact school improvement. I encourage you to disseminate
the results of your study to many different audiences so that other teachers,
administrators, parents, and academic researchers can learn from the important
work you have done. I also encourage you to teach your colleagues to use the
action research process. Pass on the knowledge and skills you now have, and
mentor other educators so that they can benefit from studying their practice.

REFERENCES

Adelman, C. (1997). Action research: The problem of participation. In R. McTaggart (Ed.), *Participatory action research* (pp. 79–112). New York: State University of New York Press.

Allen, L., & Calhoun, E. F. (1998). Schoolwide action research: Findings from six years of study. *Phi Delta Kappan, 79*(9), 706–710.

Anderson, G. L., Herr, K., & Nihlen, A. S. (1994). *Studying your own school: An educator's guide to qualitative practitioner research*. Thousand Oaks, CA: Corwin Press.

Anderson, G. L., Herr, K., & Nihlen, A. (2007). *Studying your own school: An educator's guide to practitioner action research* (2nd ed.). Thousand Oaks, CA: Corwin Press.

Baskerville, D., & Goldblatt, H. (2009). Learning to be a critical friend: From professional indifference through challenge to unguarded conversations. *Cambridge Journal of Education, 39,* 305–221. doi:10.1080/03057640902902260

Berg, B. L., & Lune, H. (2012). *Qualitative research methods for the social sciences* (8th ed.). Upper Saddle River, NJ: Pearson.

Blum, H. T., Lipsett, L. R., & Yocum, D. J. (2002). Literature circles: A tool for self-determination in one middle school inclusive classroom. *Remedial and Special Education, 23,* 99–108.

Bogdan, R. C., & Biklen, S. K. (2007). *Qualitative research for education: An introduction to theories and methods* (5th ed.). Boston: Allyn and Bacon.

Bolton, G. (2010). *Reflective practice: Writing and professional development* (3rd ed.). London: SAGE.

Bottomley, D. M., Henk, W. A., & Melnick, S. A. (1998). Assessing children's views about themselves as writers using the Writer Self-Perception Scale. *The Reading Teacher, 51,* 286–296.

Bullough, R. V., & Gitlin, A. D. (2001). *Becoming a student: Linking knowledge production and practice of teaching* (2nd ed.). New York: Routledge.

Burns, A. (2010). *Doing action research in English language teaching: A guide for practitioners.* New York: Routledge.

Buysse, V., Sparkman, K. L., & Wesley, P. W. (2003). Communities of practice: Connecting what we know with what we do. *Exceptional Children, 69,* 263–277.

Calhoun, E. F. (2002). Action research for school improvement. *Educational Leadership, 59*(6), 18–24.

Carr, W. (2006). Philosophy, methodology, and action research. *Journal of Philosophy of Education, 40*(4), 421–435.

Carr, W., & Kemmis, S. (2009). Educational action research: A critical approach. In S. Noffke & B. Somekh (Eds.), *The SAGE handbook of educational action research* (pp. 74–84). Thousand Oaks, CA: SAGE.

Chiu, L. (1997). Development and validation of the School Achievement Motivation Rating Scale. *Educational and Psychological Measurement, 57,* 292–305.

Clancy, D. (2001). *Studying children and schools: Qualitative research traditions.* Prospect Heights, IL: Waveland Press.

Cochran-Smith, M., & Lytle, S. L. (1993). *Inside outside: Teacher research and knowledge.* New York: Teachers College Press.

Cole, A. L., & Knowles, J. G. (2009). *Researching teaching: Exploring teacher development through reflexive inquiry.* Nova Scotia: Backalong Books.

Costa, A. L., & Kallick, B. (1993). Through the lens of a critical friend. *Educational Leadership, 51*(2), 49–51.

Creswell, J. W. (2011). Mixed methods research. In N. K. Denzin & Y. S. Lincoln (Eds.), *The SAGE handbook of qualitative research* (4th ed., pp. 269–283). Thousand Oaks, CA: SAGE.

Creswell, J. W., & Plano Clark, V. L. (2011). *Designing and conducting mixed methods research* (2nd ed.). Thousand Oaks, CA: SAGE.

Daniels, H. (2002a). *Literature circles: Voice and choice in book clubs and reading groups* (2nd ed.). Portland, ME: Stenhouse Publishers.

Daniels, H. (2002b). Resource for middle school book clubs. *Voices from the Middle, 10*(1), 48.

Daniels, H., & Steineke, N. (2004). *Minilessons for literature circles*. Portsmouth, NH: Heineman.

Day, J. P., Spiegel, D. L., McLellan, J., & Brown, V. B. (2002). *Moving forward with literature circles: How to plan, manage, and evaluate literature circles that deepen understanding and foster a love of reading*. New York: Scholastic.

Denzin, N. K., & Lincoln, Y. S. (2011). The discipline and practice of qualitative research. In N. K. Denzin & Y. S. Lincoln (Eds.), *The SAGE handbook of qualitative research* (4th ed., pp. 1–19). Thousand Oaks, CA: SAGE.

Dewey, J. (1933). *How we think: A restatement of the relation of reflective thinking to the educative process*. Boston: D. C. Heath.

Dinkelman, T. (2003). Self-study in teacher education: A means and ends tool for promoting reflective teaching. *Journal of Teacher Education, 54*, 6–18.

DuBois, D. L., Felner, R. D., Brand, S., Phillips, R. S. C., & Lease, A. M. (1996). Early adolescent self-esteem: A developmental-ecological framework and assessment strategy. *Journal of Research on Adolescence, 6*, 543–579.

Duckenfeld, M., & Swift, K. (Eds.). (2002). *A gallery of portraits in service learning: Action research in teacher education*. Clemson, SC: National Dropout Prevention Center.

Eisner, E. (1991). *The enlightened eye: Qualitative inquiry and the enhancement of educational practice*. New York: Macmillan.

Elliot, J. (2009). Building educational theory through action research. In S. Noffke & B. Somekh (Eds.), *The SAGE handbook of educational action research* (pp. 28–38). Thousand Oaks, CA: SAGE.

Elliot, J. (2010). Educational action research and the teacher. *Action Research in Education, 1*, 1–3.

Fecho, R. (1992). Reading as a teacher. In M. Cochran-Smith & S. L. Lytle (Eds.), *Inside outside: Teacher research and knowledge* (pp. 265–272). New York: Teachers College Press.

Finley, M. (2003). Fugue of the street rat: Writing research poetry. *International Journal of Qualitative Studies in Education, 16*(4), 603–604.

Fishman, S. M., & McCarthy, L. (2000). *Unplayed tapes: A personal history of collaborative teacher research*. New York: Teachers College Press.

Flores-Kastanis, E., Montoya-Vargas, J., & Suárez, D. H. (2009). Participatory action research in Latin American education: A road map to a different part of the world. In S. Noffke & B. Somekh (Eds.), *The SAGE handbook of educational action research* (pp. 453–466). Thousand Oaks, CA: SAGE.

Fontana, A., & Frey, J. H. (2009). The interview: From neutral stance to political involvement. In S. Noffke & B. Somekh (Eds.), *The SAGE handbook of educational action research* (pp. 695–727). Thousand Oaks, CA: SAGE.

Freire, P. (1997). *Pedagogy of the oppressed* (20th Anniversary Edition, trans. M. B. Ramos). New York: Continuum.

Friedman, I. A. (1994). Conceptualizing and measuring: Teacher-perceived student behaviors: Disrespect, sociability, and attentiveness. *Educational and Psychological Measurement, 54*, 949–958.

Fullan, M. (2002). The change leader. *Educational Leadership, 59*(8), 16–20.

Fullan, M. (2010, March/April). The awesome power of the principal. *Principal,* 10–15.

Greenwood, D. J., & Levin, M. (2007). *Introduction to action research: Social research for social change* (2nd ed.). Thousand Oaks, CA: SAGE.

Harris, A. S., Bruster, B., Peterson, B., & Shutt, T. (2010). *Examining and facilitating reflection to improve professional practice.* Plymouth, UK: Rowan and Littlefield Publishers.

Henk, W. A., & Melnick, S. A. (1995). The Reader Self-Perception Scale (RSPS): A new tool for measuring how children feel about themselves as readers. *The Reading Teacher, 48,* 470–479.

Hill, G. W. (2002). *Critical friendship.* Brisbane, Australia: Mottram D'Hill & Associates.

Hobson, D. (2001). Action and reflection: Narrative and journaling in teacher research. In G. E. Burnaford, J. Fischer, & D. Hobson (Eds.), *Teachers doing research: The power of action through inquiry* (pp. 7–27). Mahwah, NJ: Lawrence Erlbaum Associates.

Huberman, A. M., & Miles, M. B. (1998). Data management and analysis methods. In N. K. Denzin & Y. S. Lincoln (Eds.), *Collecting and interpreting qualitative materials* (pp. 179–210). Thousand Oaks, CA: SAGE.

Johnson, B., & Christensen, L. (2012). *Educational research: Quantitative, qualitative, and mixed approaches* (4th ed.). Thousand Oaks, CA: SAGE.

Kemmis, S. (2006). Participatory action research and the public sphere. *Educational Action Research, 14,* 459–476.

Kemmis, S., & McTaggart, R. (2000). Participatory action research. In N. K. Denzin & Y. S. Lincoln (Eds.), *Handbook of qualitative research* (2nd ed., pp. 567–605). Thousand Oaks, CA: SAGE.

Kemmis, S., & Wilkinson, M. (1997). Participatory action research and the study of practice. In B. Atweh, S. Kemmis, & P. Weeks (Eds.), *Action research in practice: Partnerships for social justice in education* (pp. 21–36). London: Routledge.

Kong, A., & Fitch, E. (2002/2003). Using Book Club to engage culturally and linguistically diverse learners in reading, writing, and talking about books. *The Reading Teacher, 56*(4), 352.

Lather, P. (1991). *Getting smart: Feminist research and pedagogy with/in the postmodern.* New York: Routledge.

Lather, P. (1993). Fertile obsession: Validity after poststructuralism. *Sociological Quarterly, 34,* 673–693.

LeCompte, M. D., & Goetz, J. P. (1982). Problems of reliability and validity in ethnographic research. *Review of Educational Research, 51,* 31–60.

Lincoln, Y. S., & Guba, E. G. (1985). *Naturalistic inquiry.* Newbury Park, CA: SAGE.

Lyons, N. (2010). Reflection and reflective inquiry: Critical issues, evolving conceptualizations, contemporary claims, and future possibilities. In N. Lyons (Ed.), *Handbook of reflection and reflective inquiry* (pp. 3–22). New York: Springer.

Maxwell, J. A. (2009). Designing a qualitative study. In L. Bickman & D. J. Rog (Eds.), *The SAGE handbook of applied social research methods* (2nd ed., pp. 214–253). Thousand Oaks, CA: SAGE.

McNiff, J. (2002). *Action research: Principles and practice* (2nd ed.). London: RoutledgeFalmer.

McNiff, J., & Whitehead, J. (2006). *All you need to know about action research.* London: SAGE.

McNiff, J., & Whitehead, J. (2010). *You and your action research project* (3rd ed.). New York: Routledge.

Merriam, S. B. (2009). *Qualitative research: A guide to design and implementation.* San Francisco: Jossey-Bass.

Mills, G. E. (2011). *Action research: A guide for the teacher researcher* (4th ed.). Upper Saddle River, NJ: Pearson.

National Academy of Education (NAE). (1999). *Recommendations regarding research priorities: An advisory report to the National Educational Research Policy and Priorities Board.* Washington, DC: Author.

National Board for Professional Teaching Standards (NBPTS). (2001). *NBPTS standards for early childhood generalist* (2nd ed.). Arlington, VA: Author.

National Research Council. (1999). *Improving student learning: A strategic plan for educational research and it usability.* Washington, DC: National Academy Press.

Noffke, S. E. (2009). Revisiting the professional, personal, and political dimensions of action research. In S. Noffke & B. Somekh (Eds.), *The SAGE handbook of educational action research* (pp. 6–23). Thousand Oaks, CA: SAGE.

Norlander-Case, K. A., Reagan, T. G., & Case, C. W. (1999). *The professional teacher: The preparation and nurturance of the reflective practitioner.* San Francisco: Jossey-Bass.

Palincsar, A. S., Magnusson, S. J., Marano, N., Ford, D., & Brown, N. (1998). Designing a community of practice: Principles and practices of the GIsML community. *Teaching and Teacher Education, 14,* 5–19.

Pan, M. L. (2004). *Preparing literature reviews: Qualitative and quantitative approaches* (2nd ed.). Glendale, CA: Pyrczak.

Peidong, L., & Laidlaw, M. (2006). Collaborative enquiry, action research, and curriculum development in rural China: How can we facilitate a process of educational change? *Action Research, 4*(3), 333–350.

Phillips, A. K., & Carr, K. (2010). *Becoming a teacher through action research: Process, context, and self-study* (2nd ed.). New York: Routledge.

Pintrich, R. R., & DeGroot, E. V. (1990). Motivational and self-regulated learning components of classroom academic performance, *Journal of Educational Psychology, 82,* 33–40.

Richards, L. (2005). *Handling qualitative data: A practical guide.* London: SAGE.

Rossman, G. B., & Rallis, S. F. (2012). *Learning in the field: An introduction to qualitative research* (3rd ed.). Thousand Oaks, CA: SAGE.

Rudduck, J. (1988). Changing the world of the classroom by understanding it: A review of some aspects of the work of Lawrence Stenhouse. *Journal of Curriculum and Supervision, 4,* 30–42.

Ryan, G. W., & Bernard, H. R. (2000). Data management and analysis methods. In N. K. Denzin & Y. S. Lincoln (Eds.), *Handbook of qualitative research* (2nd ed., pp. 769–802). Thousand Oaks, CA: SAGE.

Schön, D. A. (1987). *Educating the reflective practitioner.* San Francisco: Jossey-Bass.

Schubert, W. H., & Lopez-Schubert, A. (1997). Sources of a theory for action research in the United States. In R. McTaggart (Ed.), *Participatory action research* (pp. 203–222). New York: State University of New York Press.

Seidman, I. (1998). *Interviewing as qualitative research: A guide for researchers in education and the social sciences* (2nd ed.). New York: Teachers College Press.

Shank, G. D. (2002). *Qualitative research: A personal skills approach.* Upper Saddle River, NJ: Merrill Prentice Hall.

Shosh, J. M., & Zales, C. R. (2005). Daring to teach writing authentically, K–12 and beyond. *English Journal, 95*(2), 77–81.

Simons, H. (2009). *Case study research in practice.* London: SAGE.

Singer, N. R. (2007). Taking time for inquiry: Revisiting collaborative teacher inquiry to improve student achievement. *English Leadership Quarterly, 29*(3), 7–10.

Skillings, M., & Ferrell, R. (2000). Student-generated rubrics: Bringing students into the assessment process. *Reading Teacher, 53*(6), 452–455.

Smiles, T. L., & Short, K. G. (2006). Transforming teacher voice through writing for publication. *Teacher Education Quarterly, 33,* 133–147.

Sparks-Langer, G. M., & Colton, A. B. (1991). Synthesis of research on teachers' reflective thinking. *Educational Leadership, 48,* 37–44.

Stenhouse, L. (1981). What counts as research? *British Journals of Educational Studies, 29,* 103–122.

Stevens, D. D., & Cooper, J. E. (2009). *Journal keeping: How to use reflective journals for effective teaching, learning, professional insight and positive change.* Sterling, VA: Stylus.

Stinnett, T. A., Oehler-Stinnett, J., & Stout, L. J. (1991). Development of the Teacher Rating of Academic Achievement Motivation (TRAAM). *School Psychology Review, 20,* 609–622.

Stringer, E. T. (2007). *Action research* (3rd ed.). Los Angeles: SAGE.

Swaffield, S. (2005). No sleeping partners: Relationships between head teachers and critical friends. *School Leadership and Management, 25*(1), 43–57. doi:10.1080/13632430802292191

Taggart, G. L., & Wilson, A. P. (2005). *Promoting reflective thinking in teachers: 50 action strategies* (2nd ed.). Thousand Oaks, CA: Corwin Press.

Wolcott, H. F. (1994). *Transforming qualitative data: Description, analysis, and interpretation.* Thousand Oaks, CA: SAGE.

Yin, R. K. (2011). *Qualitative research from start to finish.* New York: Guilford Press.

Zeichner, K., & Liu, K. Y. (2010). A critical analysis of reflection as a goal for teacher education. In N. Lyons (Ed.), *Handbook of reflection and reflective inquiry* (pp. 67–84). New York: Springer.

Zeni, J. (Ed.). (2001). *Ethical issues in practitioner research.* New York: Teachers College Press.

Zeni, J. (2009). Ethics and the "personal" in action research. In S. Noffke & B. Somekh (Eds.), *The SAGE handbook of educational action research* (pp. 254–266). Thousand Oaks, CA: SAGE.

INDEX